HF1602.15.C2 H65 2002

Holroyd, Carin.

Government,
  international trade, and
    c2002.

DATE DUE	RETURNED

Government, International Trade, and Laissez-Faire Capitalism

Government, International Trade, and Laissez-Faire Capitalism

Canada, Australia, and New Zealand's Relations with Japan

CARIN LEE HOLROYD

McGill-Queen's University Press
Montreal & Kingston · London · Ithaca

© McGill-Queen's University Press 2002
ISBN 0–7735–2336–7

Legal deposit second quarter 2002
Bibliothèque nationale du Québec

Printed in Canada on acid-free paper that is 100%
ancient forest free (100% post-consumer recycled),
processed chlorine free.

This book has been published with the help of a grant
from the Humanities and Social Sciences Federation of
Canada, using funds provided by the Social Sciences
and Humanities Research Council of Canada.

McGill-Queen's University Press acknowledges the
financial support of the Government of Canada through
the Book Publishing Industry Development Program
(BPIDP) for its activities. We also acknowledge the
support of the Canada Council for the Arts for our
publishing program.

National Library of Canada Cataloguing in Publication Data

Holroyd, Carin
   Government, international trade and laissez-faire capitalism:
   Canada, Australia, and New Zealand's relations with Japan

   Includes bibliographical references and index.
   ISBN 0–7735–2336–7
   1. Commercial policy.   2. Japan—Commercial policy.
   3. Canada—Commerce—Japan.   4. Japan—Commerce—
   Canada.   5. New Zealand—Commerce—Japan.   6. Japan—
   Commerce—New Zealand.   7. Australia—Commerce—Japan.
   8. Japan—Commerce—Australia.   I. Title.

   HF1601.H64 2002   381.3   C2001–903750–3

Typeset in 10/12 Baskerville by True to Type

To Ken and to my parents

Contents

Tables

Acknowledgments

There are many people without whose assistance and support this book would not have been possible. Many government officials, business people, academics, journalists, and friends in New Zealand, Australia, Japan, and Canada agreed to be interviewed (often for many hours), read drafts of various chapters, allowed me to discuss my ideas and findings, and gave freely of their knowledge, information, analysis, ideas, and support. In Australia (or working for the Australian government in Japan), I am profoundly grateful to Leonie Muldoon, Peter Harrison, Jamie Anderson (particularly for his incredible generosity in sharing his research materials with me), Ian Wing, Jane Madden, and Ian Marsh. In New Zealand (or working for the New Zealand government in Japan), I received much valuable help from Ken McNeil, Ken Henshall, Richard Nottage, Simon Tucker, Eugene Bowen, Sachiko Suzuki, Ifor Ffowcs Williams, Roger Peren, Nils Holm, John Jenner, Phil Lindsay, Celia Ryan, Becky Robson, Innes Moffat, Joanna Scott-Kennel, Rod Gates, Ian Kennedy, Kerry McDonald, Gary Hawke, Roger Kerr, Cathy Trewby, Alan Norton, and John Arathimos. In Japan, I would like to thank the Japanese Ministry of Foreign Affairs for a much appreciated research grant, James Yellowlees, and Eamonn Fingleton.

My research in Canada was aided significantly by contributions from Neil Ridler, Mohammed Kabir, Larry Woods, Greg Poelzer, the Japan Studies Association of Canada, Robert Collette, Robert Eberschlag, Tamara Beatty, Sarah DeVarenne, Jennifer Rosebrugh, Alan Virtue, John Skeggs, Maurice Hladik, Patricia Cronin, Bruce Christie, Peter Campbell, Klaus Pringsheim, Martin Thornell, John Tak, Jim Anholt, David Beardsall, Ralph Reschke, John Spence, and Jim Seciccone.

On a personal level, I would like to express my appreciation to family and friends who supported me throughout the writing of the manuscript. Thank you Ann McEwan, Lin Min, Maria Galikowski, Jennifer Hammond, Cheryl Douglas, Jenny Daubeny, Nobuhiko Kawai, Mae Sagar, Emiko Matsuo, Akiko Nakayama, Carolyn Willick, Sylvain Allyson, Lisa Holroyd, Mark Coates, Laura Coates, and Bradley Coates.

In particular, I would like to thank Alan Simpson, my supervisor at the University of Waikato, for agreeing to be my thesis supervisor and for his careful reading and analysis of the manuscript and his excellent ideas and suggestions. I am also extremely grateful to the University of Waikato for its most generous post-graduate scholarship. Special thanks go to Auréle Parisien at McGill-Queen's University Press, who believed in the manuscript right from the beginning and was unfailingly helpful and supportive. Thank you also to Joan McGilvray and the rest of the staff at McGill-Queen's for helping in the transformation of this work from a manuscript into a book. The book is much stronger as a result of the helpful professional advice I received from editor Lesley Barry. The anonymous reviewers provided excellent comments and suggestions; I hope that I have done justice to their useful advice.

I would also like to express my thanks and appreciation to my parents, Les and Beth Holroyd, for their love, support, and unwavering confidence that I would indeed finish the book.

My deepest thanks go to my husband, Ken Coates. Thank you, Ken, for your belief in me, your interest in the topic, your willingness to allow me to ramble on about my ideas endlessly, your unflagging support through the good and bad times (how many times did the computer crash?), your hours of proofreading, and your constant love. Thank you for making everything worthwhile.

Abbreviations

AJBF   Australia-Japan Business Forum
AMC   Australian Manufacturing Council
APEC   Asia Pacific Economic Cooperation
ASEAN   Association of Southeast Asian Nations
Austrade   Australia Trade Commission
BCNI   Business Council on National Issues (C)
BIE   Bureau of Industry Economics (A)
CER   Closer Economic Relations (NZ & A)
CIBS   Canada's International Business Strategy
DFAIT   Department of Foreign Affairs and International Trade (C)
DFAT   Department of Foreign Affairs and Trade (A)
EPA   Economic Planning Agency (J)
FDI   Foreign Direct Investment
FDIAG   Foreign Direct Investment Advisory Group (NZ)
GATT   General Agreement on Tariffs and Trade
GDP   Gross Domestic Product
GNP   Gross National Product
IBDR   International Business Development Review (C)
IPFP   Investment Promotion and Facilitation Program (A)
ITAC   International Trade Advisory Committee (C)
JAG   Joint Action Group (NZ & A)
JETRO   Japan External Trade Organization
MFAT   Ministry of Foreign Affairs and Trade (NZ)
MFP   Multifunctionpolis (A)
MITI   Ministry of International Trade and Industry (J) (known as of 2001 as METI, the Ministry of Economy, Trade and Industry)

MOF Ministry of Finance (J)
NRI Nomura Research Institute (J)
OECD Organization for Economic Cooperation and Development
OPEC Organization of Petroleum Exporting Countries
SAGIT Sectoral Advisory Groups on International Trade (C)
TCS Trade Commissioner Service (C)
Tradenz Trade Development Board (NZ)

A – Australia, C – Canada, J – Japan, NZ – New Zealand

Government, International Trade, and Laissez-Faire Capitalism

Introduction:
Japan's Dominions

Governments matter, or so people used to believe. In the heady years of post-World War II economic growth, governments were actively involved in managing national economies. Japan and the "Asian Tigers" popularized the "development state" model while Cuba and the former Soviet Union adopted centralized state planning. Most industrialized countries opted for a more moderate track, like the free enterprise system that, subsidized and enriched by military spending, fueled America's growth, and the state socialism that found adherents from Australia and New Zealand to the United Kingdom, Germany, and Sweden. Canada, ever indecisive and worried about the reaction from its powerful southern neighbour, flirted with state intervention at a variety of levels, but opted largely for the welfare state model of personal transfer payments. Whatever the approach, governments and political decision-makers played a pivotal role in the management of national economies and international trade environments.

The last two decades of the twentieth century witnessed a veritable collapse in public confidence in the value and reliability of state management. Highlighted by the Soviet Union's disintegration and China's introduction of selected elements of the free market, state-centred approaches seemed to topple in a capitalist variant of the long-feared domino effect. As welfare states in the west wallowed in a mire of individual and regional dependency, accelerating national debts, and open-ended expectations, politicians from the right offered a vision of an economic environment with a level international playing field unfettered by excessive state regulation. As countries edged toward economic catastrophe – with New Zealand hanging over the edge of the fiscal precipice in 1984 – a new economic consensus emerged. Not since the age of imperialism early in the twentieth century was there as broad an agreement on the best approach to the operation of national and international economics. In *The End of History and the Last Man*, one of the first bibles of the new era, Francis Fukuyama confidently declared the permanent ascendancy of capitalism and its political partner, democracy.[1]

This emerging consensus – celebrated in western industrial circles and roundly critiqued by those attempting to maintain the social welfare state model – focused on the liberalization of trade and a sharp reduction in the size and influence of government. Capitalism won the day; totalitarian communist regimes had lost, and milder forms of state socialism had to adapt or wither. Headed by the unrepentant capitalists Ronald Reagan and Margaret Thatcher in the 1980s, the United States and the United Kingdom led the way in challenging the power of the state, with its high taxes, strong bureaucracy, and management ethos, and spread the gospel of the new economic order. The dramatic economic success of countries like Japan and Singapore, both of which relied on powerful, high quality civil services to guide national economic development, was something of a mystery and a concern to proponents of the free market approach. But, as though to anoint the non-Asian nations who had followed the lead of Reagan and Thatcher, the "Asian flu" of the late 1990s undercut the Asian "miracle."

Nonetheless, obituaries for state interventionism appeared too soon. In several European states, most notably France, Italy, and Germany, social democratic parties fought their way back into office by the end of the century. In England, Tony Blair led the Labour Party to a massive victory over John Major's Conservatives, albeit with a capitalist-friendly version of social democracy marketed under the label "New Labour," and was re-elected in 2001. The November 1999 election of the Labour Party in New Zealand, complete with promises of increased taxes on the "rich"[2] and a return to state-driven economic planning, was perhaps the most dramatic indication of the re-emergence of the old ideas, made more notable by the fact that New Zealand had been the poster child of neo-classical economics for the previous decade. Similarly, the 2000 decision of Canada's Liberal government to "re-invest" part of the annual budgetary surplus in a new round of national social and economic initiatives signaled a change in the country's hitherto strong retreat from state involvement in the economy. Even so, the imperatives of free trade and economic liberalization have become widespread and powerful. The ascendancy of the

World Trade Organization, International Monetary Fund, and World Bank, the agencies charged with promoting this approach to economic development around the world, indicate the growing power of the free market ideology. Perhaps the best illustration of the uneasy balance between the old and new orders was the debate over the 1998 Multilateral Agreement on Investment (MAI). That the agreement proceeded as far as it did – to the status of a treaty requiring final amendment and ratification – suggests that national governments and business leaders were committed to trade and investment liberalization. That the MAI was stopped by intense grassroots lobbying by nationalist groups, trade unions, and social democratic parties – facilitated by the easy access to both information and mass communication provided by the internet – shows that the advocates of state control of the economy had not folded their tents and surrendered the struggle. The debate over the MAI was for many people in a range of countries their first introduction to the realities and possible impacts of globalization. As if to accentuate the growing tension between the two sides, the 1999 World Trade Organization meetings in Seattle, Washington attracted large numbers of anti-free trade protesters, and one of the most raucous and confrontational international protest rallies of the 1990s.

Analysts addressing the issue of the management of national economies in this new era have focused on two issues: the growing power of the forces of globalization and the role of the state in economic management. Globalization exists at a variety of levels, from the increasing influence of arms-length international financial and trade agencies to the spread of western-style mass culture. It is also the subject of intense debate, a victim to excessive hype and uncritical commentary. Scholars have demonstrated, for example, that the world's economy was more "international" in the late nineteenth and early twentieth centuries, albeit through the unequal and Eurocentric systems of imperialism.[3] There is considerable evidence, as well, that national economies retain considerable independence and autonomy despite increasing integration – and the integration that has occurred has been more through regional blocs and trade alliances, like the North American Free Trade Agreement, the South American Mercosur agreement, and the European Union, and less the result of creative expansion of international trading networks. Researchers from various disciplines are attempting to define both what this means for the nation-state and what it means for individuals.[4] Some see increased prosperity for all; others envision powerless individuals in the grasp of multinational corporations; still others question whether globalization is even occurring to the extent that both promoters and critics claim.[5] What has become clear is that governments are increasingly concerned about international competition for markets, services, capital, and labour, that transnational and multinational organizations and corporations are exerting increased economic influence, and that non-commercial international influences (including the illicit drug trade and organized crime) play an increasingly important role within national economies. Further, continued advances in information technology have compressed distance to the point of near irrelevance and allowed companies to search for workers, supplies, services, and markets in widely dispersed countries. Economic globalization is not a myth – to reject the reality of international integration goes too far – but neither is it inevitable nor the sole determinant of national prosperity.

The implications of the free market economy are far from being well understood, but the strength of the western economies, led until the winter of 2000–01 by America's continuing and surprising performance, hardened political resolve in favour of liberalization. Few politicians are prepared to tinker with "success," even though it is not at all clear that the economic policies of the past two decades have produced domestic economic rewards or that the benefits of increased trade have been distributed equitably. To a degree that shocks some observers and heartens supporters, a surprisingly strong consensus has emerged on the inevitability of freer trade, the shortcomings of national regulation and economic management, and the need to open borders to increase trade and investment. Even Japan, once known for the complexity and seeming impenetrability of its formal and informal trade barriers, has taken substantial strides toward trade liberalization, albeit with a peculiarly Japanese twist.[6]

The lack of confidence in government intervention springs in large part from the substantial failure of government-managed enterprises and the massive deficits created by western governments during the 1970s and 1980s. In country after country, political and social pressures resulted in ill-advised national investments, driven more by political than business considerations, and in the continued expansion of a voracious welfare state. This was certainly the case in Australia, Canada, and New Zealand, where governments stepped in to purchase ailing businesses deemed to be in the national interest and companies in order to protect jobs. As national debts piled up and taxes increased, demands from the left for further government involvement in the economy fell on disbelieving ears. Business leaders, emboldened by the inability of state-owned enterprises and government commercial incentives to boost the national economy, broadened their attack on any political part of the centre or left that proposed to maintain the old order. Demands for a reduction in government economic management escalated to the point that formerly interventionist politicians and civil servants became, in many western nations, among the leading advocates for liberalization and a "hands off" approach. The few public voices calling for a more compassionate, less commercial approach to government policy were drowned out by reminders of failed national initiatives and massive government debt.

Without necessarily arguing that the premises underlying contemporary western industrial economies are wrong, it is important to begin the process of assessing the significance, impact, and contributions of the free market model. In each of the three dominions studied here – Australia, Canada, and New Zealand – government policy shifted dramatically from state-driven economic management in the 1970s to laissez-faire, internationalist policies by the mid-1990s. In all three countries, governments cut taxes, reduced regulatory regimes, privatized state-owned enterprises, reduced government-funded subsidies to regions and individuals, and actively promoted foreign investment and international trade. In each country, regardless of whether the governing party was Labour or National (New Zealand), Progressive Conservative or Liberal (Canada), Labour or Liberal-National coalition (Australia), national priorities focused on a business-friendly agenda. The social welfare policies that were long credited with bringing prosperity and equality receded in importance, and politicians and civil servants largely abandoned the long-standing belief in the efficacy of intervention. The turnaround, stunning in its speed and intensity, remains substantially unstudied, in part because of the worldwide nature of the transition in political and economic thinking. How has the new approach to government affected the economy, and civil society? National governments have made key assumptions in shifting from a state-centred to a business-driven economic order, and the electorate, in supporting or insisting upon this change, believes that the free market approach will bring greater prosperity and provide for a better future than the old interventionism did.

A CASE STUDY ASSESSMENT

The broad purpose of this study is to examine the impact of neo-classical economic ideology on the role and activity of governments in the contemporary global economy, by way of a three-country comparative investigation within a specific time frame: Canada, New Zealand, and Australia's international trade and investment activities, specifically with Japan, between 1985 and 1997. The study encompasses the practical, political, and administrative issues associated with international trade, the mobilization of national government action, and the business-government relationship as seen in each country's economic relationship with Japan.[7] Comparing and contrasting how the three countries responded to the dramatic changes that occurred in Japan in the twelve years after the 1985 Plaza Accord enables us to assess the nature of government involvement in a laissez-faire environment and the effectiveness of different policies and practices. Above all, it provides an opportunity to gauge the effectiveness of the limited government model, which by definition constrains the initiatives governments can undertake in an economic environment that promotes decision-making by the market place and demands flexibility and innovation.

The case study's time period of 1985 to 1997 encompasses immense and fundamental political and economic shifts throughout the world. Globalization, aided by new technology, began to change the international economy; neo-classical ideology persuaded western governments to restrict the management of their national economies; Canada's economy was transformed through extensive privatization and cutbacks and the North American Free Trade Agreement; New Zealand saw a dramatic reorientation from protectionism to the free market; Australia, like other resource-based countries, began to recognize that it needed to diversify and develop new industries to ensure long-term prosperity for its citizens; and in Japan the Plaza Accord set in motion changes that would have enormous implications for its trading partners.

The three dominions have much in common. All three are relatively young countries, born of the same British parent and with continuing strong ties, through immigration and commerce, to the English-speaking world. Britain was, for many years, the primary market for many of the products these nations produced. Preferential purchasing agreements meant that, until the 1970s, New Zealand and Australia in particular felt little need to look for other purchasers. Canada retained a strong bond with Britain through to the 1960s, but then found easy access to American markets. Economic links with the United Kingdom have declined in importance, but emotional ties remain to varying degrees in each country. Over the last thirty years, trade and investment links between the three dominions and the U.S. have expanded dramatically.

All three countries are wealthy and possessed of vast quantities of land relative to their populations. Development emerged from individual hard work and a hardy, much-celebrated frontier spirit. Sheep and cattle stations in the Australian outback and farms and ranches on the Canadian prairies were often large and operated by single families. New Zealand built off a tradition of small farmers, dictated by the topography and the prosperity of the sheep and dairy industries. In Canada and Australia, the weather is often harsh and even dangerous. The newcomers, who competed with indigenous peoples for the land and who typically shouldered them aside, had to be strong and self-reliant, or at least so national mythology has it.

These historical patterns, which emphasized independence and hard work and which downplayed economic support from the mother country and the time-limited value of their rich natural endowments, created in all three nations a sense of entitlement, in which first world status was (and is) taken for granted. Canada hosts large forests, oceans and lakes rich with fish, generous supplies of coal, oil, and minerals, and countless miles of rich farmland. Australia has large deposits of minerals (nickel, zinc, bauxite, iron ore), oil and non-oil energy resources, along with vast areas of land suitable for running sheep and raising cattle. New Zealand offers a generally benign climate combined with rich soils, which means that almost anything can grow, including all kinds of fruits and vegetables, pine trees, and grass for grazing livestock. It has excellent fishing grounds and promising supplies of natural gas. These national endowments have been both a blessing and a curse. Possession of such bounty made these nations complacent, able to rely on selling off that which is produced with relative ease. There was little incentive to develop new industries or be concerned about adding value to resources before exporting them, when their simple sale made each of these countries comfortable and, in international terms, prosperous for decades.

In the latter part of the twentieth century, however, the world changed. Canada, New Zealand, and Australia can no longer rely on the export of primary products to ensure prosperity. Increased competition with emerging nations (particularly Chile and Russia), diminished resource supply in some areas, the volatility of commodity pricing, and changes in technology have forced these nations to confront the reality of economic change. This is not an easy process. There is a general sense in each country that a prosperous past ensures a prosperous future – a faith that is not confirmed by economic history. There is both a feeling that one is owed a good future and a sense that nothing but affluence is possible. Government and industry leaders in each of these countries see that change is needed and know that a wealthy future is not assured. Governments have begun programs to get businesses working together to capture export markets, to generate a cooperative spirit, to convince the public to sacrifice now for later prosperity, and to put aside petty and historical grievances for the good of the entire nation. But, in each instance, they have been criticized as being pessimists, and have been largely ignored by those preferring the status quo.

Australia, Canada, and New Zealand are also part of the western capitalist tradition, and their national governments have embraced neoclassical economic theory. As these countries share so much in common – while maintaining distinct national political cultures and perspectives – the comparison of economic choices made and decisions taken with regard to Japan is instructive. While other countries could be chosen for this study, the similarities of these three provide an opportunity for unique insights in national differences and international commonalities, and permit an investigation of three variants of the contemporary capitalist ethos in national politics.

The opposite side of the investigation – international trade and investment ties with Japan – springs from similar considerations. By looking at the relations with one country, the impact of policies and strategies is more readily traced. While one country is not a surrogate for the entire international trade scene, Japan is of special significance: the country has been Australia's most important market since 1967, Canada's second most important export market since 1973 (and Canada's overwhelming dependence on the U.S. market makes Japan that much more important in comparative terms), and New Zealand's second largest economic partner for most of the 1980s and 1990s. In addition, as the world's second largest economy with a gross domestic product of about US$5 trillion, Japan is a major international force. Despite difficulties through the 1990s and further challenges ahead, few commentators are willing to dismiss Japan's importance. Japan will continue to be a major economic power; countries that ignore this economy do so at their peril. That Japan is difficult for westerners to understand and that it does not always react in the way they expect makes the challenge of monitoring Japan and understanding the country's impact on its trading partners that much more important.[8]

The 1985 Plaza Accord, an international financial agreement that resulted in a substantial appreciation in the value of the Japanese yen, both reflected and sparked many domestic shifts and altered Japan's trade and investment relationships dramatically. The rapid appreciation of the yen saw the Japanese move labour-intensive manufacturing offshore, stimulate domestic consumer demand, radically alter their import mix, expand investments in high technology industries, and begin economic deregulation. These changes had a direct impact on Japan's trading partners that as yet has been little studied.

The theoretical and policy implications of the emphasis on Japan are considerable. An activist state, faced with the radical changes underway in Japan, might well study the transitions, develop policies for responding to them, and implement national initiatives designed to protect or expand market share in the changing Japanese economy. A state driven by neo-classical considerations, on the other hand, might well collect market intelligence (for international affairs remains a generally accepted responsibility of national governments) but would be less likely to translate the information into concrete government action. Instead, such a national government would leave the matter of an industrial or commercial response to the business sector. As the transformation of the Japanese economy overlapped with the shift toward free market principles in Australia, Canada, and New Zealand, comparing the twelve years of trade and investment activity from 1985 to 1997 between Japan and the three dominions provides an excellent case study of the strengths and limitations of the free market order.

UNDERSTANDING THE JAPANESE ECONOMY

Any study of Japanese trade involves a series of assumptions about the nature of the Japanese economy, about which much has been written since the 1970s. Earlier writers like Ezra Vogel and William Ouchi extolled the virtues of Japanese management and "Japan Inc.," the partnership between government and industry. More extreme authors followed, including Shintaro Ishihara, whose strong and confident analysis heightened fears of Japan's future progress, and Jon Woronoff, who highlighted the country's problems and predicted Japan's imminent economic and social decline. More recent writing reveals a similar range of opinions, although there appears to be agreement that Japan will remain a potent global economic force despite a number of short- and medium-term problems.

Japan's challenges include a rapidly aging population, concerns about the education system, disarray in financial institutions, public disillusionment with politicians and a newfound distrust of bureaucrats, ongoing tensions in relations with the U.S., and the potential "hollowing" out of the economy as manufacturing is relocated overseas. In other words, Japan faces many of the same problems as other leading industrial nations. Commentators point to the Japanese ability to work together to overcome diversity as the key to continued economic strength. Christopher Wood suggests that "Japan as a society has a tremendous record for pulling together in a crisis, as opposed to the dog-eat-dog behaviour normal in Anglo-Saxon countries"; the country also uses long-term planning and industrial policy effectively. A number of the books that discuss these Japanese attributes in detail were written by Americans striving to show what the United States, in particular, could learn from Japan. Clyde Prestowitz and William Holstein have both encouraged America to consider developing some form of industrial policy along Japan's lines.[9]

This investigation concurs with the analysis that the Japanese economy will remain strong and that the country will continue as a world leader in the short and long term. Western commentators, particularly those with little detailed knowledge of Japan, have been far too quick to dismiss Japan in the past. Predictions of Japan's uncertain future were inaccurately offered after World War II, after the oil shocks of the 1970s, after the yen increased in value in the mid-1980s, and again during the recession of the late 1990s. Despite the difficulties at the end of the twentieth century, there remains much in Japan's economic make-up to justify anticipating a strong future.

NATIONAL GOVERNMENTS AND INTERNATIONAL TRADE

International trade is all about the interplay of politics and economics. As Susan Strange observed, "exchanges in international trade are not simply the outlines of market forces, of relative supply and demand. Rather, they are the result of a complex and interlocking network of bargains that are partly economic and partly political."[10]

The decisions of the governments of Australia, New Zealand, and Canada regarding trade and investment relations with Japan were made in a specific ideological and intellectual context. As we have seen, that context was the increasing attack on state intervention in the management of national economies. While the primary emphasis in this study is on specific government programs and initiatives, it is important to examine intellectual debates about the appropriate role for government in the economy. These issues have been placed in stark relief by the financial and economic transitions that followed the Asian monetary crisis of 1997-98. The rapid collapse of the economies of Thailand, Malaysia, and Indonesia, and the flow-through difficulties in Hong Kong, Japan, and other major regional trading partners, provided a graphic illustration of the interdependence of contemporary economic systems and of the inherent uncertainties involved with international trade. The crisis showed the importance of monitoring, understanding, and responding quickly and accurately to changes in the international trading environment, and it tested the ability of national governments to guide their domestic economies. The marked, but by no means dominant, resurgence of the welfare state and the belief in the importance of state intervention, most evident in the re-election of the Labour Party in New Zealand in November 1999 and in a less pronounced fashion in the increased statist approach of the Liberal government of Canada, underscores the importance of understanding the interplay of politics, ideology, and economic assumptions. Moreover, understanding this interplay in the larger context of increasing globalization is vital for accurate analysis of the best methods of governance – domestic, regional, and international – for the future.

The underlying argument advanced in this study is that the action and inaction of governments do matter in economic affairs. As this book documents, by adopting a neo-classical approach to economic leadership, national governments do not assume a primary role in responding to changing international economic circumstances, but rely on the business community to take responsibility for shaping international trade relations. The evidence drawn from economic relations between Japan and Australia, Canada, and New Zealand demonstrates that the largely leaderless business response did not result in the national economies responding creatively to the dramatic changes in the Japanese economy. Left to their own devices, and without strong government direction, the business sector adhered to traditional markets and long-standing approaches, resulting in a reduced presence in the economy of the world's second wealthiest nation. Governments were not completely inactive, and some of the initiatives brought positive results. In general, however, business and government in Australia, Canada, and New Zealand adhered to the neo-classical agenda – and their national economies paid through a less than impressive adaptation to economic changes in Japan.

Chapter 1 places this study within the context of writings on government and international trade, and chapter 2 explores the history of the trade and investment relationships that Canada, Australia, and New Zealand developed with Japan. Chapter 3 then describes the changes in the Japanese economy following the 1985 Plaza Accord and assesses the impact of these changes on Japan's trading partners. This establishes a foundation for the subsequent assessment of national administrative and policy responses to the Japanese economic transitions. Chapters 4, 5, and 6 describe the national government policy and administrative strategies of Canada, Australia, and New Zealan respectively for encouraging trade and investment with Japan, and show the state of their exports to Japan and of Japanese investment between 1985 and 1997. Chapters 7 and 8 analyse the differences among the three countries in their commercial relations with Japan and discuss the options available for future trade and investment relations, while chapter 9 updates the study through the year 2000. My primary emphasis is on the background to, and the impact of, specific national policies and trade and investment initiatives, but the underlying purpose is to consider the intersection of trade and government initiatives by way of a three-country comparison within a fixed time frame. Within the context of current scholarship, this book explores the arguments for government involvement in the management of national economies in an era of economic globalization.

1 Governments and International Trade: An Intellectual Analysis

It is easy to forget how recently western nations shared, both intellectually and politically, a firm belief in the efficacy of the activist state. With only a few exceptions, like Hong Kong, capitalism was expected to operate within firm boundaries, and the public expected government to play a major role in economic management. Over the last two decades of the twentieth century, the analysis that underscores political economy changed dramatically. Where academics once defended and explained state-managed economies, they now led the way in supporting the free market approach. Where there was once almost unanimous agreement on the need for state intervention on the personal, regional, and national level, theories of laissez-faire economics began to rival, if not exceed, the old arguments in popularity and impact. Voices of protest could be heard, more from journalists than from mainstream academics, and arguments in favour of state intervention have never died out completely. In fact, by the end of the century, a steady stream of new books heralded something of a rebirth – or was it a last gasp? – of the central ideology of the post-World War II western world.[1]

NEO-CLASSICAL ARGUMENT

Neo-classical economists believe in the primacy of market forces in allocating resources and setting prices. When the market is completely unfettered and there is perfect competition, the argument goes, then the market is at its most efficient and society's resources are distributed most effectively. Market imperfections can exist, but these are seen as being of relatively minor importance. The activities of government should be restricted to essential economic functions, such as creating macroeconomic stability, providing the nation with proper physical infrastructure, supplying national security, education, and other "pure public goods," and redistributing income so that the poor can meet basic needs. Nevertheless, Milton Friedman, one of the most famous neo-classicists, wrote that "any use of government is fraught with danger."[2] For this reason, "the scope of government must be limited. Its major function must be to protect our freedom both from the enemies outside our gates and from our fellow citizens: to preserve law and order, to enforce private contracts, to foster competitive markets."[3] He conceded that there may be times when it is appropriate for government to undertake projects that benefit all citizens (the building of roads, for example) and which would not make economic sense to be undertaken by each person individually; beyond this, Friedman argued, the private sector must remain a check on the government and ensure that individual freedoms are protected.

Most neo-classical economists would also agree that government may step in when price distortions occur because of market failure. The difficulty comes in determining what constitutes legitimate market failure. Even when market failure is recognized, some economists do not believe that government intervention, particularly sectoral industrial policy, is of any value. In many cases, they blame market imperfections on previous government actions and are pessimistic about the ability or willingness of governments to use their economic powers wisely or to detect industrial opportunities the private sector has missed.[4]

The neo-classical argument is based on the theory of comparative advantage. This theory states that each country would do best if it concentrated on producing those products and services to which it is best suited. As Adam Smith stated in his famous *The Wealth of Nations* treatise of 1776, market forces, not government controls, should determine the direction, volume, and composition of international trade. He noted that some countries, owing to the skill of their workers or the quality of their natural resources, produce the same volume of a particular good with less labour than do other countries. He argued that under free, unregulated trade, each nation should specialize in producing those goods it produces most efficiently. The sale of some of these goods would pay for imports that are produced more efficiently elsewhere. Smith and others who followed him believed that trade can be a positive game whereby all parties benefit, as long as the market is allowed to work unencumbered.

As the market knows best, interference by governments distorts the rational decisions made by corporations and consumers. Governments that believe in neo-classical economics (such as the United States, Canada, New Zealand, and Australia) therefore see little role for themselves in promoting one industry over another, as this would distort market forces. (There are exceptions to this, however. For example, most countries, including those listed above, intervene in the agricultural sector and have substantially distorted free market trade in food products. This issue was the focus of the controversial and unsuccessful WTO meetings held in Seattle in 1999.) While many of the Asian governments agree with the importance of the market in principle, they also believe that the market does not always know best. Too much domestic competition or a short-term crisis can eliminate firms that, provided they had a little support at the crucial time, would be successful in the long term. Not all industries are created equal; not all industries guarantee the same economic future for a nation. It therefore makes sense for governments to promote one over another. Some neo-classical economists partially agree and can be convinced that policies to promote manufacturing can be beneficial, but they would not agree to policies that favour particular manufacturing sectors.[5]

In the 1980s, when a conservative counter-revolution challenged the ascendency of interventionist governments, economists moved beyond their long-standing celebration of the fundamental primacy of the marketplace and emphasized both the limitations of state-driven intervention and the basic incapacity of states to direct economic development. While some economists acknowledged that the activism of East Asian governments had assisted in regional expansion, they often dismissed this model as being irrelevant or difficult to assess accurately. Some have argued that the success in Asia occurred *despite* rather than *because of* government involvement in economic planning and development.[6]

INDUSTRIAL POLICY

Other economists, however, believe that governments should be more active and should promote some form of industrial policy. Industrial policy has been defined as "programs adopted by the government to promote the growth and competitiveness of companies and workers."[7] The idea of government or national action to encourage economic development has been around a long time. One of the first to argue in its favour was Friedrich List (1789–1846), a German political economist. List explored the role of nationality and/or collective action as an intermediary between individuals and the human race generally. While François Quesnay, the originator of the idea of universal free trade, and Adam Smith wrote about worldwide freedom of commerce, List did not believe this would benefit all countries equally. He believed "that free competition between nations which are highly civilized can only be mutually beneficial in cases when both of them are in a nearly equal position of industrial development."[8] A nation that is industrially or commercially underdeveloped must strengthen itself before competing on a free basis with advanced countries. List believed that the state's coordinating role should apply while a nation is, for example, developing expertise in a certain industry. Once that expertise is fully developed, the state's role should begin to decline.

Many of the recent writings about industrial policy have stemmed from interest in the spectacular growth of the East Asian economies, beginning with Japan. In 1982 Chalmers Johnson identified Japan as a "capitalist developmental state," in contrast to the American-style "capitalist regulatory state."[9] By this he meant that the Japanese state "had played primarily a developmental role in its economy, rather than the regulatory role prescribed by Anglo-American theory."[10] Capitalist development states are plan-rational and thereby concerned with "the structure of domestic industry and with promoting the structure that enhances the nation's international competitiveness."[11] This is most often illustrated by the existence of an industrial policy and clear goal-oriented strategies for its implementation. Market-rational economies, on the other hand, focus on rules and concessions; trade policy is often subordinate to foreign policy.[12]

Johnson describes industrial policy as "the initiation and coordination of governmental activities to leverage upward the productivity and competitiveness of the whole economy and of particular industries in it. Above all, positive industrial policy means the infusion of goal-oriented, strategic thinking into public economic policy."[13] He goes on to explain that it does not mean that the market is replaced or that government tells business what it must do. Instead it "reflects the cooperative efforts by the public and private sectors to understand the nature of technological change and to anticipate its likely economic effects."[14] In capitalist development states, economic growth is a priority. Close ties between government and business are encouraged to facilitate the exchange of information and coordinated decision-making. A central government agency like the Ministry of Finance or the Ministry of International Trade and Industry in Japan or the Industrial Development Board in Taiwan is usually involved.

Following Johnson, other authors have also studied the Asian economies and evaluated the role of government in their economic success. Those who argue that government was decisive in that success include Robert Wade, whose study focused primarily on Taiwan, and Alice Amsden, who examined the activities of the Korean government.[15] A number of authors, many of them American, and specialists in East Asia, have continued on this theme, and encouraged the United States to begin to look seriously at some form of industrial policy.[16] One of the first was Clyde Prestowitz, former counselor for Japan Affairs to the U.S. Secretary of Commerce. He wrote:

The real question is what kind of environment do we want to create for our economy. At issue is not pure free trade or total protectionism – we never have had and never will have either one; but rather what combination of free and managed trade we will have. It is not a matter of whether the U.S. government intervenes in the economy – it does and will intervene, massively; but whether it will do so in a way that helps or hurts. Some commentators argue that we cannot copy the Japanese. Of course not, but there is a difference between copying and learning from others. We must learn what we can from Japan in order to make our system work better.[17]

William Dietrich set forth a similar argument in 1991. His thesis was that Japan's success was based on the comprehensive and system-wide use of industrial policy and that the only way for America to counter the Japanese challenge and regain world economic leadership was for America to develop its own industrial policy. To develop that industrial policy required a strong central state and a top professional bureaucracy. He wrote, "How long and how hard a beating do we have to take at the hands of the Japanese until we recognize that something is seriously wrong, until we understand that Japan has a superior economic system?"[18] He continued on to say that trade talks focusing on getting Japan to remove non-tariff or structural barriers to the entry of U.S. goods will not work because that is asking Japan to change its economic system and play by America's rules. "But they are now playing by their rules and winning the game. It is we who must change.... Today's game is managed trade. Japan is not going to open its markets, not going to eliminate its trade surplus, not going to halt its pursuit of technological dominance... We can engage and contain the Japanese only by means of an American industrial policy. We can open Japan's markets only by means of managed trade."[19]

This message, with different emphasis, was also delivered by Eamonn Fingleton, who argued that "for the most part these difficulties can be addressed only by an effective industrial policy. The problem for Washington is that America at present does not have the organizational resources needed to administer an ambitious industrial policy. In particular it lacks the strong government agencies of East Asia."[20]

All of these authors made it clear that they believed Japan's approach to trade was different than America's and that it was time the U.S. lost its fixation on its utopian ideals of free trade. While free trade may be beneficial to the world as a whole, it does not benefit those countries that practise it while their competitors do not. While Japan and many of the Asian countries might profess to believe in free trade, their definition is radically different from the American definition. As Marie Anchordoguy wrote, "a free market, to the Japanese, means a market without such formal constraints as tariffs, quotas, and prohibitions on foreign investment; it has nothing to do with whether competitive foreign products are actually purchased."[21] Daniel Drache argued in the same vein. "It is not good enough for a government to subscribe uncritically to the dictates of free trade that require it to open its markets regardless of cost and consequences. Rather it should not give more than it is getting from the globally driven system."[22] Drache pointed out that governments still need to look out for their national interest, and although he did not advocate a return to protectionist policies, he suggested that states should "have strong policy instruments that will let them plan and finance their strategic goals including job creation, science and technology policy, R&D, environmental policy, affirmative action programmes and the like."[23] This is neither protectionism nor free trade but managed trade.[24]

Linda Weiss and John Hobson focused on "the role of political institutions in economic development,"[25] asserting that a strong state is vital for national economic development and industrial transformation. They believed that this is as applicable to highly developed nations as it is to those newly developing. They looked at the various kinds of state structures and government-business relations and advanced a theory of East Asian political economy called "governed interdependence." In brief, their theory states that government and business are interdependent, that there are rules for how this interdependence is managed, and that the state takes the lead in managing the relationship.[26] They wrote, "The important point is not that East Asian bureaucrats are omniscient or infallible ... But if error-free management were a useful criterion of effectiveness, it is hard to know how even the private sector would qualify. The point is that, by exacting performance standards in exchange for support, and by focusing resources on key technologies, East Asian policies look quite different from those pursued elsewhere in the industrialized world."[27]

As Japan's economic expansion has slowed down, less has been published that celebrates the accomplishments of the Japanese or East Asian "miracle." Instead, the balance has shifted toward journalists and commentators who see the current difficulties as a sign that the underlying economic model of government-managed economies was and is flawed. Nonetheless, analysts who believe that state-guided economies have considerable potential remain. Robert Kuttner is one who does not trust "the unfettered market-place," nor "its ability to increase wealth, promote innovation, and 'optimize outcomes' – and to regulate itself flawlessly all the while."[28] He makes the case for a mixed economy in which government steps in to override markets for a variety of reasons. Nobody has the time to calculate, much less optimize, each decision, Kuttner says, and cites examples of situations and experiments in which people did not behave rationally. He discusses economic development and the state and how what might be initially more efficient – importing goods from another country – may not turn out to be the most efficient in the long term.

In a similar vein, Paul Omerod observes that while Adam Smith argued that free markets, in which everyone, whether a buyer or a seller, followed his or her self-interest, would lead to outcomes that were to the benefit of all, his analysis was much more complex than is now remembered: "Smith's insistence on the importance of the institutional framework and the overall set of moral values in which free markets operate was neglected, for such concepts do not convert readily into the language of mathematics. Neither was his deep interest in the process of economic growth and the processes by which some nations become rich while others remain poor addressed by the new system of economic analysis."[29]

So deeply entrenched are western sentiments about the primacy of the individual and of individual companies to act as they see fit, that it is often difficult to even discuss industrial policy or specific government roles with business or government people in North America. James Fallows, an American journalist, describes it this way:

The Anglo-American system of politics and economics, like any system, rests on certain principles and beliefs. But rather than acting as if these are the 'best' principles, or the one that their societies 'prefer,' Britons and Americans often act as if these were the *only possible* principles and that no one else, except in error, could choose any others. That is, political economics becomes an essentially religious question – leading to the standard drawback of any religion, the failure to understand why people outside the faith act as they do.[30] [italics in original]

The Cold War helped consolidate this position by pitting state-led command economies against laissez-faire economies. Now that Asian economies appear to be foundering, critics are quick to assert that this was inevitable and that industrial policy never worked in the first place.[31]

Those who believe in some kind of government industrial policy or economic leadership make a number of points. First, they point to the need for government or a branch of government to play some kind of coordinating role to bring the various players (industry associations, state or provincial governments, academics, private think tanks) together to chart a plan for the nation's economic future. That it is better to have a strategic plan than not seems self-evident, and industrial policy advocates do not see how one can be developed without coordination. As one analyst wrote, "If 'mission statements' and 'corporate culture' are key ingredients in the quest for excellence of private sector firms, they are even more important at the nation-state level."[32] Weiss and Hobson concluded their analysis of the state's role by stating that "modern economic development generally requires a central coordinating intelligence."[33] This applies, they discovered, to all countries, no matter their level of development. In short, in order to develop a strategic effective plan government and industry must work in concert and one of those two bodies must develop ways to ensure this occurs. Government needs to stimulate the private sector, not replace it.

Another common theme advanced by industrial policy advocates is that to develop and implement a strategic plan, a nation must pull together. There must be a sense of individuals being willing (or not being given a choice) to sacrifice today for what could be tomorrow. The high savings rates that exist in most of East Asia and that have fueled its growth are a classic example. Governments have to put in place policies that force citizens to save. The nation must come first: before states, provinces, or other regional configurations, before special interest groups, before consumers, before the electorate. Paul Krugman, in arguing that there was nothing particularly complicated about Asia's earlier success, says that "the newly industrializing countries of the Pacific Rim have received a reward for their extraordinary mobilization of resources that is no more than the most boringly conventional economic theory would lead us to expect. If there is a secret of Asian growth, it is simply deferred gratification, the willingness to sacrifice current satisfaction for future gain."[34] This may not be complicated, but most forms of deferred gratification are difficult for many westerners to discuss, let alone contemplate as a serious political alternative.

Industrial policy philosophy emphasizes what is best for the group or the nation over what might be best for an individual. Neo-classical philosophy disputes the idea that there is a difference: by acting in one's own best interest, one is acting in the best interests of the country. Friedman wrote that the problem with many government initiatives is that "they seek through government to force people to act against their own immediate interests in order to promote a supposedly general interest."[35] Government should not be taking from some to benefit others or telling people what is good for them. If everyone promotes his own best interest, if the market is left alone to function, then all will benefit.

Industrial policy advocates dispute this. Government should get involved, to prevent excessive competition, for example, or to direct resources into industries that have the best long-term potential. Some new industries, particularly those in the high technology manufacturing sector, require financial backing that individual companies seldom have. Competitiveness is still demanded in the long term; firms are just given help to grow into competitiveness. Industrial policy advocates point out that proper industrial policy works closely with the market, not in opposition to it. Generally, resource allocation decisions are left to the market and the government interferes only when it believes that the market is not operating in the nation's best interest. Unfortunately, all too often the debate on the proper role of government tends to, as Pranab Bardham argued, "be restricted to the polar opposites of private market and centralized bureaucracy."[36] In fact, most industrial policy supporters believe in working closely with the market, and many neo-classical governments intervene quietly and often, when the market does not respond in the desired way.

One of the main arguments against industrial policy is that government is no good at "picking winners." How can government possibly second-guess the market and determine what products will or will not be economically successful? Kimon Valaskakis, chair of ISOGROUP (a global consulting and planning network), argued against the frequently heard assertion that the market allocates resources most efficiently and that government, by nature of being government, is automatically inefficient: "this assertion is based on a comparison of economic theory with the practice of government mismanagement. It is not, however, based on actual market practice. In fact, if one were to oppose ideal public management with actual market practice, one might get very different results."[37] Valaskakis cited examples of well-run public enterprises, like the Swiss National Railways, that are much more efficient than their private counterparts.

Robert Wade agreed. He said that selective sectoral targeting does not involve "picking winners." Instead, governments help "make" winners by selecting new technologies for development. While critics of government involvement in industrial promotion argue that governments are unsuccessful at effectively targeting industries, Wade suggested that the government record is likely not much different from that of the private sector. Criticism of government is generally made in a vacuum, with no reference to mistakes made by the private sector when it enters new industries.[38] Marie Anchordoguy, in her investigation of Japan's efforts to develop a national computer industry, outlined in detail that for the Japanese government, the decision to develop a new technology was "not a matter of picking a winner out of a hat."[39] Decisions were made carefully and based on projections of future growth areas.

While nations with a clear industrial policy believe in the neo-classical tenet of comparative advantage, they differ in their belief that a country's comparative advantages can be altered. Traditional theory takes comparative advantage as being determined by factor endowments (those attributes a country possesses, such as natural resources, an educated population, or a low-cost labour pool) that are given and unalterable. Industrial policy advocates and thinkers like Harvard economist Michael Porter argue that a nation's comparative advantages can be modified or even created. Anchordoguy's study suggests, as she wrote in her conclusion, "that nations can create comparative advantage by changing their factor endowments and that, in the computer case, industrial policy has played a key role in encouraging and facilitating this change."[40]

William Cline similarly argued that "Increasingly, trade in manufactures appears to reflect an exchange of goods in which one nation could be just as likely as another... to develop comparative advantage, and the actual outcome is in a meaningful sense arbitrary."[41] The implications of the idea that nations can and do create their own comparative advantage are enormous for countries like Australia, Canada, and New Zealand, which have tried to believe otherwise. The global economy makes the concept that nations create their own advantages even more likely. Competitive advantage, then, is not fixed. It changes both as countries make efforts to pursue advanced technologies and develop new sectors and markets, and as shifts occur in an increasingly integrated world economy.[42]

Comparative advantage, then, is not arbitrary but develops according to the strategies and activities of business and governments. If decisions are left to the market, then nations that lack strong natural comparative advantages must accept a relatively poor future: leaders like former Prime Minister Lee Kuan Yew from Singapore were determined that this would not be the case. Lee Kuan Yew decided that natural resources could include human capital and aimed to develop a skilled, educated, and hard-working population well suited for knowledge-intensive industries.

GOVERNMENT'S ROLE WITHIN THE NEO-CLASSICAL FRAMEWORK

Scholars who challenge the value of a neo-classical approach to economic management rarely advocate a return to major social-democratic state intervention. Instead, they argue that relatively small shifts in government policy and action can bring dramatic results. Michael Porter has written extensively on this subject.[43] He exhorts governments to get the economic fundamentals right, with an emphasis on education, research universities, and advanced infrastructure. In keeping with, but pushing the boundaries of, neo-classical theory, he wrote: "Government should play a direct role only in those areas where firms are unable to act (such as trade policy) or where externalities cause firms to underinvest. Externalities occur where the benefits to the nation as a whole exceed those accruing to any single firm or individual, so that private entities will tend to underinvest in such areas from the perspective of the nation. Good examples are general education, environmental quality, and some types of R&D that can boost productivity in many industries."[44]

Porter describes ways he believes government can help industry become more competitive. Industry should be challenged and pushed to improve. This can be done by rewarding excellence in productivity and quality control through high profile awards and prizes (Japanese companies, for example, compete for the Deming Prize), and by ensuring that both government and the nation's firms and consumers are demanding and sophisticated buyers. Early and high level demand should be encouraged by making sure consumers (government, industry, and individual) order the next generation's systems rather than settle for whatever is currently acceptable. In this way, he writes, firms are pushed to innovate in order to satisfy demand. He discusses the ways the Japanese government gave companies incentives to purchase certain kinds of robots and arranged a leasing company to provide financing.[45]

Government also needs to pay attention to future economic trends and possibilities. Porter says that signaling, whereby government points out to firms the issues and information that it believes important, is vital. Government leaders are in a position to survey the broad picture and they have a platform from which to express opinions on important national issues and problems. Government does not tell firms how to respond, but it makes sure they are aware of emerging trends and it makes clear that their competitors are also aware. Along the same line is the sponsorship of cooperative research projects. As Porter says of Japan, "The most important role of Japanese cooperative research is to signal the importance of emerging technical areas and stimulate proprietary firm research, not to achieve efficiencies in R&D. MITI believes that Japanese firms are not always forward-looking and need highly public and visible stimuli to investigate new fields. Cooperative projects do this and enhance internal R&D spending because firms know that their competitors are investigating the field as well."[46]

What stands out from Porter's analysis is the long-term, non-partisan nature of many of his suggestions. Government's role is somewhat like that of a coach. Its decisions will not always be popular, even though it has the long-term interests of the nation at heart. He says, "The long time horizon and uncomfortable nature of the most effective policies raise difficult challenges in nations where special interest groups wield political power or where the national consensus for industrial development is not strong."[47]

Porter's has been the most prominent voice advocating more aggressive state leadership in managing national and regional economies, but he is not alone. (Where Porter clearly stands apart, incidentally, is in his ability to directly influence national governments. This will be seen in subsequent discussions of the development of Canadian and New Zealand policy.) While advocates of social-democratic approaches to economic management – state ownership, protectionism, and high levels of regulation – have been vociferous in their condemnation of current economic policy, few have done little more than suggest a return to policies that did not work all that well in the past. There are major political exceptions – Tony Blair's 'New Labour' approach in Britain, for example – and some new ideas circulating among academic analysts.[48]

Many of the tools available to governments – education and training policies, research and development priorities, labour market regulations – are already used by almost all nations, even those based on a neo-classical economic philosophy. Government use of these tools for the purposes of economic development fits with the theory of economic growth called new growth theory or endogenous growth theory. This theory states that technological change results from the resources that are devoted to it. To increase economic growth, technological change and capital accumulation must increase rapidly. The main ways in which this can occur are through the stimulation of savings, the subsidization of research and development, the targeting of high technology industries, and the encouragement of international trade. As Richard Rosencrance argued, "Intervention at an early point in the chain of development can influence results later on, which suggests that the United States and other nations can and should deliberately alter their pattern of comparative advantage and choose their economic activity."[49]

The crux of new growth theory is that the greatest profit is found in the worldwide marketing of a new technology before competitors have an opportunity to copy it. This is dynamic comparative advantage, which an introductory economics text describes as "the ability to produce a good at a lower opportunity cost than any other supplier and results from being first in the field and getting the first crack at accumulating specialized human capital to exploit a new technology. Eventually, all countries can produce all goods at the same opportunity cost (to a reasonable approximation), but the first in a field can dominate that field for some time."[50] The development of this dynamic comparative advantage requires capital, hence the need for high savings rates and subsidized research and development. High technology industries afford the greatest opportunity to develop goods that others will not be able to immediately duplicate.

The "state-as-coach" idea, writes Kimon Valaskakis, is based on the idea that government provides information and planning. However, "there is an ideological blindness, in the West, concerning planning which has become a dirty word in the wake of the prevalence of the state minimization doctrine."[51] He asks why the west has not actually compared the records of partially planned, totally planned, and completely unplanned economies, and points out that it is the partially planned economies that have done best.[52]

Although neo-classical arguments have attracted the greatest amount of political attention in recent years, advocates for planned and managed economies continue to argue that despite or perhaps because of economic globalization, the state still has a powerful role to play. The resurgence of the left, particularly in Europe, suggests that these ideas might emerge as a counter-balance to the prevailing neo-classical consensus.

IMPACT OF GLOBALIZATION AND ITS EFFECT ON THE IMPORTANCE OF THE STATE

A discussion of the appropriate role for government would not be complete without looking at the increasingly interconnected world in which governments now find themselves.[53] With few exceptions – even countries as traditionally isolationist as North Korea and Albania are reaching out beyond their borders – nations have recognized that they do not exist in a vacuum but are part of what is being called the global economy. More companies operated globally in the 1990s than in the 1970s. By the end of 1993, the stock of worldwide foreign direct investment was estimated to have reached $2.14 trillion and total sales of foreign affiliates topped $5 trillion.[54] What this means for the role and power of national governments is still unclear. Until recently, countries were relatively able to control the economic activity occurring within their boundaries.[55] Globalization has made this more difficult, although opinions on how much more difficult vary.

Much of what has been written on globalization has focused less on government direction in international business development than on what globalization means for the balance of world power. Some of those who have focused on the role of the state suggest that since countries are less able to pursue their own economic policies in the new global world, a new kind of nation-state may be emerging as the global system of business constructs a new political order. Anthony McGrew argues that although "the present global system is riven by discord, cultural diversity, economic inequality and political fragmentation ...and lacks established forms of government, [this] should not lead us to neglect the profound significance of the emergence of a global political system."[56] He describes the variety of players, beyond nation-states, that are active in the arena of global politics. These range from multinational corporations to international organizations to subnational government agencies. While McGrew believes that "processes of globalization have had and continue to have dramatic consequences for the modern nation-state,"[57] he points out that as the impact of globalization varies among states (as nation-states themselves vary dramatically in form) and across issues, generalizations are therefore risky.[58] Susan Strange notes that "the impersonal forces of world markets, integrated over the postwar period more by private enterprise in finance, industry and trade than by the cooperative decisions of governments, are now more powerful than the states to whom ultimate political authority over society and economy is supposed to belong."[59]

Strange believes that changed world circumstances has meant that states are losing their power to direct economies. Macroeconomist Robert Boyer argues that the market alone will not be a successful coordinating mechanism in the new world order: "Markets only become truly efficient when they are embedded into systems developed by the state or private corporations which then play the role of government."[60]

Kenichi Ohmae takes the view that globalization will bring significant economic benefits. As the world becomes increasingly interlinked, with the United States, Europe, and Japan at the centre, government's main role now "is to ensure that its people have a good life by ensuring stable access to the best and the cheapest goods and services from anywhere in the world."[61] To him, "In the interlinked economy, it does not matter who builds the factory or who owns the office building or whose money lies behind the shopping mall or whose equity makes the local operation possible. What matters is that the global corporations that, one way or another, do business within a set of political borders, act as responsible corporate citizens. If they do, no matter what their home country, they will treat the people fairly, give them good work to do, and provide them with valuable products and services. If they do not, the people will neither work for them nor buy what they produce."[62]

Ohmae's view was too optimistic for some. Who builds the factory or owns the office building does make a difference, critics have said. Ownership, in fact, can determine a corporation's commitment to the community in which it operates and whether or not the company treats its employees fairly. While far from perfect, local corporations tend to be more committed to their community because it is home to those who manage the corporation, and they plan to be there over the long term. Corporations from far away are more likely to pull out as soon as circumstances change. Anti-globalization protesters, in particular, think that views like Ohmae's are naive at best, given the many examples, past and future, of companies that have not treated their workers fairly, given them good work to do, or provided them with valuable products and services. The statement that people will not work for bad companies nor buy what they produce assumes that workers have a choice, when in many instances they do not.

Former U.S. Secretary of Labour Robert Reich had a slightly different outlook. While he agreed that companies operate globally and that it does not matter much which country owns what, he believed that it is important to enable a country's citizens to add value to the world economy and thereby improve their standard of living.[63] Reich thought it incumbent on a government to maximize the national economic benefits that companies can bring, no matter where they are headquartered. Reich saw globalization as an opportunity for nations to work together, "to enhance global welfare rather than to advance one nation's well-being by reducing another's."[64]

In writings like those of Reich and Ohmae, there is often a sense that globalization, free trade, and an unfettered marketplace are a "done deal," that there are no alternatives, that governments no longer have any power nor are likely to have any in the future. Linda McQuaig, in discussing this phenomena (primarily in the context of inflation and unemployment), argues that the Canadian government has accepted neo-classical doctrines so profoundly that it has abandoned its role, right, and responsibility to work in the best interests of its citizens. To those who say that world economic forces have rendered the state powerless, McQuaig responds that the willingness of national governments to respond to the dictates of the financial marketplace indicates that the state is anything but powerless, that it can act decisively to meet the needs of certain economic interests, and can have substantial influence: "The obstacles preventing us from gaining control over our economic lives have little to do with globalization and technology. Governments have backed off from taking action to fight unemployment and provide well-funded social programs not because they lack the means but because they've chosen to render themselves impotent, powerless in the face of capital markets. The technological imperative turns out to be mostly a failure of will on the part of government."[65]

Others were also unsure – both of the reality of globalization and of its benefits. Daniel Drache has pointed out that after four decades of liberalized trade, less than one-quarter of all trade can be considered free.[66] Political economist Manfred Bienefeld did not believe that globalization will increase prosperity. Rather, he said globalization "is far more likely to yield instability, conflict and polarization ultimately leading to stagnation and decline."[67] In a detailed examination of the mythology and free enterprise euphoria surrounding globalization, Paul Hirst and Grahame Thompson acknowledge that internationalization is occurring but argue that it is "well short of dissolving distinct national economies in the major advanced industrial countries."[68]

Paul Doremus with his colleagues discovered in a study of multinational corporations that a strong link exists between corporate behaviour and national cultures and operating styles. The United States, Germany, and Japan are the home bases for a large proportion of the globe's multinational companies. In each case, "enduring national political structures continue to shape the operations that most decisively determine the futures of those corporations – their internal governance and long-term financing operations, their research and development (R&D) programs, and their direct investment and intrafirm trading strategies. At the core of the world's leading multinationals, in short, there is no such thing as globalization."[69]

Martin Carnoy of Stanford University has shown that multinationals are closely tied to their home countries. He pointed out that American parent operations hold approximately 78% of all assets, 70% of sales, and 74% of employment of U.S. multinationals (1988 figures).[70]

Japanese figures could well be higher. In addition, most multinationals depend on their home markets for acquiring capital and for high end research and development.[71] The nation-state, therefore, remains crucial as the future of a multinational company is closely tied to the strength of its home economy.

THE FUTURE OF THE NATION-STATE

While there is a considerable literature that critiques contemporary assumptions about globalization and advocates a return to government-directed economies, it is important to consider briefly a related body of analysis on the future of the nation-state. Scholars have been observing a variety of competing trends in recent years, including economic and cultural globalization,[72] declining support for the integrity of the nation-state, a rise in ethnic nationalism and regionalism (with consequent threats to the integrity of the territorial state), the continued power of multinational corporations,[73] and the emergence of new technologies that, in their complexity and speed, defy the ability of national governments to regulate or control them.[74] At their most extreme, these analysts argue that the nation-state, as currently configured and understood, will dissolve over time, retaining at best minimal functions and providing limited direction for the citizenry.[75] Less dramatic interpretations argue that nations are losing their territorial imperative and no longer exercise tight control over a defined physical space, that the role of government will decline in many non-essential areas, that devolution to local or regional authorities will accelerate.

Peter Drucker nicely tied together the concerns about globalization, the changing nation-state, and the role of government in the management of national economies when he argued that "Despite all its shortcomings, the nation-state has shown amazing resilience ... So far, at least, there is no other institution capable of political integration and effective membership in the world's political community. In all probability, therefore, the nation-state will survive the globalization of the economy and the information revolution that accompanies it. But it will be a greatly changed nation-state, especially in domestic fiscal and monetary policies, foreign economic politics, control of international business, and, perhaps, in its conduct of war."[76]

Vincent Cable, contending that national functions are increasingly being overtaken by international governance and regulation, suggests that "It is tempting to conclude that economic globalization has made the traditional nation-state redundant. The truth is much messier ... National economic sovereignty is being eroded, slowly and differentially, not eliminated."[77]

Thus the debate about the role of the state in the management of economic affairs will continue in a different context, one in which the basic functions, operations, and even existence of the nation-state are questioned. The somewhat short-term outlook of much of this writing is best exemplified in Francis Fukuyama's argument, made on the basis of the brief euphoria that surrounded the collapse of the former Soviet Union, that liberal democracy and capitalism had carried the great struggle of the twentieth century and would remain ascendant thereafter.[78] The continued crises in Russia, the fall-out from the economic turmoil in East Asia, and the re-emergence of the left as a political force in the western industrialized world suggests that the old order, including the nation-state, might well prove more resilient than some analysts have assumed.

OTHER INFLUENCES: CULTURE, DOMESTIC POLITICS, CORPORATE-GOVERNMENT RELATIONS, AND INTERNATIONAL BUSINESS

While this study focuses on national governments, policy-making, and the national experience in international trade, it is simplistic and inaccurate to assume that ideological, policy, and political considerations represent the sum total of the major influences on a nation's international trading activity. Canada, for all its rhetoric about being a global trading nation, has performed poorly by international standards, for reasons that are as much cultural as economic. Much the same can be said for New Zealand and Australia. Assessing the nature and impact of cultural influences on national business and economic development is, however, a separate project, albeit one that proceeds logically from this study. Scholars are just beginning to explore the influence that culture has on business. This study shows that the responses of Canada, New Zealand, and Australia to the Japanese market reflect elements of their history and contemporary political systems; it offers only preliminary observations on the degree to which national culture influenced these trading relationships. While it is widely recognized that culture has an impact on business, in what way and why is much more difficult to measure. Analysts in marketing and advertising have struggled for years with the more superficial aspects of culture and language to determine what influences purchasing decisions, but determining the reasons and value orientations behind those decisions is even more challenging. As business people increasingly recognize that, as Lisa Hoecklin observed, "Business and culture are not discrete, rational domains of activity separate from a society's particular cultural beliefs and values,"[79] interest in understanding differences in value orientations has grown.

The way in which value orientations combine to form a nation's business culture has been explored in only a few studies, although scholars have been noting the different forms of capitalism in European, North American, and Asian settings for some time. The hesitation in researching national business cultures is probably due to the necessity of using very large sample sizes from numerous countries to reach reliable conclusions. The most well-known study was that conducted by Geert Hofstede, who analysed over 116,000 individual responses from 67 countries to a questionnaire circulated by IBM in 1968 and 1972. His analysis, documented in *Culture's Consequences*, led him to identify four dimensions of work-related value differences: power distance, uncertainty avoidance, individualism vs. collectivism, and femininity vs. masculinity.[80] His second book, *Cultures and Organizations*,[81] re-examines this material in a style more suitable for a general audience and adds material on Michael Bond's Chinese Value Survey[82] as well as that on organizational culture differences conducted by the Institute for Research on Intercultural Cooperation.[83]

A later work by cross-cultural management consultants Charles Hampden-Turner and Alfons Trompenaars explores the business cultures of the U.S., Britain, France, Germany, Japan, Sweden, and the Netherlands. They discuss how each nation has a unique combination of values: "This value set is an economic fingerprint, which, we believe, correlates with specific types of economic achievement and failure."[84] Hampden-Turner and Trompenaars show that, while it is important to know the cultural make-up of other nations to determine how best to do business with them, a nation must also understand its own cultural make-up if it is to take control of its economic future and realize the barriers to economic growth.[85]

Business and economics scholars, most of them rooted in the western academic tradition, have focused their culture-based studies on "other" (i.e. non-western) countries and conducted relatively little research on the cultural foundations of Anglo-American business. Much has been written about Japanese culture and its influence on how Japanese people approach business and government; little has been written about similar issues in countries like Canada, New Zealand, and Australia. Scholarly and journalistic investigations of Japan's trading relationships generally emphasize the manner in which Japanese culture and commercial structure constrain imports and investment through both formal, direct methods and informal, often underlying factors (e.g. language, long-term business focus, convoluted distribution systems).[86] A much smaller body of work shifts the emphasis from cultural and structural barriers in Japan to those factors within western industrialized nations (like Canada, Australia, and New Zealand) that limit their ability to seek or seize international economic opportunities in Japan. Most of the Canadian, New Zealand, and Australian writing on culture emphasizes a search for identity and sense of self and for an explanation of what makes them different from each other and their noisier British and American cousins.[87]

Academic work on international trade and related policy developments does not give extended attention to the impact of domestic political consideration on trade initiatives, although change in the national government can, and often does, have marked effects on economic policy. In all three countries, and in fact in any democratic nation, the ebb and flow of electoral politics and internal political considerations can have a profound impact on the development of international relations. The structure of the domestic legislative and constitutional system itself helps determine this impact: New Zealand's unicameral system has the potential for providing the country with an opportunity for more decisive political action than in Canada and Australia, where power is divided between federal and provincial/state governments. Leaders are empowered in a way that Canadian and Australian leaders are not.

There are a number of ways in which rivalries between internal political jurisdictions manifest themselves. Inter-state or inter-province fighting can result in domestic decisions being made for political rather than practical reasons, and the country then loses or diminishes an opportunity to develop or increase its production of a desired product. The location of new government-sponsored industrial projects, for example, is often determined by which province or state's turn it is, or which place yells the loudest, rather than by which location makes the most practical sense. Michael Porter made this point when discussing Canada, and explained that it has meant new industries are located far from other related companies or plants, making it more difficult for them to become viable: "Competition among provinces to be the chosen location for federal development or procurement initiatives has often resulted in projects being located in areas distant from any cluster of related industries. Again, short-term job creation has usually been a higher priority than the fostering of viable industries and industry clusters."[88]

In other instances, multiple layers of government, rules that vary by jurisdiction, and competition within a country for the same offshore resources leaves potential international partners or customers at best confused, and more likely to turn their attention elsewhere. Australian industry analyst Jenny Stewart pointed out that the different Australian states even have different regulations about labeling and packaging.[89]

Inter-provincial/state battles for investment monies from abroad clearly work to the detriment of the federalist nation. Rather than a concentrated effort to bring an investment project to Canada, time, energy, and money are devoted to fighting about where this investment should go. Provinces or states work to out-bid each other to lure investment to their territory. There is no sense of a national objective or vision; the country appears fragmented, disorganized, and acrimonious. State and provincial governments often offer more in incentives to the investing company than that company had ever contemplated requesting. Money is spent unnecessarily and Canada and Australia appear, at times, to potential investors to be ridiculously desperate.

Examining the impact of domestic politics on international business development can encourage a nation to think of what is possible if it pulls together, particularly if it sees more clearly what it loses by pulling apart. Ian Marsh has proposed developing a national purpose for Australia: "the idea of a national vision or purpose would ... be differentiated from the electoral strategies that might be adopted by the major parties. A central requirement for a national vision is that it be bipartisan at least in its major elements."[90] Responsibility for developing this national vision, Marsh suggests, could be given to an independent agency like one of Australia's many think tanks.[91]

Business-government interaction sits at the centre of any consideration of international trade development. In the neo-classical economies, business keeps a careful, often critical, eye on government actions and priorities, and governments in turn look to business to support and sustain new programs initiated under the current approach to economic development. Organizations like the Business Roundtable in New Zealand purport to provide a business response to government policy proposals, although such groups tend to represent larger businesses (and often multinational business interests) and do not always have a broad, national constituency. Moreover, these organizations often speak only for one side of business and only on a limited range of issues. In Canada, Australia, and New Zealand, discussion focuses much more frequently on what governments should not be doing rather than on what positive contributions government can make. It is difficult to find examples of business encouragement for specific government initiatives, beyond cutting taxes and reducing regulatory burdens.

Nonetheless, business has long played a crucial role in national economic development and, under the neo-classical approach, now has an even more central function. Rosabeth Moss Kanter discusses ways in which towns or cities can get their populations working together to create what she calls world class regions. Business and government can participate in civic forums in which they identify the core skills of an area and the investments needed to increase the region's stock of world class concepts, competence, and connections.[92] A classic example of a company working to improve the domestic economy, Kanter says, was Wal-Mart's "Bring it Home to the USA" suppliers program, which began in 1985 when imported goods made up over one-third of Wal-Mart's sales.

To encourage manufacturers to produce goods in the United States, founder Sam Walton issued a mandate: 'Find products that American manufacturers have stopped producing because they couldn't compete with foreign imports.' Buyers targeted import items and gave lists to state industrial development agencies to find manufacturers for conversion to Wal-Mart's program. Walton wrote three thousand domestic suppliers, asking them to commit to improving facilities, machinery, and employee productivity; some 1,800 suppliers agreed. Southwest Missouri University conducted evaluations to help suppliers qualify for Wal-Mart business."[93]

Such corporate altruism is, however, relatively rare; few Canadian, Australian, or New Zealand companies wear their national pride as overtly as does Wal-Mart.

In fact, one of the themes that runs through the country comparisons that follow is the arms-length approach that business routinely takes to government policy-making and program implementation. Even in an era where the national polity has indicated a willingness to delegate considerable economic leadership to the business community, the evidence from Canada, New Zealand, and Australia is that the business sector has been reluctant to accept the responsibility. Under the neo-classical model, the business community is expected to set the direction, provide leadership, and ensure national prosperity by responding creatively to the commercial opportunities that arise in a globalized economy. The corporate response to efforts by the governments of New Zealand, Canada, and Australia to promote international trade suggests that the business sector has not yet fully accepted its role in the new economic order.

THE AMERICAN "MIRACLE" AND MANAGEMENT OF NATIONAL ECONOMIES

Through the 1990s, the sustained and remarkable performance of the American economy raised serious doubts in many quarters about the value of government-led industrial policy. Public and political discussion about the role of government in the economy has been shaped by international understanding of the United States government's limited role in economic management. With the Cold War over, and the accompanying decline in U.S. military spending, the American government accepted a far less active role in the direction and management of the national economy. Instead, under the direction of Federal Reserve Chairman Alan Greenspan, the United States administration focused on underlying economic conditions. Greenspan worked to keep inflation in check, lower interest rates, and thereby use macroeconomic monetary policy to shape the American economy. The administration of President Bill Clinton, locked in a series of messy personal and political conflicts with the Republican-dominated House and Senate, offered little in the way of proactive industrial policy. The result – to the delight of neo-classical economists the world over – was a decade-long economic expansion and one of the most prosperous periods in U.S. history. While Greenspan received a great deal of credit for his skillful handling of American monetary policy, there was general agreement in the United States and abroad that the hands-off approach to economic policy had aided in the expansion of the world-leading American economy.[94] The major government initiatives in this period, including the negotiation of the North American Free Trade Agreement with Canada and Mexico, clearly assisted economic growth but were not responsible for it.

The high technology sector stood at the forefront of the United States' economic miracle of continuing low unemployment, negligible inflation, low interest rates, and soaring business expansion. Capitalizing on the country's risk-taking investment climate, dot-com and high technology companies saw their market capitalization and stock prices soar to unimagined levels. Companies like Microsoft, Sun Systems, Cisco, Intel, Yahoo!, Amazon.com, e-Bay, and the like became the darlings of an investment boom that generated thousands of overnight millionaires and brought great optimism throughout the country. Average personal incomes rose dramatically, and if the distribution was skewed and if the gap between rich and poor escalated significantly, the country nonetheless celebrated its role as the world's strongest, fastest-growing, and most dynamic economy. Political leaders, in office and in opposition, offered no strong vision of government-led industrial development, but rather spoke with enthusiasm about maintaining the status quo on the economic front and focusing on such "fundamentals" as education, crime, and social security.

America's continued economic success through to the winter of 2000–01 offered a compelling counterpoint to those who advocated – largely for other countries – a more interventionist approach. Japan, for example, faced a steady barrage of advice, from inside and outside the country, about how it should shelve its government-directed approach to economic development in favour of deregulation, privatization, freer trade, looser investment rules, and low taxation. The arguments seemed compelling as the American economic machine continued moving forward. At the end of 2000, however, major cracks began to appear. The fiasco around energy deregulation in California left the country's most populous state and a key leader in the "new economy" with rotating blackouts and great uncertainties about private sector energy management. More dramatically, the collapsing prices for high technology and dot-com stocks in 2000–01 stripped much of the vitality from the risk-capital sector, reduced the wealth of "paper" millionaires, and added new stresses and uncertainties into the American marketplace. The decline – either the foreshadowing of a major economic change and, potentially, a recession, or a normal adjustment related to an overheated investment climate – might result in a rethinking of American economic policy, although that is unlikely. The United States, like most western countries, appears wedded to the idea of laissez-faire economics and the concept of limited state involvement in the management of the national economy – even though a more critical evaluation of American economic policy shows that the U.S. government was actually quick to intervene when it thought American economic interests were threatened. Canadians were particularly sensitive to American self-interest on economic issues as they contended with government-led attacks on everything from softwood lumber to the film industry.

This review of the major intellectual currents relating to the role of the state in the managing of national economies reveals both the complexity and intensity of the issue. For politicians and analysts alike, this question strikes at the heart of contemporary discussions about the political process, the relationship between government and business, national responsibility for economic prosperity, and ongoing debates about the power – or powerlessness – of the state in an era of globalization. These debates have been pushed forward by the pressures of contemporary events, including the formidable rise of Asian economic power, Japan's ascendancy as an economic superpower, and the East Asian financial crisis of 1998. The lengthy run of economic prosperity in major western industrial nations, capped by the continued strength of the American economy, the seeming success of the New Zealand "experiment" in national economic liberalization, and the continued power of multinational corporations give practical evidence of the potential value of the neo-classical approach to economic management. But many observers are less sanguine about a globalized economy run according to the dictates of international business, and worry about regional and national economic disparities, about state systems that place trade liberalization ahead of pressing domestic social and cultural needs, and about the seemingly widespread western political acceptance of the idea that national governments can no longer aspire to control and manage state economies.

Analysis of the contributions of leading thinkers on this topic demonstrates that much remains unanswered about the received wisdom concerning neo-classical economic approaches, and that even basic assumptions about the shape and nature of the nation-state and of globalization need to be carefully considered. For the purposes of this study, arguments advanced by Robert Wade, Ian Marsh, Jenny Stewart, John Hobson, Daniel Drache, and Linda Weiss, and approaches to state involvement advocated by Michael Porter illustrate the strong body of analysis and interpretation that supports continued state involvement in the management of national economies. While many of these authors would argue that the social-democratic structures of the 1970s and 1980s limited economic flexibility and interfered with the ability of national economies to respond to developing opportunities, they (and others) share a common view that business-led, laissez-faire economics is rarely in a country's best interest. Moreover, many scholars agree that the issues of globalization, the changing role of the nation-state, and national government responsibility for economic management will have a profound and direct influence on the prosperity of individual nations and on the level of citizens' satisfaction with their national governments.

2 Patterns of Japan's Trade and Investment with Canada, New Zealand, and Australia before 1985

Much of the debate surrounding the current and future role of the nation-state in the management of economic affairs is based on only partial understanding of past government actions. Understanding the manner in which governments historically interceded in the creation and maintenance of international trading opportunities helps place more recent activities in context. For much of the twentieth century, national governments in Canada, New Zealand, and Australia provided only the most basic assistance to companies seeking to expand overseas; laissez-faire economics of the type advocated for the present period has a long history in the western industrial world. Only for a relatively brief period, from the 1960s to the 1980s, did truly activist states seek to control and direct commercial and economic affairs – and, even then, most governments acted within a very narrow range of options and considerations, most of them based on historical trading opportunities.

Thus, although the nature and scale of trade with and investment from Japan changed markedly in the final fifteen years of the twentieth century, the opportunities now available to Canada, Australia, and New Zealand owe much to the links established before the 1985 Plaza Accord. Just as surely, today's narrowness of vision, political and administrative stumbling blocks, and cultural impediments standing in the way of commercial success and stronger ties with Japan likewise originated in earlier decades of contact and exchange.

Despite the similarities among the three countries, each has had its own unique relationship with Japan. A look at their respective initial contacts with the Japanese is instructive. The first known Canadian in Japan was Ranald MacDonald, born of a Hudson's Bay Company trader father and a west coast aboriginal mother. In 1848 he signed on to a whaling ship heading to the Far East, asking in advance to be let off near the island of Hokkaido. He was held under quasi-arrest by Japanese authorities in Nagasaki and pressed into service as an English teacher. One of his students, Enosuke Moriyama, eventually served as an interpreter for U.S. Commodore Perry. (Given the large number of Canadians teaching English in contemporary Asia, it is appropriate that the first English teacher was a Canadian.) One of the earliest Japan-New Zealand connections was two American brothers from New Zealand who operated a paddle steamer between Yokohama and Tokyo in the late 1860s. It is also thought that these two men established a coach service between the same Japanese cities for the Australian company Cobb and Co.[1] An early example of Kiwi entrepreneurship, it is also fitting that the New Zealanders were working for a non-New Zealand company. The most famous early Australian in Japan was Henry Black, a *rakugo* or vaudeville performer. Around the turn of the century, he traveled the country with his troupe of six and his Japanese wife, telling stories and doing impersonations. He was famous enough to be asked to recite for the Crown Prince.[2] While these examples demonstrate a certain amount of style and courage, it is interesting to observe, in the context of future trends, that all the individuals involved were selling a service, not a product, and that their objectives and the benefits were personal, and not for king or country.

CANADA

Until the 1930s, Canada was a diplomatic satellite of Great Britain, relying on the mother country for overseas representation. Only slowly did Canada establish missions abroad and develop its foreign service. Japan, in contrast, moved fairly rapidly in the early twentieth century to create an international presence, largely to encourage overseas trade, to counter the entrenched stereotypes about Japanese society, to learn more about the industrial advances in the western world, and to defend the interests of Japanese nationals emigrating to foreign countries. Not surprisingly, then, Japan created a diplomatic presence in Canada before Canada developed one in Japan.[3]

The Japanese Consulate General in Vancouver was established in 1889 and was followed in 1903 with an additional office in Ottawa. Both offices were opened primarily in response to the growing number of Japanese immigrants to British Columbia and the mounting hostility against them. Tensions exploded with the Vancouver riot of 1907 and in 1908 a 'Gentleman's Agreement' was signed in which Japan voluntarily slowed emigration to Canada.

In other matters, the existence of treaties between Britain and Japan, accords to which Canada was, as a member of the British empire, automatically tied, set the parameters for Canadian actions. The Anglo-Japanese Alliance, signed in 1902 and renewed in 1911, made Japan an ally of Canada, at least through the troubled years of World War I. When the accord came up for renewal again in 1921, Prime Minister Arthur Meighan was instrumental in having the agreement scrapped in favour of a new Four Power (Britain, Japan, United States, and France) treaty. Canada signed as a member of the British delegation.

The Canadian government appointed its first trade representative to Japan in 1897 and opened a trade office in Yokohama in 1904. Gradually, the country realized that it should not continue to rely on British diplomats to handle Canadian consular matters and decided it needed a more direct presence in Japan. In 1928 an exchange of ministers between Canada and Japan was negotiated and the following year Herbert Marler became Canada's first minister to Japan. The Japan station was only the fourth mission Canada had established overseas (after Washington, London, and Paris) and was therefore of considerable significance in Canada's embryonic international operations.

The first Japanese minister to Canada, Prince Iyemasu Tokugawa, arrived in Ottawa in the fall of 1929 and remained for five years. Tensions between the two countries increased as Japanese militarism escalated through the 1930s. Canada supported the League of Nations' statement of censure over the Japanese invasion of Manchuria, but the growing importance of Canada's trade with Japan kept diplomatic relations on a relatively even keel. However, when Canadians in Asia found themselves in the path of Japanese armies or attacked by anti-foreigner mobs in Japan, feelings hardened, and when Japan joined Germany and Italy to form the Axis alliance, the cries for a cessation of Canadian trade with Japan and further restrictions on Japanese immigration grew louder.

Japan figured minimally in Canadian plans for the twenty years following the Second World War, although a liaison mission was re-established. (Canada was, through much of this time, also coming to terms with the manner in which it had treated Japanese-Canadians during the war, including the forced evacuation from their homes on the British Columbia coast and the confiscation and sale of their goods at rock-bottom prices.) Japan's historic ties to the Canadian resource sector, combined with the demands of its rapidly growing industrial economy, ensured that trade links between the two countries would resume and then expand. Most of this expansion took place with relatively little assistance from the Canadian government or business community. The Japanese identified what they needed and Canadians were pleased to sell to them, provided the price was right.

The Trudeau government of the 1970s, worried that Canada was becoming too dependent on the United States, made some efforts to expand economic and diplomatic contacts with the European Community and with Japan. A strong personal relationship developed between Prime Minister Trudeau and Yasuhiko Nara, the Japanese ambassador to Canada, resulting in 1976 in a 'Framework for Economic Cooperation.' However, within the following decade, it was apparent that little had changed in Canada-Japan relations. The civil service and the Canadian business community were not prepared to put substance into the political rhetoric and Canada moved toward increased integration with the United States, culminating in the Canada-United States Free Trade Agreement (1988) and later, with Mexico, the North American Free Trade Agreement (1992), a blazingly clear indication that Canada saw its future as inextricably tied to the United States.

Trade between Canada and Japan began a decade before Japan established its Vancouver consulate: ironically, given Canada's future resource-dominated trade with Japan, a shipment of manufactured goods sent from Canada to Japan is recorded in 1878. It was around 1885–86, however, with the completion of the Canadian Pacific Railway and the establishment of shipping connections between the two countries, that regular trade began to grow steadily.

Canada sought markets for its traditional trading goods, primarily forest products, grain, and fish, hoping to offset declining trade with Britain and to avoid too great a dependence on the United States. Lumber and wooden ships' masts went to Japan in 1886, a small amount of coal was sent in 1891, the first shipments of wheat and salted herring were exported in 1892, followed by salted salmon in 1896 and Douglas fir lumber in 1903. Japanese immigrants to Canada were among the first to identify the potential trade opportunities across the Pacific, and these small traders led the way in establishing business connections with Japan.

Japan's first entrée into the international marketplace was with tea and silk. The initial shipment of silk from Japan reached Canada in 1887. Silk was to Japan as wheat was to Canada in the late nineteenth century, earning 40% of Japan's foreign exchange and therefore a crucial resource, along with tea, in enabling the country to purchase foreign technology and manufactured goods. Japan's rapid industrialization rested, therefore, on the exports of this most traditional of Japanese products. By the late 1920s, silk represented over 60% of Canada's imports from Japan. 'Silk Expresses,' Canadian Pacific Railway trains running the raw product to textile mills in New York where most of it was turned into ladies' stockings, burst into prominence. The west coast port of Vancouver and the Canadian Pacific rail system owes much of its early prosperity to the steady flow of silk from Asia to North America.

Over the years, Canada found ready markets in Japan for its raw materials, but this seldom resulted from Canadian initiative. Early in the century, the Japanese consul general in Canada, Tatsugoro Nosse, observed that Japanese buyers had difficulty finding Canadian firms interested in selling into the Japanese market. Instead, large Japanese trading companies actively sought out Canadian products, particularly raw materials, often guaranteeing or financing part of the cost of extracting the resources. Canadian business devoted more energy to restricting imports in textiles and other manufactures, for example, than it did promoting its exports to countries such as Japan, which were clearly eager to buy.

Sir Wilfrid Laurier, prime minister from 1896 to 1911, was the first Canadian leader to become truly enthusiastic about the prospects for Canadian trade with Japan. Laurier and his ministers believed Canada could export pulp and paper, fresh and canned fruit, preserved beef, pork, butter, cheese, and fish to this newfound market. Their most hearty enthusiasm was reserved for the export potential of wheat, as the prime minister felt that bread could replace rice as the staple food of Japan. The Japanese failed to fit into Laurier's grand scheme, but his vision of transcontinental prosperity ensured that the Canadian government began to take Japan seriously.

Japan's rapid industrial expansion during World War I created additional opportunities. Canada began to export lead, nickel, zinc, and aluminum on a relatively large scale and Japan became a primary customer for these products. By 1929, the year that Canada established a diplomatic presence in Japan, Japan had become Canada's fifth largest trading partner, with 3.1% of Canada's exports going to Japan and 1% of its imports coming from there.[4] Canada's exports then consisted mostly of wheat and flour (51% of total exports to Japan in 1929), fish, and wood products.

In the pre-World War II period, when Canada was either slightly ahead of, or on par with, Japan in industrial terms, markets also existed for Canadian manufactured products. A few items – shoes, tires, automobiles, and electrical equipment – found Japanese purchasers, and in 1935, manufactured goods represented 24.5% of Canadian exports to Japan, although this was due at least in part to the reduction of resource exports caused by trade conflicts between the two countries. Problems began in 1931 when Canada increased tariffs on certain imports, duties that fell disproportionately on Japanese imports. In retaliation, the Japanese government soon placed an additional 50% duty on Canadian wheat, flour, lumber, wood pulp, and wrapping paper. Canada again responded in kind, levying a duty of 33 1/3% on all Japanese imports. The 1935 Canadian election resulted in a change of government and the introduction of a less protectionist trade policy. New regulations saw a return to pre-existing trade arrangements, and manufactured products dropped to less than 2% of total Canadian exports.

Canada-Japan trade leveled off at the end of World War I, but three years later, in 1922, Canadian exports to Japan surpassed Japanese exports to Canada for the first time. Canadian import markets remained the domain of American and British traders, and Japanese exports languished through the 1920s and 1930s as cotton and manufactured textiles took over from silk and the traditional Japanese trade evaporated. Canadian businesses imported a small volume of household and novelty goods, but Japan had very little to sell that Canada could not get more cheaply or more reliably elsewhere. At the same time, Canadian sales to Japan grew substantially. In 1929 Canadian exports hit a pre-war high of over C$42 million, almost C$30 million more than Japan managed to sell to Canada that same year.

Japan's aggression in the Far East in the late 1930s slowed pre-war commercial relations considerably. Canadians reacted to Japanese expansionism and military prowess by clamping on a series of trade restrictions, only to have Japan retaliate in kind. When Japan joined the Second World War in 1941, trade ceased for the duration of the conflict. Only in 1947, with the Allied Occupation fully in place in Japan and most of the wartime leadership relegated to the sidelines, did Canada re-establish trade contacts with Japan. Lingering wartime stereotypes and hostilities in conjunction with the devastation wrought on Japan's economy prevented a rapid expansion of commercial links.

By the end of the war, Japan was physically and psychologically flattened. Brought to its knees by the final American bombardments, Japan faced the formidable task of rebuilding. The country desperately needed food and the raw materials necessary to revive its crippled industries. Traditional Asian suppliers, who were themselves recovering from the war or, as in China, were engulfed in revolution, could not readily supply Japan's needs. But Canada could. It had abundant grain, forest products, and minerals. It also had a sizable industrial base, hastily retooling from the production of military materials to consumer goods. Japanese authorities were soon worried about an over-dependence on Canadian resources, particularly since Canada appeared reluctant to purchase Japanese goods. Anxious to continue selling, Canadian politicians and business leaders recognized Japanese concerns and soon began to open the Canadian market to Japanese imports – principally inexpensive manufactured goods and textiles.

The Korean War had a tremendous impact on Japan's economy. U.S. purchases of Japanese goods escalated dramatically and sparked a major expansion of Japanese industry. The Japanese turned to the revitalization of their economy with the same drive and determination they had committed to the war effort and, by the mid-1950s, cheap imports from Japan flooded into western markets. Canadian consumers benefitted from the importation of cheap Japanese trade goods, which capitalized on abundant, hard-working, and inexpensive Japanese labour. Competing Canadian industries, particularly a beleaguered domestic textile industry long sustained by protective tariffs and government benevolence, suffered serious losses. But the Canadian appetite for cheap imports had been whetted, and there was little prospect of closing off these trade ties. Canadians could scarcely complain – exports to Japan topped C$127 million in 1956, more than three times higher than the best pre-World War II annual trade. Even though imports sky-rocketed from slightly more than C$3 million in 1948 to over C$60 million by 1956, Canada maintained a very favourable balance of trade with Japan.

Over the following three decades, until the dramatic reorientation of Japanese trade in the mid-1980s, Canada-Japan trade followed along the basic track laid down in the post-war period. Canada sold an ever-increasing volume of raw materials to Japan – minerals, lumber, pulp and paper, and foodstuffs – and purchased an equally rapidly growing quantity of manufactured goods from Japan. Canada maintained a healthy surplus throughout this period (except for 1972 when imports from Japan exceeded Canadian exports), supporting Canada's continued belief that its seemingly inexhaustible supply of resources would sustain prosperity indefinitely.

The principal change in this period occurred on the Japanese side. Through the 1960s, Japan's exports to Canada consisted of low-priced, inexpensively produced consumer goods – the type that gave the label 'made in Japan' an unappealing public image. Canadian competitors, particularly in the textile trades, maintained their criticism of 'unfair' Japanese trade, but limited consumer interest placed a cap on the value and impact of Japanese trade goods. But then Japan began the transformation of its economy that became the country's hallmark.

Table 2.1   Canadian exports to and imports from Japan, selected years 1961–1985 (US$m)

Year	Exports			Imports		
	Japan	Total	Canadian % of Total	Japan	Total	Canadian % of Total
1961	232	5,865	4.1	117	5,786	2.0
1965	293	8,107	3.6	213	7,987	2.7
1970	762	16,179	4.7	557	13,357	4.2
1975	2,081	33,990	6.1	1,185	35,140	3.4
1980	3,751	67,730	5.5	2,384	61,004	3.9
1985	4,222	90,780	4.7	4,475	78,673	5.7

Source: International Monetary Fund, *Direction of Trade Statistics Yearbooks*, various editions 1960–89

Table 2.2   Commodity composition of exports, Canada to Japan, 1970–1980

Commodity	1970 (%)	1975 (%)	1980 (%)
Live animals	0.1	0.1	0.2
Food, feed, beverages, and tobacco	16.1	25.5	17.5
Crude materials, inedible*	50.1	55.4	44.7
Fabricated materials, inedible**	31.1	15.9	35.2
End products, inedible***	2.5	3.1	2.4

   *Grains, ore, pulp, and natural gas
  **Leather, lumber, pulp, wood products, metals, organic and inorganic chemicals
***Machinery, transportation and communication equipment, personal and household goods, miscellaneous end products
Source: Statistics Canada, *Exports-Merchandise*, various editions, Catalogue 65-202 Annual

The production of low-end products was handed over to new low-wage economies in Southeast Asia, and Japan reoriented its industrial plant to focus on new technologies, particularly steel, automobile manufacturing, and ship-building.

The first automobiles matched the Japanese reputation for exporting 'cheap' goods. The early Datsun (Nissan), Toyota, and Honda products were inexpensive, lightly built, and small, and were quickly adopted as commuter vehicles and second family cars. North American manufacturers paid little attention, scarcely perceiving the Japanese cars as much of a threat, so confident were they of their market share. They were wrong, for although consumer loyalty to the Big Three North American automobile manufacturers (Chrysler, Ford, and General Motors) has proved reasonably strong, the quality of the

Japanese automobiles improved dramatically from the 1960s to the mid-1970s, moving from low-end commuter vehicles to high quality, reasonably priced, and eminently reliable mid-range vehicles. Cars like the Honda Civic, Toyota Corolla, and Datsun 610 became familiar on Canadian roads, and higher cost cars – Datsun 240Z, Mazda RX7, and even four-wheel drive vehicles – competed favourably with North American products.

Japan quickly capitalized on other commercial opportunities. Although the Japanese, at this point, developed few new products on their own, they perfected the art of copying and adapting expensive items for mass consumption. Miniaturization and the use of transistors sparked a veritable flood of Japanese electronic products into North America, pushing many North American producers out of the market and establishing a Japanese ascendancy. By the late 1970s, Japan had transformed its commercial image from an exporter of cheap trade goods to the manufacturer of the world's most reliable and inexpensive automobiles, and the best electronic products. Japanese manufacturers and traders had completed a stunning reversal of corporate and national imagery, establishing Japanese products at the forefront of the consumer electronics revolution.

Japanese investments in Canada have traditionally been made to support Japan's internal industrial requirements. Beginning early in the twentieth century but accelerating in the 1960s, Japanese companies invested in Canadian resources to guarantee themselves access to timber, minerals, and food supplies. Forest products, copper, and coal were the chief areas of investment. Many of the agreements came in the form of joint ventures with Japanese trading companies (*sogo shosha*). Japanese companies also often took minor equity positions in Canadian companies whose products they desired, copper being a prime example. Almost fifty per cent of the Japanese investment made in Canadian resource development came in the form of loans, including corporate bonds and debentures. Initially, the amount of money involved was small because, prior to the 1960s, Japan was not particularly active in foreign investments and because Canada was not deemed a prime investment market.

The initial wave of resource investment peaked in the early 1970s when, according to geographer David Edgington, "investments in local assembly industries were also made to facilitate the continued exports of parts and components from Japan and to overcome Canadian tariffs and other forms of trade protection. Throughout this period, Japanese trading companies and banks set up offices in Canada to assist both exports and imports."[5] Throughout the 1980s Japan steadily increased its presence in Canada, moving from being the eighth largest foreign investor in Canada to the third largest, behind the United States and the United Kingdom. As discussed in chapter 4, the vast majority of this increase occurred after 1985. From 1980 through 1982, pulp and paper and mining were the primary recipients of Japanese investment capital. Investment in both sectors declined after 1982, but pulp and paper investment experienced a resurgence of activity after 1986.

Canada's relationship with Japan until 1985 was, overall, a positive one. The two countries became involved early on in their respective diplomatic lives, each establishing a presence in the other's country before the turn of the century. Canada had a seemingly limitless supply of many of the resources Japan needed in order to industrialize, and Japan was not only willing to buy but, in many instances, Japanese companies were prepared to help finance the costs of obtaining the resources they needed. Japan moved from selling silk and tea to selling automobiles and electronics, but Canada made few changes in its export mix, content with the status quo and reassured as the balance of trade between the two countries remained in Canada's favour from 1886 to 1984.[6] Canada remained focused on the United States and put little effort into pursuing the Japanese market or diversifying its exports.

It is not surprising then, but it should be upsetting for Canadians, that, as analyst Klaus Pringsheim concluded, "Japan remains unwilling to regard Canada as anything more than a resource hinterland of the United States and is as yet not disposed to consider Canada as a major potential supplier of manufactured and processed goods for the Japanese market, nor as a sophisticated industrial nation, distinct and separate from the United States."[7] He might have added that this approach has generally been acceptable to Canada.

NEW ZEALAND

New Zealand-Japan relations were extremely limited prior to the Second World War. This was partly because prior to 1945, New Zealand did not have much of an international presence. Indeed, it did not have a Department of External Affairs until 1943, and much of its foreign relations were conducted for it by Britain. The first contacts, therefore, were the result of agreements between Japan and Britain, like the agreement regarding 'the expenses incurred for shipwrecked subjects' from 1878 to 1911 to which New Zealand was a party. As with Canada, the Anglo-Japanese Alliance of 1902 made Japan and New Zealand allies during World War I; battlecruiser HIJMS *Ibuki* escorted New Zealand troops to war in Europe in 1915.[8]

The first Japanese official responsible for New Zealand, K. Ueno, was the Japanese consul, who arrived in Sydney in 1908. The first Japanese consul-general in Wellington, Kiichi Gunji, arrived in April 1938, although there was an honorary consul for Japan in Wellington from 1897 (Alfred Aldrich, originally from Britain, worked on the railways in Japan and then retired to New Zealand in this position)[9] and in Auckland from 1919.[10] Japanese emigration to New Zealand was minimal; prior to the Second World War, only twelve Japanese people became New Zealand citizens.[11]

The Japanese consulate closed in December 1941 upon the declaration of war. New Zealand played a limited role in the Pacific War against Japan (most of the country's troops were committed to Europe), but it was part of the occupation forces and a signatory to the Japanese terms of surrender. Indirectly, however, the war of Japanese aggression had a profound impact on the country. New Zealanders feared a Japanese invasion and prepared an extensive network of civil defense positions. They welcomed the large American armed forces to their country and followed the Allied advance across the Pacific Islands with rapt attention and growing confidence. New Zealanders developed a strong antipathy toward the Japanese, one influenced by government wartime propaganda, and the effects of this anger lingered long after 1945. After the war, New Zealand was worried about future security in the Pacific and pushed unsuccessfully for a more restrictive settlement with Japan.[12] In 1947, a non-diplomatic trade representative, R. Challis, was appointed to Tokyo. His trade office became the first New Zealand legation in Japan upon the signing of the San Francisco Peace Treaty in 1952. The next year, the Japanese opened an office in Wellington.

Bilateral political relations improved quickly. Sir Sydney Holland's visit to Japan in 1956 was the first official visit by a New Zealand prime minister. Prime Minister Nobusuke Kishi made a return visit to New Zealand in 1957 and set the pattern for a relatively regular schedule of visits of the leaders of the two countries. Over the following twenty-five years, official relations expanded. Various accords were signed, including an Agreement on Commerce (1958), an Exchange of Notes on Full Relationships under the GATT (1962), a Double Taxation Convention (1963), Fisheries Agreements (1967 and 1978), and an Air Services Agreement (1980).[13] Direct flights from Auckland to Tokyo began in 1980, and in 1985 New Zealand opened a Consulate General in Osaka.

Trade between New Zealand and Japan began in the 1880s but was extremely limited until well into the 1920s. New Zealand produced a relatively limited range of products and only some of these – wool and sheepskins particularly – were of much interest to the Japanese. New Zealand's other main exports, dairy products and frozen meat, were not part of the average Japanese diet. Transportation of goods was an additional challenge as, until the mid-1930s, there was no direct shipping service between New Zealand and Japan; all goods had to be sent via Australia and reloaded there with all the costs and delays that involved.[14] New Zealand was not too concerned, however, as it was primarily interested in maintaining its share of the British and, to a lesser extent, American markets. New Zealand had the opportunity in 1895 and again in 1911 to become party to the Anglo-Japanese Commercial Treaty but declined both times, primarily out of fear of possible Japanese immigration.[15] Nonetheless, small quantities of wool, sheepskins, butter, and tallow were exported to Japan and larger amounts of silk, cotton, footwear, clothing, glassware, and toys were imported.[16]

Japan's period of rapid industrial expansion during and after World War I stimulated trade between New Zealand and Japan. In 1928 Japan dramatically increased its purchases of New Zealand wool, and for the first time in the history of the relationship, the balance of trade tipped in New Zealand's favour.[17] In this same year, the two nations signed a limited trade agreement, New Zealand's first with a non-Commonwealth nation.[18]

Exports to Japan as a percentage of New Zealand's total exports fluctuated considerably during the 1930s. In 1930 only 0.3% of New Zealand's exports went to Japan but by 1937 this had reached 4.7%, making Japan New Zealand's third most important customer, after Britain and the United States, for a brief period of time. An increase in sales of wool, partly due to a trade dispute between Australia and Japan, was the main reason for the surge, but sales of tallow, casein (a protein found in milk that forms the basis of cheese), dried and preserved milk, scrap metal, and even butter and meat expanded. Imports from Japan also increased in 1936 and 1937, with cotton and linen clothing, toys, and hosiery making up the bulk of the increase while purchases of silk and linen declined.[19]

Trade began to drop after 1937. The New Zealand government strongly encouraged the growth of domestic industries and restricted the importation of non-essential goods, which included the majority of Japanese imports. This, combined with wartime restrictions on Japanese industry and a boycott of Japanese goods in New Zealand following Japan's invasion of Manchuria, further limited the trading relationship. Even wool exports were down as Japan purchased most of what it needed from Australia.[20]

After World War II, trade between New Zealand and Japan did not resume in earnest until 1948. Britain and Japan signed a Sterling Area

Agreement designed to boost non-American trade with Japan. New Zealand, Australia, India, and South Africa were also parties to the agreement, which saw the signatories agree to increase trade significantly.[21] Wool continued to be New Zealand's major export, along with smaller quantities of sheepskins, casein, and seeds. In return, Japan sent over textiles, timber, and wood manufactures.[22] For the first two years of the agreement, however, New Zealand and the other signatories to the agreement had difficulty finding enough Japanese goods to import to balance the value of goods being exported. In New Zealand, this was exacerbated by the country's import restrictions. Japan became frustrated that Britain and the other nations were not buying sufficient Japanese products and in 1950 stopped purchasing New Zealand and Australian wool temporarily.[23]

From 1949 to 1951 the value of Japanese exports to New Zealand increased in value by almost sevenfold and the variety of products expanded considerably.[24] Nonetheless, New Zealand did not see Japan as a particularly important trading partner, as Britain continued to purchase all of New Zealand's surplus dairy produce and meat. Wool was the only major New Zealand export sold on the open market. As long as the relationship with Britain was strong, there was little need to look for markets further afield.[25]

During the early 1950s, exports to and imports from Japan hovered around 1% of the New Zealand total. By 1960 this had increased to almost 3%, still a small amount but growing.[26] Japan and New Zealand signed a trade agreement in 1958 that allowed New Zealand to compete for "all of the Japanese foreign exchange available for meat imports, and 90 percent of that for wool."[27] Wool remained New Zealand's most important export, followed by frozen meat and then casein, scrap iron, timber, sheepskins, and a few other products. In comparison, Japan was exporting almost one hundred different items, none, with the exception of cotton fabrics, of much importance or value on their own.[28]

As can be seen in table 2.3, Japan's importance as a trading partner for New Zealand increased significantly between 1960 and 1985. In 1962 the two nations granted each other most favoured nation trading status.[29] Exports to Japan increased from just over 5% of New Zealand's total exports in 1961 to 14.5% in 1985, while imports soared even more dramatically from 2.9% to 20.5% over the same period. In 1972 Japan became New Zealand's third most important trading partner for both exports and imports.[30]

New Zealand's exports to Japan consisted predominantly of crude materials (primarily wool and pulp) and food products (dairy produce and meat), although basic manufactures (paper and non-ferrous

Table 2.3   New Zealand exports to and imports from Japan, selected years 1961–1985
(US$m)

Year	Exports			Imports		
	Japan	Total	New Zealand % of Total	Japan	Total	New Zealand % of Total
1961	42	794	5.3	23	804	2.9
1965	52	1,002	5.2	60	968	6.2
1970	120	1,211	9.9	112	1,163	9.6
1975	278	2,157	12.9	420	3,148	13.3
1980	680	5,407	12.6	784	5,472	14.3
1985	828	5,714	14.5	1,220	5,944	20.5

Source: International Monetary Fund, Direction of Trade Statistics Yearbook, 1960–89

Table 2.4   Commodity composition of exports, by New Zealand to Japan, 1970–1980

Commodity	1970 (%)	1975 (%)	1980 (%)
Crude materials	54.65	39.30	40.60
Food products	35.47	35.54	33.54
Chemicals	5.10	3.44	4.28
Basic manufactures	2.61	19.63	19.93
Oils and fats	1.64	1.68	.03
Machinery	.05	.14	.23
Beverages	.01	.00	.01
Energy	.00	.10	.70
Misc. manufactures	.12	.05	.21
Other goods	.35	.12	.48

Source: Bureau of Industry Economics, *Australia and New Zealand in Asia – an analysis of changes in the relative importance of Australia and New Zealand as suppliers of goods to East Asia 1970–80*, Australian Government Publishing Service, Canberra 1984

metals) increased dramatically as a percentage of New Zealand's exports to Japan between 1970 and 1980, and comprised almost 2% of Japan's imports in this commodity in 1975.[31] Imports from Japan were primarily manufactured products: communications equipment, cars, machinery, textiles, and chemicals.[32]

As New Zealand's trade with Britain declined in the 1970s, Japan's importance as a destination for exports increased dramatically. New Zealand purchases from Japan increased even faster, suggesting that Japanese firms capitalized on the opportunities presented by the new trade relationships much faster than did New Zealand companies. In both imports and exports, the range and variety of commodities changed relatively little over the decades.

Historically, New Zealand has not been particularly successful at attracting foreign investment. Many offshore investors believed that New Zealand's small internal market limited its economic development potential and were unimpressed by the country's regulatory environment, which they felt would make doing business there difficult and unprofitable. In addition, while New Zealand governments sought to attract foreign direct investment, the general populace was much less supportive, so many potential investors felt that other countries presented better opportunities.[33] Nonetheless, the United Kingdom invested a substantial amount of money in agricultural and industrial development early in New Zealand's history, and Australia and the U.S. later became the country's largest investors.[34]

The first Japanese investment in New Zealand occurred relatively early. Kanematsu-Gosho, a major *sogo shosha*, opened its doors in New Zealand in 1937. Following this, other companies entered the field: Sanyo electrical manufacturing (1948), YKK zipper producers (1959), and Brother Distributors and Toyomenka trading companies (1959). A small number of additional new ventures built on these early developments, so that by 1987 there were about sixty Japanese-owned or partially owned companies operating in New Zealand. These firms covered a wide spectrum, from automobiles and computers to tourism and pulp and paper, forestry, fishing, and transportation. Trading houses made up one-third of the companies; another third were directly involved in manufacturing. Most of the Japanese firms were relatively small, employing ten people or fewer, and only ten had more than fifty employees. The largest Japanese-based firms were New Zealand Aluminum Smelters (with over 1,000 employees), Mazda Motors (NZ), Mitsubishi Motors (NZ), Nissan Motors (NZ), Toyota (NZ), and Carter-Oji Kokusaku Pan-Pacific.[35] Japan's NEC Corporation and the New Zealand Post Office (now Telecom Corporation of New Zealand Ltd) formed a software-production joint venture company called Telecommunications System Support in 1982.

It would be fair to say, in conclusion, that until the 1980s, while the diplomatic relationship swung from friendly to fearful and back again, the trading relationship between New Zealand and Japan was characterized by relative indifference on both sides. New Zealand did not produce many products, and of those it did produce, only wool and sheepskins were of interest to Japan until the 1960s. For New Zealand, maintaining preferential access to the British market was of the greatest importance, while, as far as Japan was concerned, New Zealand was a tiny market that never bought even 1% of its total exports. Japan gradually became a more important market for New Zealand, and the focus of greater attention, from the mid-to-late 1970s on, as New Zealand began to realize it was overly dependent on Britain.

AUSTRALIA[36]

D.C.S. Sissons, who has written extensively on early Australian-Japanese relations, writes that "Contacts between Australia and Japan are as old as the treaties that marked the end of Japan's seclusion."[37] To illustrate, he points to some of the early Australians who went to Japan: Alexander Marks, a young merchant from Melbourne, who moved to Yokohama in 1859; J.R. Black, who arrived in Japan in 1862 and became active in the newspaper business (Black's son Henry was the *rakugo* storyteller mentioned earlier); and J.H. Brooke, a political leader from Victoria, who went to Japan in 1867 and became the proprietor and editor of the Japan *Daily Herald*.[38] By the 1880s a small number of Australians had settled in Japan, teaching, establishing businesses, or preaching Christianity.[39]

The first Japanese who arrived in Australia for whom there are records was Sakagawa Rikinosuke, an acrobat who came in 1871, married an Australian woman, became naturalized, and purchased land.[40] In 1886 an Englishman toured Australia for fifteen months with 'The Japanese Village,' a Japanese group of traditional craftsmen, acrobats, and jugglers, who proved very popular with Australian audiences.[41] As early as the late 1800s there were already a few Japanese living in the remote ports and towns of north and west Australia. The majority of these were fishermen, mainly pearl fishermen, workers in the Queensland sugar cane fields, and poor farm women from the remotest parts of Japan who were brought to Australia to be prostitutes. The Yoshisa Emigration Company sent the first group of fifty contract labourers to work on sugar plantations in Queensland in 1892.[42] The flow of immigrants continued, and Australians began to fear that the Japanese would take over their jobs. The result was the Immigration Restriction Act of 1902, which aimed at keeping Australia 'white' and the Japanese out. The only Japanese allowed in, other than a few tourists and students for short-term stays, were businessmen, who moved to the larger centres.[43] One of the earliest honorary Japanese consuls in the British Empire was Alexander Marks, mentioned above, who upon returning to Australia from Japan served as honorary Japanese consul for Victoria from 1879 to 1902.

Like Canada and New Zealand, Australia was included in the Anglo-Japanese Alliance of 1902 because of its ties to Britain, and Australian troops were also accompanied by Japanese navy escort as they sailed to war in Europe in 1915. The first economic ties between the two countries began in 1902 when the government of New South Wales stationed a trade commissioner to the Far East in Kobe.[44] A Japanese consul arrived in Sydney in 1908. Until 1935 Australia did not have much trade representation abroad, nor a separate Department of External Affairs, instead relying, like Canada and New Zealand, on British representation. One of the earliest trade commissioner posts established was in Tokyo in 1935. The Australian legation in Tokyo established in late 1940 was also one of Australia's first foreign diplomatic posts. The legation closed upon the outbreak of war, re-opened as a mission in 1947, and became an embassy in 1952.[45]

The Australia-Japan Agreement on Commerce was signed in July 1957. According to Alexander Downer, discussing the treaty forty years later as Australia's minister for foreign affairs, it heralded an era of unprecedented growth in trade relations between Australia and Japan. For Australia, the treaty was a clear vote of confidence in Japan's ability to sustain its impressive post-war economic growth. The treaty was also a constructive way of encouraging Japan's inclusion in regional and global deliberations – of facilitating, where possible, an international role for Japan more commensurate with its growing economic prowess.[46]

Also in 1957, the first reciprocal prime ministerial visits took place. Australian Prime Minister Sir Robert Menzies went to Japan in April and Prime Minister Nobusuke Kishi visited Australia in December. Following on from the commerce treaty and prime ministerial visits, relations between Australia and Japan improved steadily. The treaty was re-negotiated in 1963 and commercial and social ties strengthened in succeeding decades. The Basic Treaty of Friendship and Cooperation was signed in 1976, serious negotiations having taken place as the two countries worked to resolve differences on resource policy.[47] The successful conclusion of the Basic Treaty was followed by the Australian government's formation of the Australia-Japan Foundation, an organization that promoted various forms of cooperation and interaction.[48] The Joint Declaration on the Australia-Japan Partnership was signed in 1995 and followed up in 1997 by the Australia-Japan Partnership Agenda, in which it was agreed, among numerous other items, that the two countries would hold annual prime ministerial meetings.[49]

As with Canada, Japan's involvement with Australia was spurred on by the Japanese desire for resources. Australia has vast quantities of minerals and non-oil energy resources, as well as sugar, wheat, coal, nickel, zinc, bauxite, wool, beef, veal, lamb, mutton, and iron ore and concentrates. Japan began importing many of these resources long before 1945. Ease of shipping between Japan and Australia made the country a common supplier.[50]

Japan first began trading with Australia in the later part of the nineteenth century. *Sogo shosha* were instrumental in forging the trading relationship, and their primary interest was wool. Changes in clothing styles and the desire for new military uniforms created a wool industry in Japan in 1876. By about 1879, Australian merchants had set up shop in Yokohama and Kobe and were selling wool to Japanese traders who in turn sold it to the Japanese government. The first Japanese trader to set up shop in Australia was Teiji Akiyama, who established a store in Melbourne in 1881. In 1890 Kanematsu Shoten, whose *sogo shosha* would be considerably involved in trade between Japan and Australia, opened an office in Sydney.[51] Although it appears that Kanematsu had initially hoped to import Japanese rice into Australia, he instead began exporting Australian wool to Japan.[52] Japanese trading companies rushed to enter this new market. Until the 1920s, however, the wool trade was primarily controlled by Australian merchants (some based in Japan), who sold wool on consignment to Japanese trading houses. By 1941 there were thirty-one *sogo shosha* in Australia.[53]

During the early 1900s about 1% of Australia's trade was with Japan. The relationship grew slowly but steadily, and by the late 1920s, 7% of Australia's exports went to Japan and 3% of imports came from there.[54] During the early 1930s, trade between the two countries began to flourish. The Japanese occupation of Manchuria in 1931 spurred an increase in the need for warm winter uniforms and therefore for Australian wool.[55] By 1936 Japan had become Australia's second largest export market, behind the United Kingdom, taking 13% of Australia's exports, and was the third most important source of imports (6%) behind the U.K. and the U.S.[56] Japan's primary exports were silk and other textiles and a few household goods, such as dishes, toys, and glassware. In return, Australia supplied 95% of Japan's wool and 75% of its wheat during the 1930s.[57]

Japan approached Australia for a trade agreement several times (in 1911, 1915, 1926, and 1935) but Australia was reluctant, primarily due to its strong loyalty to Britain. In fact, as many of Japan's exports to Australia competed with British goods, Britain soon applied pressure on Australia to purchase less from Japan. The formation of the Australian Trade Diversion policy in 1936 contained import licensing requirements and punitive tariffs designed to reduce imports from Japan.[58] Japan responded in kind, imposing tariffs or restricting Australian imports altogether. Many Australians, particularly those involved in exporting to Japan, successfully lobbied their government

Table 2.5   Australian exports to and imports from Japan, selected years 1961–1985 (US$m)

Year	Exports			Imports		
	Japan	Total	Australian % of Total	Japan	Total	Australian % of Total
1961	420	2,376	17.7	110	2,096	5.2
1965	495	3,014	16.4	329	3,374	9.8
1970	1,254	4,789	26.2	577	4,540	12.7
1975	3,471	11,899	29.2	1,759	9,986	17.6
1980	5,871	22,031	26.6	3,477	20,335	17.1
1985	6,295	22,611	27.8	5,430	23,499	23.1

Source: International Monetary Fund, Direction of Trade Yearbook, 1960–89

to drop the tariffs and even, after the Japanese invasion of China, to forgo any punitive measures whatsoever. Although by the late 1930s relations between the two countries were strained, as late as 1941 the Australian prime minister said that "Australia wanted to draw closer to Japan and the Minister for the Army said Australia had no quarrel with Japan."[59] The eventual outbreak of full-scale hostilities did result in a cessation of Australian-Japanese trade for the duration of the war.

Wool continued to dominate Australian exports to Japan (and cotton textiles made up the largest share of Australia's imports from Japan) up to the Second World War and even up until the 1960s. Australia's exports diversified after the war and the country began selling a rapidly increasing volume and variety of goods to Japan. In the early 1950s the Australian-Japanese balance of trade was substantially in Australia's favour, with Japan taking 14% of Australia's exports but providing only 2% of its imports.[60] The Japanese need for resources was part of the reason for the imbalance, but a significant factor was Australia's discriminatory import tariffs and reluctance to buy Japanese goods. Japanese leaders recognized this and pressed for access to the Australian market. In 1957 the Australia-Japan Commerce Agreement was concluded and Japanese goods began to flow into Australia, while Japan increased its purchases of Australian wool, wheat, and barley. Again, the sogo shosha were instrumental in this increase in trade.[61] During the 1960s Australian exports of wool and agricultural products remained strong and were joined by exports of mineral ores and metals. By the following decade, aluminum, coal, and natural gas were also being shipped to Japan.

Trade with Japan was of significantly more importance to Australia from the 1960s through to 1985 than it was for either Canada or New

Table 2.6   Commodity composition of Japanese imports from Australia, 1970–1980

Commodity	1970 (%)	1975 (%)	1980 (%)
Crude materials	56.9	43.2	36.9
Food products	18.0	22.3	21.5
Energy	16.6	26.1	32.1
Basic manufactures	5.0	5.6	6.1
Chemicals	2.1	1.8	2.7
Oils and fats	.6	.5	.1
Machinery	.4	.2	.2
Misc. manufactures	.2	.1	.1
Beverages	.0	.0	.0
Other goods	.2	.1	.2

Source: Bureau of Industry Economics, *Australia and New Zealand in Asia – an analysis of changes in the relative importance of Australia and New Zealand as suppliers of goods to East Asia, 1970–80*

Zealand. As early as 1961, almost 18% of Australia's exports went to Japan and by the mid-1970s that percentage had risen to almost 29%. Imports (primarily manufactured goods and machinery and vehicles)[62] increased from 5% to 23% over the same period, making Australia a significant market for Japan. Japan became an important trading partner for Australia, and because of the key materials Australia supplied (bauxite, coking coal, iron ore, meat, wheat), Australian exports were important to Japan.[63] However, while Japan's importance to Australia as a source of imports increased over this twenty-five year period, the reverse was not the case. In 1961 Australia supplied 7.8% of Japan's imports but by 1985 it was only supplying 5.8%. To analyse the reasons for this decline, it is necessary to look at the kind of goods purchased by Japan from Australia: crude materials, energy, food products, and, to a lesser extent, basic manufactures. During this twenty-five year period, Japan's need for crude materials declined. Although Australia increased its share of the Japanese market for crude materials, that market had significantly decreased in size, causing Australia's overall trade with Japan to suffer. During this period, Japan worked hard to diversify its sources of supply for most of its import categories. Pressure from other trading partners and the Japanese desire to ensure competitive and secure access to food products, energy, and crude materials drove the Japanese to buy from competing suppliers.[64]

The composition of Japanese imports from Australia (table 2.6) changed relatively little over the 1970s. Energy shipments (primarily coal) increased substantially and crude material sales to Japan declined (as they did in New Zealand). In most areas, the decade saw a maintenance of Australia's trade composition with Japan, with a continued reliance on unprocessed or partially processed items. The scale of trade with Japan increased dramatically, befitting the rapid expansion of the Japanese economy, which had the effect of convincing many Australian observers that trade with Japan was flourishing. Only a few observers recognized the long-term importance of diversifying their trade with Japan and of developing better markets in Japan for Australian manufactured goods.

Japanese investment in Australia really began in the middle of the 1960s, when the *sogo shosha* began investing in and lending to a number of mineral and other resource projects. (In 1960 a federal government ban on the export of iron ore was lifted and exploratory work soon discovered vast reserves of high grade ore.) Australia had vast supplies of minerals and limited international trading contacts, and the Japanese trading companies capitalized on this opportunity.

Initially, Japanese involvement was as a customer for Australian mines, signing long-term sales contracts that enabled exploration and development to begin in the Pilbara (Western Australia) and in Tasmania.[65] The Japanese steel industry, which had begun importing small amounts of Australian coking coal in the 1950s, was such an eager customer that it was the catalyst for the development of coal mining in central Queensland. The steel industry was aided by state governments, which, anxious to assist the development of their hinterland regions, made large investments in ports and roads and provided generous incentives to overseas investors willing to exploit iron ore and coal deposits for sale into Japanese markets. This was particularly the case in the isolated Pilbara region of northwest Australia, where mining towns and new port facilities were constructed at Dampier, Port Headland, and Cape Lambert.

By the early 1970s, Japanese companies reached beyond iron ore and coal and were investing in other mineral projects including solar salt, coal char, bauxite-alumina, and manganese. The major buyer of all of these minerals was Japan. Soon Japanese investors moved into exploration for nickel, uranium, and oil and natural gas. The Japanese also looked to Australia for aluminum as the high energy requirements for aluminum smelting meant Japan was forced to reduce its own aluminum industry.

After the two oil shocks of the 1970s Japanese trading corporations and processing industries became concerned about being too dependent on a limited number of resource-suppliers and began to diversify their sources of supply. In some areas, this change in thinking was to Australia's detriment, as Japan began to look to other countries for alternative sources of iron ore, beef, natural gas, and even coal. (It was

at this time that the Japanese steel producers and the British Columbia government first entered into discussions about a major coal
project.) For its non-oil energy needs and for iron ore, though, Japan
continued to focus on Australia. Between 1979 and 1982, nine steam-
ing coal projects were established with Japanese equity in New South
Wales and Queensland and many others were under discussion.[66]
Japanese companies such as Mitsui, C. Itoh, and Mitsubishi were
involved in iron ore development projects in northwest Australia. By
the early 1980s the Japanese steel industry was buying almost 45% of
their iron ore from this area. Japan's purchases represented approximately 65% of the total iron ore production of Western Australia.[67]

It is important to note that while Japanese trading companies and
steel mills invested in numerous mining projects, their investments
were seldom of any significant size. What the Japanese brought to the
projects was a long-term commitment to purchase the coal and the
iron ore. Bank loans were based on the security these purchase contracts provided. After 1982, however, Japan needed less of Australia's
resources. The decline in oil prices and a global recession were part of
the reason, but more significant were the decisions Japan had made to
diversify supplies of the resources it needed and to focus on less
resource-dependent industries.

Japanese manufacturers moved into Australia toward the end of the
1960s. They hoped that, by producing locally, they could get around
Australian import tariffs and thereby maintain or even increase their
share of the market.[68] Some companies began by establishing representative offices (staffed by Japanese engineers who could assist the
sogo shosha or the Australian distributors, both of whom lacked technical knowledge) while others, particularly those companies that produced products where more contact between the manufacturer and
the customer would be desirable and that no longer wanted to rely on
a sogo shosha, started with sales and distribution companies. Fuji Electric (1967) and Bridgestone (1970) began with representative offices
while Industrial Sewing Machines (1958), NSK (ball bearings) (1956),
and Koyo ball bearings (1964) initially set up sales and distribution
offices.

Toyota was one of the first Japanese companies to actually begin producing in Australia. It began limited production in conjunction with Australia Motor Industries in 1962 and then established a representative
office the following year. In 1966 Nissan, which had been marketing in
Australia since the early 1960s, arranged for cars to be manufactured by
the Pressed Metal Corporation in Sydney. The Australian government
put in minimum local content rules and Toyota and Nissan raised their
levels of local content. (Toyota also encouraged a Japanese component

manufacturer, Nippon Denso, to built an Australian manufacturing subsidiary.) By the early 1970s, the Australian government demanded 85% local content and the auto makers had to decide whether to abide by the regulations or withdraw from the market. Both companies decided to stay. Toyota built an engine factory and Nissan began manufacturing after its purchase of Motor Producers Ltd from Volkswagen.[69]

A number of Japanese colour-TV manufacturing plants were also opened in Australia. By 1983 there were five colour-TV plants wholly or partially owned by Japanese companies: Sharp (100% Japanese owned), Sanyo (100%), Matsushita (100%), Rank-NEC (40% in 1983, 100% owned by NEC in 1985) and AWA-Thorn (15% in 1983, 60% in 1985).[70] At the end of the 1970s, two existing Australian companies were purchased by Japanese manufacturers. The Chrysler Motors subsidiary was purchased by Mitsubishi Motors (1979) and the Uniroyal Tire Subsidiary was taken over by Bridgestone Tires (1981).

Japanese involvement in the capital-intensive chemical, petroleum, and basic metal production industries did not occur, with the exception of industrial salt processing in Western Australia, until the early 1980s. In 1981 Japanese companies invested A$225 million in the Boyne Island aluminum smelter at Gladstone in Queensland. In the same year, other Japanese businesses invested in a coal to oil liquefaction pilot plant in Victoria.[71] Again, the ultimate market for the products of these investments was Japan. In 1985 Sumitomo Electric and Australian producers formed a joint venture to capture a portion of Telecom Australia's demand for long distance fibre-optic cable.

The commercial relationship between Australia and Japan evolved with more deliberate thought than the relationships between either Canada or New Zealand and Japan, where trade and investment developments were more a result of happenstance or commercial action by the Japanese. At the end of the nineteenth and beginning of the twentieth centuries, *sogo shosha* played a definitive role in forging trading relationships between the two countries. Australian merchants were not left behind here, though, as they quickly controlled most of the wool trade and sold on consignment to Japanese traders. When pressure from Britain resulted in the Australian Trade Diversion policy, many Australians successfully lobbied the government to drop the punitive tariffs against Japan. Australians had quickly realized the importance of the Japanese market. Australia diversified its export mix (although it did remain with primarily resource products) and by 1970 over one-quarter of all Australian exports went to Japan.[72]

This brief historical overview cannot do full justice to the complex interplay of politics, culture, business, and international markets that

Table 2.7   Japanese exports to Australia, Canada and New Zealand, selected years
1961–1985 (US$m)

Year	Total	Australia	% of Japanese total	Canada	% of Japanese Total	New Zealand	% of Japanese Total
1961	4,234	100	2.4	117	2.8	22	0.5
1965	8,456	319	3.8	215	2.5	61	0.7
1970	19,318	590	3.1	563	2.9	114	0.6
1975	55,728	1,738	3.1	1,151	2.1	393	0.7
1980	130,435	3,407	2.6	2,449	1.9	680	0.5
1985	177,189	5,430	3.1	4,559	2.6	1,082	0.6

Source: International Monetary Fund, *Direction of Trade Statistics Yearbook*, selected years

Table 2.8   Japanese imports from Australia, Canada and New Zealand, selected years
1961–1985 (US$m)

Year	Total	Australia	% of Japanese total	Canada	% of Japanese Total	New Zealand	% of Japanese Total
1961	5,810	452	7.8	266	4.6	50	0.9
1965	8,168	552	6.8	355	4.3	61	0.7
1970	18,881	1,508	8.0	929	4.9	158	0.8
1975	57,846	4,154	7.2	2,498	4.3	367	0.6
1980	141,284	7,018	5.0	4,752	3.4	834	0.6
1985	130,516	7,516	5.8	4,802	3.7	910	0.7

Source: International Monetary Fund, *Direction of Trade Statistics Yearbook*, selected years

underlies the commercial relations between Japan and Australia, Canada, and New Zealand. Several key characteristics stand out from the pre-1985 period, however, and their significance will become even more evident in the following chapters. The experience of these three countries reveals the degree to which deeply entrenched habits of business and politics, themselves in turn rooted in the cultural assumptions of the country at large, influence international trading options. Countries seeking to break into new markets, to identify new opportunities in the 'new world order,' inevitably find themselves struggling with their history as they attempt to re-order operative cultural assumptions and break well-established habits and commercial traditions.

1 Relative importance of Japanese trade: Prior to the late 1970s only Australia had definitely decided that Japan would be an important

market. Canada was focused on the United States and New Zealand on Britain; both made little effort to look any further afield. Despite the fact that limited attention was given to their relationships with Japan, for a good deal of their trading history, Japan was among the top five and often even top three of their trading partners.

2 Mix of trade goods: All three countries relied on the export of their resources and made little or no effort to trade manufactured goods. Canada exported forest products, wheat, fish, and minerals, while New Zealand's primary export was wool followed by sheepskins, tallow, casein, and later dairy products and meat. Australia's main export was also wool, although wheat, barley, minerals, coal, and natural gas were also important. The resource wealth of these nations appears to have made them complacent. Over the decades Japan made and exported a whole range of products, but the other three countries remained content to rely on the sale of their resources.

3 Comparative balance of trade: Except for 1920 and 1921, the balance of trade between Canada and Japan was continually in Canada's favour from 1886 to 1984. From the 1880s until 1928, the balance of trade for New Zealand and Japan was in Japan's favour. From 1928 until World War II, trade fluctuated and the balance of trade shifted. From the end of the war to 1957, the balance of trade was in New Zealand's favour. Since then New Zealand's imports from Japan have far outweighed its exports. Australia's balance of trade position reflects the country's more active involvement in promoting Japanese trade. By the 1970s Australia had established a trade surplus with Japan, and it maintained this favourable arrangement into the next decade.

4 National attitudes toward Japanese trade: In all three cases, although less so in Australia, national attitudes towards Japanese trade mirrored a resource-first, protectionist approach to international trade generally. All three countries moved slowly out of the umbrella of the British empire, in Canada's case only to rush for the protective cover of the American economy. At the national level, governments saw certain benefits in encouraging trade with Japan, which quickly emerged as an important commercial actor on the international stage, but they rarely made an effort to sell this vision to the business community or country at large. Japan's cultural distinctiveness and a deeply entrenched Anglo-Imperial anti-orientalism made it easier for Canada, Australia, and New Zealand to turn their backs on the country's trade potential; Japanese aggression before and during World War II reinforced existing negative stereotypes and made it more difficult to con-

vince business people and investors to consider targeting the Japanese market.

As Japan emerged as an economic superpower in the 1960s and 1970s, and as established protectionist trade arrangements collapsed in the face of changing international trading regimes, Canada, Australia, and New Zealand found themselves scrambling to capitalize on the new trade and investment opportunities. Australia, not surprisingly, was first and best in the race, able to capitalize on several decades' worth of the careful cultivation of Japanese prospects (albeit in a narrow range of products) and because of its willingness to sell natural resources to the growing industrial nation. Canada followed suit, somewhat more reluctantly and with even less certainty of purpose. But the Canadian government and business community was prepared to sell to Japan and to accept Japanese investment, provided the Japanese took the initiative. Lagging behind, New Zealand clung to the comfort of its long-standing trade relationship with Britain and its dependence on a very slim range of resource exports (meat, dairy, fish, and lumber). Only a major financial shock at the end of the period in question – the much-debated financial crisis that hit New Zealand in 1984 – broke the country's complacency and made New Zealanders consider a major shift in economic direction.

It is important to remember that Japan's emergence as an international trading power was not restricted to the post-World War II period. Before the war *sogo shosha* had made significant inroads overseas and the Japanese government was encouraging greater involvement with diverse foreign markets. For each of Australia, Canada, and New Zealand, Japan represented a considerable market and therefore a potentially valuable trading partner. But the three countries, brought into economic maturity under the protection of Britain, remained largely content with trading relationships with the English-speaking world and averse to the cultural and social adaptations necessary to capitalize on trading opportunities in Asian markets. They took a passive approach to the possibilities of Japanese trade and quickly turned to national protectionism in the face of economic turmoil. This created an opening for Japanese companies to move first to open trade ties and to begin to exploit the possibilities for resource and manufacturing investments. In the dance of capital and market share that is the international trading world, Japan had taken the lead, thus ensuring that its priorities, needs, and vision of the future dominated commercial relations with New Zealand, Australia, and Canada in the period before 1985.

3 Japan's Economic Transition after 1985

If governments are to be effective in managing national economies, they must anticipate and capitalize on changes in international trade. New Zealand's near bankruptcy following Britain's reorientation to the European Community was the disastrous consequence of one government's failure to stay alert to the shifts in other economies. Japan, as one of the world's most dynamic economies, has presented its trading partners with a variety of challenges and opportunities since the 1960s, particularly following the 1985 Plaza Accord.

The country's phenomenal powers of economic adaptation and resilience have been evident throughout its history, but despite their decades of trade and diplomatic ties stretching back to the nineteenth century, Canada, New Zealand, and Australia have not understood Japanese economic and social evolution particularly well. The stereotypes of Oriental exoticism, tinged with strong streaks of cultural ethnocentrism and anti-Asian racism in each of the settler dominions, kept the Japanese at arm's length and prevented Canadians, New Zealanders, and Australians from appreciating Japan's commercial potential, business culture, and political realities. The implications of this lack of insight became particularly evident during the period of the case study, when a failure to comprehend internal Japanese transformations meant that none of the three countries fully capitalized on the opportunities that attended the restructuring of the Japanese economy. Understanding Japanese business culture and the evolution of the Japanese economy before 1985 is pivotal to our analysis of the manner in which the three countries attempted to react to Japanese business opportunities from 1985 to 1997.

Japan's first economic transformation began in the mid-nineteenth century with the Meiji Restoration, a period of phenomenal change and industrialization. Economic modernization continued through to the 1930s and formed the foundation for the country's military expansion in the latter part of that decade.[1] By 1945, Japan was in ruins.

The San Francisco Peace Treaty of April 1952 signaled the end of the Allied Occupation of Japan and, among other things, the resumption of Japan's control over its economic policies. Earlier, in 1949, the official yen-dollar exchange rate had been set at ¥360 to U.S.$1. By the end of 1955 the Japanese Economic Planning Agency announced the first of its five-year plans, outlining targets for the GNP growth rate.[2] Between 1955 and 1970 the Japanese government regularly underestimated the growth of the economy, which typically reached the five-year goals in two or three years. These government plans encouraged investor confidence and consumer optimism and thereby sparked growth.[3]

From 1953 to 1957 Japan had a trade deficit, although the severity of the deficit declined over time. Pre-war per capita production levels were regained by the mid-1950s[4] and by the end of the decade the economy was soaring. Prime Minister Hayato Ikeda put forward his ten-year Doubling Income Plan in 1960 and achieved it in seven years. Japan sustained growth rates of about 10% through the 1960s. The government selected industries perceived to be important to Japan's economic future and supported them with export subsidies and low-interest loans and by limiting imports of similar products. While 'made in Japan' once meant inferior and unreliable, Japanese products soon began to earn a reputation for being of good quality at reasonable prices. Japan reoriented its economy, handing over the manufacture of low-end products (inexpensive textiles, plastic toys, dishes) to its Asian neighbours and focusing on new technologies like steel, automobile manufacturing, and ship building. In just over twenty years after the Second World War Japan had re-emerged as a major economic power: by the late 1960s it had become the largest or second largest trading partner of most nations in the Western Pacific and East Asia.[5]

As Japan's economy grew so did its trade surpluses, and it became evident that the yen was undervalued. As the yen was not the only currency to need realigning, the Bretton-Woods fixed-exchange rates were converted to floating exchange rates in early 1973, and the yen quickly appreciated to ¥300 to U.S.$1 from its fixed rate of ¥360. Naturally, this imposed difficult adjustments on Japanese exporters.

Little did they know that a larger challenge was right around the corner – the quadrupling of OPEC oil prices in the fall of 1973 and another dramatic rise in the late 1970s.

Western observers assumed that the 1973 OPEC oil crisis would stop the Japanese 'miracle' in its tracks, and in the short term this prognostication proved correct. Imported oil accounted for over 60% of Japan's energy resources[6] and many of its industries were heavy consumers of energy. The oil shocks hit Japan hard and inflation spiraled. Japan adjusted quickly, however, and learned the valuable lesson of its vulnerability. Government and business worked hard to make industry more energy efficient and to find other sources of supply, and the country remained economically formidable.

Japan's next challenge came in the mid-1980s with the Plaza Accord. As Japan's trade surplus continued to increase through the 1970s and early 1980s, international frustration began to mount. The United States, in particular, complained that the Japanese yen was heavily undervalued and pushed for exchange rate corrections to be made. The Americans believed that the trade deficit was the fault of exchange rates; there was nothing wrong with the U.S.-Japan trade deficit that a rate of ¥180 to the dollar would not solve.

In September 1985, at the Plaza Hotel in Washington, the leaders and finance ministers of the G5 nations agreed to put in place mechanisms that would see the yen and the German mark increase in value and the dollar decrease. The resulting agreement, called the Plaza Accord, signaled to speculators and investors that it would be unwise to continue to bet on the dollar increasing in value. In the first day of trading after the Plaza Accord was announced, before any intervention whatsoever, the yen increased in value by five yen to the U.S. dollar.

On this front, the Plaza Accord was extremely successful: the yen appreciated rapidly after September 1985 (see table 3.1). The main purpose of the accord, however, was to address the United States-Japan trade imbalance by making American goods less expensive and Japanese goods more expensive, so that Japanese customers would buy inexpensive American goods and Japanese companies would have to raise their prices in dollar terms and therefore lose customers. Initially, Japanese companies did reel from the shock of such a rapidly strengthening yen and the Japanese economy experienced a brief recession until late 1986. But manufacturers worked hard and quickly to adjust, and the economy bounced back and began to expand.[7] A look at Japan's balance of trade statistics (see table 3.2) provides no clues that the yen had doubled in value between the fall of 1985 and the summer of 1987.

Table 3.1   Japan's exchange rate, 1965–1997

Year	Yen per US$1
1965	360
1970	360
1975	297
1980	227
1985	239
1986	169
1987	145
1988	128
1989	138
1990	145
1991	135
1992	127
1993	111
1994	102
1995	94
1996	109
1997	121

Source: International Monetary Fund, *International Financial Statistics Yearbook, 1995*, 468–9

There were a number of reasons why Japan's balance of trade did not behave as western economists expected. The first was that the benefits of a strong yen had been overlooked. The resource products Japan purchased to fuel its industries were suddenly half as expensive as they had been months earlier. These lower priced inputs made a substantial difference to an energy- and resource-hungry Japan. Second, Japanese companies were willing to take minimal profits or even sustain a loss to maintain their market share over the long term. This reaction had not been anticipated by the more short-term focused Americans. A good part of the reason why Japanese companies were able to contemplate such a strategy was government support; companies knew that they could depend on the government to ensure that Japanese industry got the financial backing it needed to remain competitive.

The time from 1986 until the middle of 1990 in Japan is often referred to as the 'bubble economy.' This period saw massive expansion, primarily due to a rapid surge in domestic demand – a growth in capital investments and in personal spending.[8] Stocks and real estate prices skyrocketed. People and companies borrowed large sums of money to purchase or invest in other properties, using real estate as equity. Land prices, particularly in downtown Tokyo, were so high that,

Table 3.2   Japanese balance of trade, 1965–1997 (US$b)

Year	Exports	Imports	Surplus
1965	8.33	6.43	1.90
1970	18.96	15.00	3.96
1975	54.65	49.71	4.94
1980	126.74	124.61	2.13
1985	174.02	118.03	55.99
1986	205.59	112.77	92.82
1987	224.62	128.20	96.42
1988	259.77	164.77	95.00
1989	269.55	192.66	76.89
1990	280.35	216.77	63.58
1991	306.58	203.49	103.09
1992	330.87	198.47	132.40
1993	351.31	209.74	141.57
1994	384.18	238.25	145.93
1995	429.32	297.24	132.07
1996	400.28	316.72	83.56
1997	409.24	307.64	101.60

Source: International Monetary Fund, various issues of the International Financial Statistics Yearbook

as one author commented, "Narrow slivers of property in central Tokyo served as collateral for the acquisition of vast estates overseas."[9] Japanese homes, previously derogatorily referred to as 'rabbit hutches,' were now worth more than palaces in Beverly Hills. The press was filled with stories of wild excess, with Japanese banks at the centre. As Taggart Murphy comments, "The great names of Japanese banking – Sumitomo, Fuji, the Industrial Bank of Japan – shoveled vast amounts of credit at the flimsiest of ventures, often managed by the yakuza, the Japanese underworld."[10]

This could not last, and eventually the price of real estate peaked and fell. As the collateral they were holding decreased in value, banks began calling in loans and limiting further expansion. Investors who could no longer count on receiving substantial capital gains began to worry about the profitability of companies and started selling shares. The bursting of the bubble led to numerous bankruptcies and a banking sector that was seriously overstretched.

A number of financial commentators argue that the entire bubble economy – its boom and its bust – was engineered: the Ministry of Finance (MOF) set up the crash to move money from wealthy individuals to Japan's large companies. Eamonn Fingleton wrote that "the

MOF never lost its grip on the markets: it engineered the crash as a counterintuitive piece of industrial policy to effect the transfer of wealth from rich private citizens to corporate Japan."[11] The MOF inflated the financial markets (by increasing the money supply, thereby inducing a fall in interest rates and cutting borrowing costs for industry) and this triggered a boom in real estate purchases as the banks financed speculators who bought real estate and then used that real estate as collateral to buy even more.[12] Murphy quotes a Bank of Japan official as saying "We intended first to boost the stock and property markets. Supported by this safety net – rising market – export oriented industries were supposed to reshape themselves so that they could adapt to a domestic-led industry."[13]

By this criterion, the bubble economy appears to have worked. Corporations profited by selling large numbers of shares at exaggerated prices to unwise speculators. When securities prices fell, the victims were not the issuing companies but the purchasers, who were generally wealthy individuals or small companies.[14] In the eyes of the Japanese government, this evened out some of the inequalities of personal wealth and transferred money to corporate Japan so that companies would reshape themselves and adjust to a domestic-led economy. By the time the bubble was over, Murphy wrote,

Japan had added to its GNP an amount equivalent to the GNP of France. Most of its industries were fully competitive in world markets at rates of 110 yen to the dollar and beyond. Most important, Japan's administrators believed they had achieved the goal of the century, a wholly integrated industrial structure under Japanese control. Hardly a key manufactured component for any downstream manufactured product was not being made by a Japanese company. Japan depended on foreigners only for commodities, commercial aircraft (for which most components were manufactured or could be manufactured by Japanese companies) and certain kinds of software.[15]

As the Plaza Accord transformed numerous aspects of Japan's economy, so did these changes affect the country's trading partners. One of the more obvious results of the rapid rise in the value of the yen was the equally rapid increase in Japanese direct overseas investment. While the Japanese government had discouraged foreign direct investment (FDI) in the 1950s and then been relatively neutral toward FDI in the 1960s and 1970s, in the 1980s it encouraged companies to invest abroad.[16] This was not difficult, as Japanese manufacturers wished to take advantage of lower labour costs abroad and use local production to avoid the increasing protectionism in Europe and the United States. As table 3.3 illustrates, the scale of foreign investment

Table 3.3   Japanese direct foreign investment, 1965–1997

Year	Foreign Direct Investment (US$b)
1965	.03
1970	.26
1975	1.53
1980	2.39
1985	6.45
1986	14.48
1987	19.52
1988	34.21
1989	44.16
1990	48.05
1991	30.74
1992	17.24
1993	13.74
1994	17.97
1995	22.66
1996	23.44
1997	26.06

Source: International Monetary Fund, International Financial Statistics Yearbook 1994, 1995, and 1997

increased dramatically. In 1985, the first year of the re-valued yen, Japanese overseas investment reached almost US$6.5 billion. It almost tripled over the next two years and more than doubled again by 1989. FDI peaked at over US$48 billion in 1990 and thereafter began a precipitous decline. This pattern reflected the artificial wealth of the bubble economy, based on the vast increases in the value of Tokyo real estate, and the consequent Japanese enthusiasm for buying up overseas properties and businesses.

With the bulk of overseas investment initially in manufacturing, many of the affiliated parts makers for the automobile industry also set up production lines in North America. In North America, in particular, however, the first surge of investment in manufacturing was followed from 1988 with investments in non-manufacturing businesses like real estate companies, financial institutions, insurance companies, and resort properties. A number of high profile investments such as Sony Corporation's purchase of Columbia Pictures in 1989 and Mitsubishi Estate Company's purchase of Rockefeller Center in 1990 were met with American anger and fear. In Hawaii and Australia, Japanese investors also bought large numbers of homes and commercial properties, driving up local land prices. In many cases, the new home owners often remained in Japan, leaving the houses empty for much of the year and contributing little money or energy to the community. While the high prices pleased the sellers, many Hawaiians and Australians were resentful.

Direct overseas investment had an impact on Japan's total trade surplus (although, as seen in table 3.2, the total surplus remained at about 1986/87 levels) and its surpluses with individual countries. The anticipated decline in Japan's trade, however, did not occur. Overseas production by Japanese companies of automobiles and electrical equipment also resulted in 'reverse importing,' whereby Japanese manufacturers ship their products back to Japan. In 1989, 10% of all of Japan's finished product imports were reverse imports.[17]

More production moved offshore after 1993 when the value of the yen again began to climb. For many manufacturers, an exchange rate of ¥100 to the dollar meant that they were simply not viable if they did not find new ways to survive. For most of the larger companies this meant increased overseas production. In the early 1990s Sony announced plans to move nearly half of its electronics production overseas by 1997; Matsushita Electric Industrial Co. planned to increase overseas output to 50% of total overseas sales by fiscal 1996[18] and to transfer production of playback-only VCRs and radiocassette players to Malaysia; Sanyo moved its production of North America-bound VCRs to Indonesia; Nikon arranged for half of its camera production to be done overseas; Toyota boosted its overseas production; and Nissan increased its U.S. production.[19]

What was most significant about this shift of manufacturing investment abroad was that substantially more of it was going to Asia and less to North America and Europe. (This was sometimes masked by the fact that Japanese direct investment in non-manufacturing sectors in Europe and North America remained strong.) In 1988 67% of Japanese foreign direct investment in manufacturing went to North America; by 1993 this had dropped to 37%. Investments in Europe followed a similar pattern (see table 3.4). In the same period, investment in Asia went from 17% to 33% of Japan's total.[20] China showed a particularly dramatic increase, growing from around 1% of total manufacturing FDI in the mid-1980s to over 12% in 1993. This transfer of manufacturing to Asia tended to be accompanied by a reduction of facilities in Japan[21] and occurred not just to take advantage of cheap labour but also to capitalize on growing consumer markets in the region.[22]

Japan and the Asian countries appeared to be following a regional division of manufacturing.[23] As incomes rose in the newly industrializing countries, production shifted from Japan to them. Production of middle range value-added products (cellular phones, standard fax

Table 3.4   Japanese manufacturing FDI to Asia and the world (US$m and %)

	1981–1985	1985	1986	1987	1988	1989	1990	1991	1992	1993
World	2,365	2,352	3,806	7,832	13,805	16,284	15,486	12,311	10,057	11,132
	(100)	(100)	(100)	(100)	(100)	(100)	(100)	(100)	(100)	(100)
North America	1,056	1,223	2,199	4,848	9,191	9,586	6,793	5,868	4,177	4,146
	(44.7)	(52.0)	(57.8)	(61.9)	(66.6)	(58.9)	(43.9)	(44.7)	(41.5)	(37.2)
Europe	249	323	370	851	1,548	3,090	4,593	2,690	2,101	2,041
	(10.5)	(13.7)	(9.7)	(10.9)	(11.2)	(19.0)	(29.7)	(21.9)	(20.9)	(18.3)
Asia	589	460	804	1,679	2,370	3,220	3,068	2,928	3,104	3,659
	(24.9)	(19.6)	(21.1)	(21.4)	(17.2)	(19.8)	(19.8)	(23.8)	(30.9)	(32.9)
NIEs	264	253	573	878	775	1,347	805	640	439	735
	(11.2)	(10.8)	(15.1)	(11.2)	(5.6)	(8.3)	(5.2)	(5.2)	(4.4)	(6.6)
ASEAN	301	166	193	704	1,360	1,553	2,028	1,945	1,808	1,474
	(12.7)	(7.1)	(5.1)	(9.0)	(9.9)	(9.5)	(13.1)	(15.8)	(18.0)	(13.2)
China	10	22	23	70	203	206	161	309	650	1,377
	(0.4)	(0.9)	(0.6)	(0.9)	(1.5)	(1.3)	(1.0)	(2.5)	(6.5)	(12.4)

Note: Figures within parentheses are percentages.
NIEs = Korea, Taiwan, Hong Kong, and Singapore
ASEAN = Thailand, Malaysia, Philippines, and Indonesia
Source: Kiyohiko Fukushima and C.H. Kwan, 'Foreign Direct Investment and Regional Restructuring in Asia,' *The New Wave of Foreign Direct Investment in Asia* (Singapore: Nomura Research Institute and Institute of Southeast Asian Studies, 1995), 4

machines, computer displays, large colour televisions) shifted from Japan to countries like Singapore and Malaysia while production of lower priced labour-intensive products (small colour televisions, lower priced audio-visual products, computer assembly, electrical parts) were being transferred from Singapore and Malaysia to Indonesia and the Philippines.[24] As is evident in table 3.4, China began to attract a significant amount of Japanese direct investment in 1993. China's huge population and the existing levels of technical knowledge gave China a strong advantage over other low-income countries in the attraction of investment monies. This also meant that while China was attracting Japanese investment in manufacturing of low-cost items, some Japanese high-technology production was also being established in China.

As Japan started to move much of its labour-intensive and middle range value-added production overseas, it worked to ensure its industrial base did not 'hollow out' and leave the country without an industrial infrastructure. Two ways to do this are to produce more value-added products domestically and to develop new industrial technologies.[25] Japan adopted both strategies.

Japan continued to produce high value-added products such as high-performance home appliances, laser disk players, high definition and digital televisions, CD-ROM multimedia products, digital compact cassette recorders, and certain computer-related parts, such as customized memory chips and high-performance work stations.[26] While the markets of the western industrialized nations remained interested in these products, Japan attached even greater importance to the large and expanding markets of Asia. As these countries become more prosperous, they represent enormous opportunities for the sale of consumer goods.

Japan also worked hard to develop new technologies. The country took the lead in the production and use of industrial robots. In 1995, over 60% of the industrial robots operating in the world were in Japan.[27] Industrial robots have been traditionally targeted at automobile and electronics manufacturers, but slow sales encouraged manufacturers to develop robots that could be used in warehousing and distribution and personal robots to do jobs such as cleaning offices or retrieving objects. Japanese companies tried to develop lower cost robots and robots with improved visual techniques and the ability to handle fragile objects.[28] While neither industrial nor personal robots have yet attracted much attention, the industry holds considerable potential.

Japan is in a good position to lead many energy-related industries, which are likely to assume additional importance as more countries industrialize and begin to draw heavily on the world's traditional energy supplies. Japan is at the forefront of the development of energy-saving applications for superconductivity, the design of energy-efficient modes of transportation like the magnetic levitation train, and the commercialization of solar power for use in consumer electronic devices, street lights, and air conditioners.[29]

Prospects for growth in the electronics industry are also strong, particularly as Japanese businesses are continually searching for new applications of existing technologies. High definition television, for example, is being used to teach medical students and has potential for use in aviation (higher definition radar screens) and architecture and engineering (for visual databases).[30] Car navigation systems, DVD systems, flat and wide screen televisions, and videophones all have considerable commercial potential as the world embraces the digital revolution.[31]

Before the Plaza Accord, Japan primarily imported raw materials and exported manufactured goods: in 1985 resource products made up two-thirds of Japanese imports. As Japan began to import basic value-added products and focus instead on the production and exportation of high technology products,[32] its need for raw materials declined; by 1991 resource products had dropped to 50% of imports,[33] and by 1995, 59.1% of Japan's imports were manufactured products. Japan's increased importation of manufactured products, particularly relatively easily manufactured products such as textiles, stemmed from a number of factors. First, as mentioned above, Japan's investment in overseas manufacturing increased greatly and imports from these overseas affiliates were quite steady. Second, consumer attitudes toward foreign products had changed: by 1988 a survey by the Manufactured Imports Promotion Organization revealed that 75% of the Japanese population would not discriminate between imports and domestic products. Third, Japan's trade surpluses with numerous countries, particularly the U.S., led to pressure on the Japanese to purchase abroad. Last, rapid industrialization in Asia meant that a number of economies became capable of supplying a range of products Japan needed at a lower cost.[34]

In their 1993 study of the Japanese market for manufactured imports, Ron Wickes and Aldith Graves concluded that virtually all of the sectors of manufactured products more than doubled in value between 1985 and 1990. In fact, one-third of the manufactured product sectors tripled in value. Clothing, road vehicles, non-ferrous metals, electrical machinery, and miscellaneous manufactures were the sectors that saw the highest growth rates.[35]

The change in Japan's import profile, as its industries moved overseas and their need for raw materials declined,[36] had dramatic implications for those nations, such as Australia, Canada, and New Zealand, whose trade with Japan was substantially resource-based. It opened up new opportunities for trade in manufactured goods, but reduced trade in resources. James Lambert, first secretary (economic) at the Canadian embassy in Tokyo, observed during the mid-1990s, "Japan's requirements for raw materials remain considerable and, in the medium term, resource exports to Japan will continue to prove lucrative. It must be recognized, however, that they will constitute a declining share of Japan's total import demand."[37] He went on to say that countries and companies needed to start exporting more processed or value-added products or they risked losing out on the potential of the Japanese market.

An important contributing factor to Japan's initial ability to cope with the rise in the value of the yen after the Plaza Accord was strong domestic demand, particularly rising personal consumption and the bubble economy's real estate boom (particularly in Tokyo).[38] To take advantage of this domestic market, new products were targeted at Japanese consumers rather than those in North America. Kenneth Courtis, strategist and senior economist for the Deutsche Bank Group in Asia, pointed out in 1994 that "From 1975 to 1985, the period of Japan's export boom, about three-quarters of innovation-related investment was targeted at the development of new products and services designed to penetrate the North American and European markets. Since 1986, however, there has been a complete reversal, with about 80 percent of innovation investment now targeting the domestic market."[39] More and more Japanese products were being introduced in Japan first, and did not appear on American shelves for months.

Many of the new products popular in Japan are high value-added and luxury products. Matsushita's New Product Centre in Osaka and Sony's Tokyo showroom showcase a wide range of high technology products, including the latest in digital audio-visual equipment, information technology devices, networked home electric appliances, and pet robots. Most of these new products are available for sale in Japan but not overseas. Popular items in the late 1990s were minidisk players (which store and play over an hour's worth of music on rewritable floppy disks), flat and wide screen televisions, notebook computers, personal handy phone system terminals (replaced in 1999 by internet-enabled mobile phones) and the Pajero Mini four-wheel drive car.[40] New models of personal computers, low malt beer (to avoid high liquor taxes), and slimming gels and soaps were also big sellers.[41]

A number of interesting consumer items are doing well in Japan but have not yet found much of a market in other countries.[42] There is a quixotic, experimental element to the Japanese consumer market. Items such as the head-cooling pillow for hot summer nights; refrigerators with five or six compartments, each with a different cooling system for a different kind of food; sensor controlled mirrors to bring natural sunlight into dark buildings; low tables with a heat source below and a quilt over to trap warm air in homes without central heating on cold evenings; and answering machines to discourage obscene phone calls (push a button and a threatening male voice yells out, or a 100-decibel blast shrieks into the caller's ear) all hold potential for markets outside Japan.[43] Those that pass the test of Japanese consumers will likely find their way to foreign stores in the years to come.

Other larger and more commercial products include temporary sidewalks (standard modular concrete curb pieces that are inexpensive and easy to install and therefore useful during road construction projects), a car wash that takes up only 360 square feet, automated downtown parking towers (a Ferris-wheel style elevator rotates cars and empty spaces up and down the parking tower), and capsule office buildings and hotels (with individual working or sleeping compartments.[44]

Unique food and restaurant ideas are also commonplace in Japan. Consumers can buy apples inscribed with personal messages that have been grown into the fruit; ice cream with flavours such as sweet potato, basil leaf, blue cheese, and oolong tea; curry donuts; and hot cocoa with chili sauce. Theme restaurants (multi-course meals all focused on one ingredient such as garlic), bars where you pay for the time spent not the alcohol consumed, rental restaurants where customers come in and cook their own food for large parties (an opportunity for company executives to show off their cooking skills), bars with nurseries, cook-it-yourself restaurants, and restaurants where noodles float down chutes in front of customers who grab them with their chopsticks are some examples of the growing variety of Japanese dining experiences.[45]

Many of these products and services have been available in Japan for a few years and represent the trend toward innovation directed at the Japanese consumer. The Japanese are well known for their insistence on quality and service, and Japanese producers have learned to satisfy these demands. Japan has an unparalleled ability to target niche markets and a strong service orientation. More new products and services are likely on the horizon as the Japanese Ministry of Finance hopes that domestic consumption will help spur the economy out of its recession.[46]

Under pressure from the Keidanren (Japan Federation of Economic Organizations) and the business community, the Japanese government began deregulating the Japanese economy in 1993. (The first action program was announced by Prime Minister Yasuhiro Nakasone in July 1985, but little progress was made.) In March 1995 it announced its 'Deregulation Action Plan,' which outlined the government's strategy for reviewing a variety of its regulations. Japanese and western perceptions of what constitutes deregulation often differ. Glen Fukushima, vice president of the American Chamber of Commerce in Japan and vice president of AT&T, writes that deregulation is often mistranslated into Japanese to mean "an easing or relaxation of regulations" rather than their elimination, which explains some of the communication difficulty. He goes on to say that "in Western systems, people tend to assume that everything is permitted unless explicitly proscribed, whereas in the Japanese system, people tend to assume that everything is proscribed unless explicitly permitted."[47] Freedom or lack of restrictions, therefore, is the exception rather than the norm.

While deregulation may occur in non-strategic industries, Japan protects those industries it deems vital. While the U.S., Canada, Australia, and New Zealand focus on leveling the playing field and making sure everyone plays by the same rules, Japan emphasizes what is best for Japan. Marie Anchordoguy summed up this difference: "Japan is much less concerned with the rules of the playground; her primary objective is to win the game."[48] At an American Chamber of Commerce in Japan forum of 1996, nine American company representatives described their company's experiences in Japan. Those in consumer products or services that were not deemed strategic reported no difficulties, while those with products in strategic sectors all expressed various degrees of dissatisfaction with trade barriers.[49]

Nonetheless, by 1997 deregulation of a number of industries (securities, banking, telecommunications) was underway or under consideration. That this occurred was not really due to foreign pressures (although deregulation of certain sectors such as the securities industry diverted attention away from the more important strategic industries) but because easing regulations in certain sectors was seen to be good for Japan by the government bureaucracy.

In 1995, government rules under review of importance to Canadian, Australian, and New Zealand firms included regulations "on housing construction materials, regulations on packaging and distribution of food products, and to a lesser extent, myriad controls on telecommunications."[50] The government put measures in place to reform its procurement system and to encourage foreign firms to enter the Japanese market.

After the October 1996 election, Prime Minister Ryutaro Hashimoto put forth "the most specific package of reforms proposed by any Japanese leader in the last decade,"[51] with the goal of making Tokyo "an international market comparable to the New York and London markets by the year 2001 by changing the laws covering banking, securities, insurance, foreign exchange and related areas."[52] The financial crisis that hit in 1998 undermined this ambitious goal. Some foreign companies entered the Japanese financial market under the new regulations, but development was significantly slower than the government had hoped. This plan, seen as a long-term strategy, had the potential to create competition in the Japanese market and thereby offer many new opportunities for foreign firms in Japan. However, many, including the chairman of the Keidanren, did not believe that the deregulation program had gone far enough; the plan was ambiguous as to which regulations would be removed and how quickly they would be dropped.[53]

1 April 1998 saw the next step in the implementation of Japan's financial reforms (often referred to as the Big Bang), aimed at liberalizing its financial markets by 2001. There were numerous changes designed to establish rules for fair and transparent transactions, develop a user-friendly market, expand options for borrowers and investors, and improve service and competition. (Opinions by business leaders and politicians on the future success of the Big Bang reform remain mixed. The numerous bank mergers [and a few bankruptcies] and the influx of foreign securities and insurance companies indicate that a shake-up has occurred in the financial services sector. Nonetheless, Japan's financial struggles in 2001 have been at least partly blamed on a failure to fully reform the sector.)

The late 1990s saw concern routinely expressed about the current level of government spending in Japan – even as the public supported and foreign governments encouraged a boost in consumer expenditures to stimulate the local economy. Similarly, public and professional confidence in Japan's political leadership dropped, and few observers expressed much confidence in its ability to lead the country out of its economic turmoil. On a more general scale, observers inside and outside Japan commented extensively on the marked impact of the country's domestic problems on the international economy – an indication of Japan's continued international importance.

As noted earlier, foreigners, particularly westerners, have a history of underestimating Japan. Japan has remade itself in the face of national crisis numerous times – at the end of the Tokugawa era when the country was forced open by the west, at the end of World War II, during the oil crises of the 1970s (no major nation was hit harder than Japan, as it relied on imported oil for about 60% of its total energy needs), and after the Plaza Accord. Each time, when an initial slowdown occurred, commentators said that this was it – Japan was in serious, long-term trouble. Westerners tend to overestimate each crisis and underestimate Japan's capacity to rebound.

In the late 1990s, western analyses varied dramatically in their interpretations of the current and future state of the Japanese economy.[54] However, many observers assumed that Japan's day had passed and that the false bubble economy of the late 1980s had given way to a more realistic future, one well represented by the late 1997 recession in the country. They consistently argued that a western-style economic regime, with more open markets, less government interference, and an improved financial system, was essential if Japan was to re-establish its economic direction. The 1997–98 round of scandals in the banking sector, the falling yen, and low business and consumer confidence all lent support to this interpretation. Given Japan's importance in the global economy (it accounted for 13% of world trade and controlled one-third of the world's savings in 1998), analysing both where Japan sat then and what its economy was likely to do in the short and long term was vitally important, and the media was filled with stories of the Japanese economy and predictions about its future. Whether or not the 1990s predictions of doom and dismay by western analysts and commentators are the latest example of their habitual underestimation of Japan remains to be seen.

In 1997, Japan was the world's second largest economy. It had a GNP of about ¥490 trillion, which at 1997 exchange rates was about US$5 trillion and about 50–60% of the U.S.'s GNP. Depending on the source, Japanese per capita GDP was calculated to be around US$30,000 to US$36,000. The more conservative estimate, adjusted for purchasing power parity, surpassed Canada, Australia, and New Zealand's per capita GDP.

A record 16.8 million Japanese went overseas in 1997. (This number of travelers dipped to 15.8 million in 1998 but increased to 16.4 million in 1999.)[55] Japan had approximately the same number of housing starts annually as the United States, despite having less than half the population.[56] The Japanese lived longer than any other nationality in the world, with life expectancy for women at eighty-three years and for men at just over seventy-seven. Ninety per cent of Japanese considered themselves to be middle class (only 5% said lower class); 98–99% of households had fridges, washing machines, colour televisions, and vacuum cleaners, while 42% had word processors and 48% new cars. Record numbers of Japanese high school graduates went on to university or junior college.[57]

Japan successfully targeted selected industries based on a number of criteria, including high entry barriers, definite economies of scale, good export prospects and research opportunities, and elastic demand. Japanese industry dominated in the production of a large range of industries and technologies (robotics, cameras, auto industry manufacturing equipment, copiers, musical instruments, superconductivity, energy-efficient transportation technologies, and more) and controlled the market for a large range of key components in certain high technology products (notebook computers, printers, compact disc players, semiconductor materials and equipment, supercomputers, cellular phones, fax machines, optical scanning equipment, etc.).[58]

Japanese business and government were continually focused on the long term and it was this shared focus and their ability to work together for the economic good of the nation that propelled the country forward. The Ministry of International Trade and Industry, the Ministry of Finance, the large Japanese corporations, and even the general population focused on what was good for the future of Japan. The Japanese bureaucracy, primarily MOF and MITI, planned and then implemented strategies that would ensure that Japan remained economically strong, even if this meant short-term sacrifice.

If the governments of Canada, Australia, and New Zealand wanted to take an active role in responding to the changes in Japan's economy after 1985, there needed to be a concerted effort to convince their private sectors that they could not afford to ignore the changes. Even more importantly, there needed be more study of what each of these countries could sell to Japan.

A misperception exists that the only manufactured products imported into Japan are "reverse imports," that is products produced by Japanese companies overseas. While Japanese overseas investment and the resulting reverse imports are significant – in 1997, about 14% of all finished product imports were reverse imports[59] – a significant market for finished products remains. Japan imported over US$300 billion worth of goods in 1997 (see table 3.2), about 60% of which were finished products.[60] Allowing for reverse imports, a market valued at US$150 billion still existed for Australian, Canadian, and New Zealand firms. The success of other nations (the U.S., Germany, China, and Taiwan in machinery and equipment, and the U.S., Germany, Ireland, and France in chemical products, for example) in the 1980s and 1990s proves this point. These countries simply seized opportunities where, as will be shown, Canada, Australia, and New Zealand did not.

As we have seen, the post-Plaza Accord changes in Japan's import profile away from resource products toward manufactured products had profound implications for nations that had been primarily resource and agricultural exporters. Japan's evolving division of labour saw it producing the most expensive and most technologically demanding products, while other nations, further down the line, produced less technically sophisticated items. Japan's direct investment in manufacturing in Asia, as discussed earlier, was evidence of this division. Leon Hollerman, in his discussion of Japan's economic strategy in Brazil, made this point in 1988 when he wrote, "the rationale of Japan's direct foreign investment may include a calculated disaggregation (or 'unbundling') of the production process, with some stages being assigned abroad and some retained at home. In arranging this allegedly 'horizontal' distribution of production between Japan and the host country, Japan retains for itself the higher value-added operations that yield the best rates of return."[61]

While a distressing prospect for a country like the U.S., which competed directly in Japan's strategic industries and had no desire to be anywhere but at the top of the manufacturing system, for Canada, Australia, and New Zealand this change heralded opportunities. If they could determine how to accommodate the needs of 125 million people, with a per capita GDP equal to that of the U.S. and an eye for quality and innovation, the potential economic benefits would be considerable. Canada, Australia, and New Zealand needed to decide if they wanted to move up the economic hierarchy, and/or whether they could afford not to make such changes. Increased competition from developing countries (in which Japan had been increasing investment in both manufacturing and resources), combined with Japan's decreasing purchases of their products, meant that to increase sales to Japan in the future, Canada, Australia, and New Zealand had to look toward exporting manufactured products.

The Japanese bureaucracy was committed to looking after Japan's best interests. Therefore, to determine what a nation would be able to sell successfully in Japan, it was worthwhile, maybe even vital, to understand how to make products or plans that would be attractive to the Japanese bureaucracy. Canadian Roger Boisvert, founder and president of Global Online Japan, had to convince the Japanese government to give him permission to start his business: "I had to present it in a way that would make the government want to do it for me. I had to think of what was in it for Japan. I told them that if Japanese companies do not have access to the most up to date information in the world, then they will fall behind and the country will fall behind."[62] The government gave Boisvert permission. If the governments of Canada, New Zealand, and Australia were to guide their private sectors in profitable directions, they had to focus on what Japan wanted. For too long, the English-speaking nations had decided that Japan could not possibly work the way it did and therefore avoided seeking to understand how the bureaucracy worked and how to use that to their advantage, as Boisvert did.

There were also issues for governments on the investment front. The general populations of Canada, New Zealand, and Australia are not always receptive to increasing Japanese foreign investment. During the 1985–97 time period of the case study, Australia's Pauline Hanson, independent member of Parliament and founder of the One Nation Party, stirred up these sentiments, as did the Reform Party in Canada and the New Zealand First Party. In all three nations, the governments tried to explain the benefits of foreign investment with varying degrees of success.

The changes in the Japanese economy following the Plaza Accord, part of a rapidly shifting international economic system, were representative of the challenges facing national governments that attempt to control, monitor, and direct international trade. For countries like Canada, Australia, and New Zealand, with substantial yet undiversified trade relationships with Japan, staying abreast of and responding to shifts in the Japanese economy was essential: failure to capitalize on opportunities or to anticipate major shifts could cause domestic economic difficulty. The Japanese economic changes occurred at precisely the time that these and other western governments were changing from a government-directed economic order to a neo-classical model of political economy. The responsiveness and adaptability of Canada, Australia, and New Zealand demonstrate whether the 'smaller government' approach worked. The following three chapters look at how the three countries responded, individually, to Japan from the time of the Plaza Accord to 1997.

4 North Pacific Partners: Canada-Japan Commercial Relations 1985–1997

Implicit in Team Canada is the recognition that the private sector – not government – is the ultimate generator of wealth. It is individual Canadians and firms that innovate, that invent, that invest and that create new jobs. The Government, however, has a clear responsibility to 'get the big picture right' – to establish a fiscal, economic and policy framework that is conducive to wealth and job creation.[1]

Although the neo-classical model has been advanced by its proponents as a solution to the economic ills of all nations, the practical reality is that each country has responded differently to the pressures to conform to a more liberalized and globalized economic order. Canada has both suffered and benefitted from its proximity to the United States, and it has been constrained by the realities of close integration with the world's largest economy. Canada's fundamental struggle has been between the relative ease of approaching the American market and the complexity and difficulty of dealing with countries outside of North America. Despite decades of rhetoric about its prominent place on the Pacific Rim, Canada has routinely wrestled with its social and economic relationships with Asia, particularly Japan.

While Japan was striving to re-orient itself in a changing world, Canada also began to recognize a need to determine its goals and direction within the new global village. At the same time, the decimation of the cod stocks in Newfoundland, the troubled west coast fishery, and declining timber resources were ringing alarm bells about Canada's future dependence on primary industries. These concerns generated public and governmental discussion, and Canada began to take more clearly proactive steps to secure its future. Michael Porter, in his 1991 analysis of Canadian competitiveness, summed up the situation. Until recently, he wrote, there was "the belief that the Canadian economy could maintain an equilibrium – based on the sheer magnitude and quality of its resources, combined with a sheltered market – without a reduction in the Canadian standard of living."[2] He concluded, however, that conditions had changed: "Increasing globalization of trade and investment, accelerating technological changes, rapidly evolving company and country strategies, and – more recently – the Free Trade Agreement with the U.S., represent significant discontinuities in the nature of international competition confronting Canadian-based industry. ... Although Canada's status as a wealthy nation is not in doubt, the risk is of a slowly eroding standard of living over the coming years."[3]

Canadians in the late 1990s were concerned about the future of their economy but unsure what steps to take to improve the situation and who should take them. The degree to which the government addressd these problems and developed a national strategy had fluctuated throughout the latter part of the twentieth century. At the centre of much of this debate was Canada's relationship to the United States.

The late 1950s saw the Conservative Diefenbaker government move in a nationalistic, pro-European/anti-American direction; plans were even made to shift about 15% of Canada's trade with the United States to Britain. The Liberals under Lester Pearson turned the country back toward the United States and signed the Auto Pact Agreement (a free trade agreement in car parts) in the late 1960s. When the U.S. economy weakened in the early 1970s, Canada again looked to Europe. The Contractual Agreement between Canada and the European Economic Union was signed but never went very far.[4]

The Liberal governments of the 1970s under Pierre Elliot Trudeau also attempted to plan a national industrial strategy. However, fighting among federal government departments and with provincial governments, each with its own agenda, along with an unsupportive private sector prevented any strategy from getting off the ground.[5] The Trudeau regime was particularly committed to regional economic development, although few of the many schemes targeted at the poorer parts of the country did much more than consume large quantities of the government's largesse. Eventually, growing dissatisfaction with the failure of Liberal economic schemes, unhappiness with the cost and ineffectiveness of Crown corporations, western anger at perceived confiscation of regional resource revenues through the

National Energy Program, and unease about the size and cost of the massive federal bureaucracy contributed to the defeat of the Liberal Party in the 1984 election and gave the Conservative administration a substantially free hand in its planned assault on government involvement in the economy.

The election in 1984 of Brian Mulroney's Progressive Conservative government represented a watershed in Canadian political life. An active campaign began to downsize the government and to privatize numerous government-owned enterprises. The Conservatives sold off PetroCanada (the national energy company), Canadian National Railways, Air Canada, and a variety of other Crown corporations. They reduced funding for regional development and slashed grants to corporations. Canada Post and some cultural agencies were the few government organizations to remain untouched. Surprisingly, this dramatic reduction in the scope and power of government elicited little protest. The general public appeared either not to recognize or not to care; the academic left, which did both, was generally ignored.

When the Liberals under Jean Chrétien took power in 1993, they promised a more interventionist government, but in fact little changed. A few small support programs, such as those for east coast fishers, remained in place, but even Crown corporations like the Canadian Broadcasting Corporation and Canada Post were required to operate on a more commercial basis. The mid-1980s to the late 1990s, therefore, saw the role for the Canadian government severely reduced, with the one exception of macroeconomic management (setting of interest rates, inflation fighting tactics, etc.). Privatization and downsizing of government stripped away the ability and willingness of the Canadian government to intervene in the economy. The Canadian government largely adopted the neo-classical approach to business management.

Canada's response to Japan's economic changes reveals the implications of this approach. As Canada's second largest trading partner and a strikingly important global trader accounting, in 1996, for 20% of world GNP,[6] Japan represented an opportunity for Canada to diversify both geographically from an over-dependence on the United States and sectorally from its historical and contemporary emphasis on resource exports. Recognition of Japan's potential for Canada resulted in the publication in 1993 of the first annual *Canada's Action Plan for Japan*, a booklet that "articulates a set of principles and initiatives which are most appropriate to realize Canada's potential in seven of Japan's highest-growth sectors."[7] Nonetheless, while the value of Canada's exports to Japan increased in the 1990s, exports to Japan as a percentage of Canada's total exports declined. Japan rapidly increased its imports of manufactured products; Canada continued to export primary and partially processed goods. By 1997, not all of Canada's initiatives had had time to achieve results, and some success stories, such as the increase in exports of prefabricated buildings, indicated that a long-term healthy trading relationship with Japan was not out of the question. However, Canada still had a long way to go to capitalize on the potential of the Japanese market.

This chapter examines the specific initiatives that formed the Canadian government's approach to international business development in the 1990s, and its investment and trade relations with Japan through to 1997; the discussion reveals the tensions between the idea of limited government and the opportunities for government leadership in the matter of international trade.

CANADA'S TRADE POLICY

Canada is comprised of ten provinces and three territories and operates under a federal political system.[8] The provincial governments have primary jurisdiction over health, education, and social welfare, and are engaged in a continual tug-of-war with the federal government over further provincial responsibilities. Several of the provinces have their own international business or trade ministries and some maintain trade offices abroad. (British Columbia, Quebec, and Alberta all have trade offices in Tokyo.) The federal Department of Foreign Affairs and International Trade (DFAIT), formerly External Affairs,[9] has primary responsibility for coordinating Canada's economic relations and expanding Canada's international trade.[10] Restructuring within DFAIT began in 1993 and by 1998 all activities relating to a country, from general relations through to trade, were coordinated out of one division. While DFAIT was responsible for Canada's international relations, Industry Canada focused on national economic issues and domestic industry sectors.[11]

As of the time of the case study, responsibility for generating foreign investment rested mainly with the Investment Development Section (also known as TBRI), in the Investment, Science and Technology, and Partnering Division of DFAIT. This section's objective was to increase Canada's share of the world's inward foreign direct investment by attracting and retaining international business investment. In concert with geographic divisions, TBRI delivered a responsive Investor Servicing Program and a proactive Promotional Investment and Corporate Services Program.[12]

An Investment Partnership Canada unit, jointly managed by DFAIT and Industry Canada, targeted and serviced specific multinational enterprises.[13] For a while, Canada had a Foreign Investment Review Agency, designed to review new investments and acquisitions and to regulate the operations of foreign corporations in Canada. The Mulroney government disbanded the agency in 1985 and thereafter only investments of over $150 million were screened.[14]

Canada had four trade policy priorities in 1997: to manage the Canada-U.S. economic relationship, to support an effective World Trade Organization, to improve international rules governing foreign direct investment and anti-competitive behaviour, and to widen Canada's network of free trade partners.[15] According to DFAIT's Trade Policy Planning Division, these priorities evolved through years of consultation with the public and private sectors.[16] There did not appear to be a clear process for the development of more specific trade policy priorities, and changes appeared to happen gradually. These priorities did not require the approval of the federal cabinet.[17]

The four priorities were an interesting reflection of the nation. While the focus on managing the country's relations with the United States was understandable, given Canada's overwhelming reliance on its southern neighbour, its other priorities, while admirable, were better suited to a country that truly was a global trader. Perhaps they reflected how Canada, or the Canadian government, liked to see itself – as one of the world's greatest trading nations – rather than as a country that exported 85% of its goods to a single destination. It is interesting that Canada did not choose to target expanding its trade with a small number of countries. The fourth priority of widening Canada's network of free trade partners would seem to address this, but the details revealed such a wide agenda – "encouraging the expansion of NAFTA," "building stronger ties with the EU," "pursuing a Free Trade Agreement of the Americas," "further the momentum of the Miami summit by initiating discussions with the MERCOSUR countries (i.e. Brazil, Argentina, Paraguay, Uruguay)," "seeking further commitments across the Pacific with Canada's partners in APEC" – that there was little focus to the goal.

Until 1990, most international business planning was done through a system of annual reporting from Canada's embassies and consulates abroad. Every post would identify the sectors holding the greatest potential for Canadian companies, the steps proposed to pursue these opportunities, and the money required. Policy issues would also be identified and passed on to the federal government in Ottawa at this time. Ottawa would then assign funds to each post, to be spent on the activities identified.

Canada's International Business Strategy (CIBS) began to develop in 1990. It consolidated the reporting from posts abroad with all the international activities of the various federal departments. Initially, CIBS began simply as a commitment among Industry Canada, External Affairs (now DFAIT), and Investment Canada (now subsumed into DFAIT) to coordinate their activities to some degree[18] and, with the private sector, to develop an international trade business plan.

This plan was sparked by an interest within DFAIT in obtaining, before the centenary of the Canadian Trade Commissioner Service in 1995, a comprehensive private sector evaluation of how well the TCS had been serving its clients. The resulting International Business Development Review Report, submitted on 30 September 1994,[19] was written by L.R. Wilson, head of Bell Canada Enterprises, and twelve other Canadian business people recruited from various provinces and industry sectors. Their task had been "to review the federal government's international business development programs and services":[20] they concentrated on DFAIT but also looked at what some of the other eighteen departments with international business-related programs and services were doing. One of the objectives of the study was to identify areas where funding could be cut.[21]

The report consisted of an introduction and then twenty recommendations, some broad and other more specific, such as the expansion of certain programs. The first recommendation was that, given the excessive duplication of programs and services related to international business development, "all federal and provincial activities relating to international business promotion be better coordinated, in part by strengthening the International Trade Business Plan by linking resource decisions within the context of this plan."[22] Recommendation 5 suggested focusing resources and attention in specific directions: "The Committee recommends the Government of Canada make difficult choices and focus, as other countries have done, on the sectors that the international marketplace is signaling as the growth industries of the future."[23]

Sectors listed as examples included advanced materials, biotechnologies, information technologies, advanced manufacturing technologies, medical, education, and health care products, and environmental industries. The recommendation goes on to say: "We must focus our business development programs on geographic markets of greatest opportunity for Canadian business." These geographic markets, however, were not identified. The report overall received a mixed but generally favourable reaction, while the recommendation regarding the selection of specific sector and geographic markets on which to focus was controversial. One DFAIT official summed it up this way: "The recommendation stirred up all the old fears both within government and in the business community that good firms were going to be short changed because they were not in the sector or the country of 'the week.'"[24]

In the end, therefore, geographic markets were not specified and the sectors listed were identified simply as growth sectors for Canada over the coming years. DFAIT then defined core services that could be provided for all sectors and markets and added an 'enhanced' level of service to the sectors that were priorities.[25] The need for a process to review the chosen countries and sectors was also discussed; International Trade Minister Roy MacLaren agreed with the general idea of choosing target markets and sectors, but he also recognized the political difficulty and felt that it was vital that the 'client' or business community be fully involved in making the choice.[26]

In any event, the government acted quickly to address the remaining recommendations in the International Business Development Review Report: one year and two days after it was submitted, MacLaren announced at the annual meeting of the Canadian Exporters' Association the start of what came to be known as the Team Canada initiatives[27] – initiatives whose first goal was to "double the number of active Canadian exporters by the year 2000."[28]

CIBS was the core of these initiatives, and its purpose was to develop the federal government's long-range plans for international business development priorities through a consultative process between the government and the private sector. CIBS attempted to streamline the promotion of international business by bringing together all of the various players involved in the export of Canadian goods: Industry Canada's knowledge of the domestic market was combined with DFAIT's understanding of offshore markets, the regional knowledge of the provincial international trade ministries, and the hands-on expertise of the private sector. Following the establishment of CIBS, representatives from Industry Canada, DFAIT, the provincial governments, industry associations, and private sector companies began to meet twice a year as members of National Sector Teams, to discuss and design sector strategies and to review proposed promotional activities for the year.[29] In 1997 there were twenty-three National Sector Teams.[30] The teams were allocated financial resources from Cabinet (the one and only blueprint for allocating financial resources for international business programs and services) and each team determined how that money would be spent.[31] All international business promotion initiatives were approved by the teams. In addition, sub-groups were started for the priority countries of every sector. Representatives from Canada's post in the country involved also had input in the process.[32]

By encouraging cooperation and assigning the National Sector Teams' fiscal responsibilities, the federal government hoped to

eliminate duplication and overlap in services. Agreements to participate in the CIBS process (a memorandum of understanding, letter of
understanding, or letter of agreement) were reached with all of the
provinces and territories,[33] with the exception of Quebec. According
to a ministry official in 1996, however, the strength of Quebec's
involvement in the National Sector Teams exceeded that of any other
province.[34] Among other items, the provinces and territories agreed to
supply their "sector strategies and initial listings of proposed activities
related to the CIBS early in the planning process" and "to provide
timely input into the CIBS development and review process."[35]

Underlying the National Sector Teams were Regional Trade Networks. The networks were "a regional equivalent of the National
Sector Teams, only they are horizontal rather than sectoral."[36] They
brought together federal and provincial governments and agencies at
the regional level to combine expertise and resources and thereby
provide better service to the business community. They offered "training and counseling, and provide companies with market intelligence
and international financing information."[37] The Regional Trade Networks also produced Regional Trade Plans, which, while containing
sectoral and market priorities, focused primarily on mechanisms for
service delivery.[38]

While the private sector was heavily involved in the National Sector
Teams, further opportunities for industry participation on a policy
level were also encouraged through Sectoral Advisory Groups on
International Trade (SAGIT), made up of people from private companies, and the International Trade Advisory Committee (ITAC),
through which senior representatives from the private sector gave con-
fidential advice to the minister of international trade.[39] SAGITs were
first created during the negotiations for the Canada-U.S. Free Trade
Agreement.[40]

The Team Canada initiatives were seen as a strong start at stream-
lining Canada's international business activities. However, while
resources and personnel became more focused, the government still
shied away from the fifth recommendation in the IBDR report, to
choose priority sectors and priority geographic areas. The political
risks of choosing one sector or geographic area over another and
alienating voters proved too great for the politicians. In July/August
1995, a DFAIT memo that outlined priority sectors and countries and
called for their adoption got as far as Cabinet before being turned
down. The second section of the CIBS overview had a few paragraphs
on the potential of many of the markets in the world, but each was presented in equally positive terms.[41] The closest the government came to
prioritizing was summed up in Roy MacLaren's comment when he

introduced the Team Canada initiatives in 1995: "Although we shall continue to offer a broad range of support to all companies in all sectors, we shall be offering enhanced support in certain key areas."[42]

This desire to streamline and focus without specifying sectors and geographic areas caused problems. For example, most of the difficulties with organizing the National Sector Teams were related to the fact that there were so many of them. Initially, DFAIT planned to have teams only for those sectors where it thought the country's strengths lay, but few well-organized sectors were excluded. Those that had been excluded could be added, at least as sub-sectors, if they lobbied hard enough.[43]

As industry associations were not the architects of the National Sector Team process, some bought into the process passively rather than taking a proactive approach. The stronger and better organized of the industry associations (such as that for automobiles), wanted to take charge of the process. Many of the teams had working groups or sector teams to cover sub-sectors. The Agriculture and Food Products National Sector Team, for example, had twenty-five working groups in 1997 covering sub-sectors such as beef, grain, wine, and dairy.[44] All meetings involved provincial and federal bureaucrats from a number of departments; twenty-three teams meeting twice a year meant a lot of meetings for the government participants, and various ways to get around this problem – conference call meetings or exchanging as much information as possible over e-mail – were tried.

Other problems with the system were not insurmountable; they simply required time to work out. Provincial budgeting schedules did not match with those of the National Sector Teams, with the result that often the provinces did not have their plans in place until after the teams' deadline for submitting their lists of approved expenditures. A more complicated challenge was making sure that everyone participated in the National Sector Team process by submitting all their planned international business expenditures to the teams for approval. Some federal departments tried to work around the system and budget for events that should have been under Sector Team approval within their own budgets. The process and the rationale here were fairly simple: government departments required funds to proceed with their own trade development activities and agendas. Waiting for the more cumbersome, consultative process to provide the necessary funds typically took a great deal more time and the results were much less certain. As a consequence, many senior officials preferred to proceed within existing departmental operations.

The IBDR report recommended financial funding cuts to DFAIT's headquarters operations, stating that "from a business perspective, the most valuable international business development service is that being performed overseas" and that the cuts should be made in both trade policy and trade promotion.[45] DFAIT, struggling under the effects of several consecutive years of budget cuts, found its resources spread very thinly over a broad and complex set of responsibilities. Given that many of its headquarters and consular activities were formally mandated and not, like most aspects of trade promotion, discretionary, DFAIT was constantly worried that additional reductions in staff and resources would further harm its ability to perform its many tasks.

CANADA-JAPAN INVESTMENT AND TRADE TO 1997

At the same time that Canada was revamping its overall international trade strategy, there was a growing recognition that the government needed to pay more attention to Japan. Prior to 1992, there was no coordinated strategy for Japan, nor a perceived need for one. Japan was still seen as a relatively insignificant trading partner by most members of the business community – and it has traditionally been the business community from which the government takes its lead – and Canadian exports to Japan were increasing even as Japan's economy was slowing down.[46] After 1993, all DFAIT activities (diplomatic, trade, and investment) related to Japan came out of one place – the Japan division – to ensure greater coordination. Until 1993, it would be safe to say that the Canadian government and the national business community did not pay much attention to the changes occurring in the Japanese economy and did little to respond to those of which it was aware. The United States was simply too large and too dominant a presence, and in the latter part of the 1980s, while Japan's economy was being transformed after the Plaza Accord, Canada was debating the pros and cons of the Canada-U.S. Free Trade Agreement, so perhaps this is not too surprising.

Canada's presence in Japan includes the embassy in Tokyo, a consulate-general in Osaka, and trade offices in Fukuoka (established in 1991) and Nagoya (established in 1992). The formalities of state between the two countries are well looked after; economic relationships and commercial possibilities have attracted less attention.[47]

From the early 1980s, the Canadian government began to strip away the remaining vestiges of economic nationalism and encourage greater foreign investment. The 1985 Investment Canada Act proclaimed that Canada was "open for business" and subsequent federal government investment policy decisions were made with this in mind.[48] Canada had limits on foreign investment in, or foreign acqui-

Table 4.1   Japanese and U.S. direct investment in Canada, 1984–1997
(C$m and %)

	Japan	United States	Total
1984	2,074	64,762	85,964
	(2.4)	(75.3)	
1986	2,679	69,241	96,054
	(2.8)	(72.1)	
1988	3,582	76,345	114,480
	(3.1)	(66.7)	
1990	5,214	84,353	131,131
	(4.0)	(64.3)	
1992	5,899	89,115	138,696
	(4.3)	(64.3)	
1994	6,552	101,514	152,784
	(4.3)	(66.4)	
1995	6,702	113,092	168,077
	(4.0)	(67.7)	
1996	7,054	118,261	174,578
	(4.0)	(67.7)	
1997	7,123	130,022	187,586
	(3.8)	(69.3)	

Note: Figures within parentheses are percentages.
Source: Statistics Canada, Canada's International Investment Position, 1994, 1995
and 1997, Catalogue 67–202

sition of companies in, financial services, broadcasting, cultural industries, fishing, uranium, telecommunications, and transportation.[49] For
the most part, however, the federal government encouraged foreign
investment and supported initiatives to open up the Canadian economy.

As described in chapter 2, Japan's investment presence in Canada
developed steadily through the 1980s. Japan became Canada's third
largest investor, behind the United States and the United Kingdom.
Following the Plaza Accord, Japanese investment in Canada began to
increase dramatically. While in 1984 Japanese invested C$2.1 billion,
by 1986 this had increased to C$2.7 billion, by 1994 to C$5.9 billion,
and by 1997 to C$7.1 billion (see table 4.1). Although these amounts
paled in comparison with the massive American investments in the
country, Japan nonetheless increased its share of total direct investment in Canada from 2.4% in 1984 to a peak of 4.3% in 1992 and
1994. (The United States' share declined during this same period
from 75.3% in 1984 to 64.3% in 1992.)[50]

This post-Plaza surge in investment saw Japanese investors begin to
move away from the traditional resource areas and into a broader

Table 4.2[53]   Japanese direct investment in Canada by industry, 1984–1994
(C$m)

	1984	1986	1988	1990	1992	1994
Food, beverages	9	9	15	38	24	25
Wood, paper	73	93	788	1,096	1,187	856
Energy	709	715	251	-63	130	194
Chemicals, textiles	15	1	7	220	240	226
Minerals, metals	124	125	415	747	927	925
Machinery, equipment	34	121	175	271	337	486
Transportation equipment	348	768	815	757	898	955
Electrical	89	182	225	281	302	278
Construction	4	4		178	270	278
Transportation services	5	5	16	50	16	50
Finance/Insurance	201	328	576	888	842	982
Consumer goods and services	372	197	100	368	285	286
Other	91	131	200	384	404	414
TOTAL	2,074	2,679	3,582	5,214	5,802	5,849

Source: Statistics Canada, *Canada's International Investment Position, 1994*, Catalogue 67-202

range of investments, including auto assembly and auto parts manufacturing, the processing of wood fiber into newsprint, and such services as hotels, banking, and construction (see table 4.2).[51] This diversification in investment was not unique to Canada. Japanese companies wished to take advantage of lower labour costs and overcome protectionist sentiments that were rising in the face of Japan's massive trade surplus, and production in Canada, particularly after the Canada-U.S. Free Trade Agreement, offered Japanese companies access to the lucrative American market without the tensions that production in the U.S. itself would bring. Most of the new Japanese investment came in the automobile sector, as Japanese firms sought to capitalize on the opportunity to secure specialized access to the American market under the Auto Pact Agreement. On a cyclical basis, key sectors (wood and paper in 1988 to 1994, chemicals beginning in 1990, minerals and metals in 1990) attracted considerable attention. Finance and other service companies followed the manufacturing companies so that they could continue to service them, resulting in sizable investments in finance and insurance. According to David Edgington, a geographer specializing in the study of Japanese business activity, in 1986, Canadian subsidiaries of Japanese banks handled close to 90% of Japanese financial activity in Canada.[52] By 1990 automotive, banking, and service sectors accounted for 36% of all Japanese investment in Canada.

Table 4.3   Major Canadian hotel and resort properties purchased by Japanese
investors, 1986–1990

Japanese Investor	Hotel/Resort Name	Location	Year
Tokyu	Pan Pacific	Vancouver	1986
Itoman	Harrison Hot Springs	Harrison	1987
Aoki	Westin Hotel	Vancouver	1988
Listel	International Lodge	Whistler	1988
IPEC/ICEC	Nancy Green Lodge	Whistler	1988
IPEC	Harbour Towers Hotel	Victoria	1988
Mutsumi	Whistler Fairways Hotel	Whistler	1988
Okabe	Coast Hotel/Motel Chain	Vancouver/B.C.	1988
Okabe	Ramada Ren Hotel	Vancouver	1988
Palios	O'Douls Hotel	Vancouver	1989
Chotokan	Radium Hot Springs	Resort Radium	1989
Yamanouchi Pharmaceutical	Chateau Whistler (80%)	Whistler	1989
Crossroads Enterprises	Royal Oak Inn	Victoria	1989
Maiami Canada	Ming Court Hotel	Vancouver	1990
Libest	Westbrook Whistler	Whistler	1990

The late 1980s saw a large number of Japanese purchases of major
hotel and resort properties in B.C. (see table 4.3) and a gradual expansion of the auto plants as they worked to serve not only the Canadian
market but the whole North American market. By 1989 there were
three Japanese-owned auto production plants in Canada: Honda
Canada (started in 1986), Toyota Motor Manufacturing (1988) and
CAMI Automotive (a Suzuki-GM Canada joint venture which com-
menced operations in 1989). All three were in southern Ontario, in
Alliston, Cambridge, and Ingersoll respectively. In 1995 these three
plants produced over 391,000 units, about 16.5% of light motor
vehicle production in Canada;[54] over 85% of the vehicles were destined for export, primarily to the United States. The Honda, Toyota,
and CAMI plants represented a combined investment of about C$2.6
billion and employed approximately 5,400 people at full production.[55]
Toyota announced plans in 1994 to invest C$600 million and build a
second Cambridge plant, which was scheduled to open in August 1997
(it opened in 2000). Early 1997 saw the announcement of the investment of an additional C$400 million to enable the Cambridge plant to
produce a new car.[56] Honda also announced plans in late 1997 to
expand its Alliston plant.[57]

Supporting these three manufacturing plants were over thirty
machine tool operations and manufacturers of auto parts and related
materials, which employed about 17,000 people. Most of these plants

Table 4.4 Japanese automotive parts-related investment and joint ventures in Canada

Company	Type of Venture	# of Employees	Year Operational	Product Line
	AUTOMOTIVE PARTS MANUFACTURERS			
ABC Nishikawa	Joint	125	1989	Panels Parts
Atoma Int.	Joint	2,500	1989	Auto Parts
Alcoa Fujikura	Joint	270	1995	Wiring Harness
Bridgestone	Direct	2,175	1990	Tires
Canadian Auto Parts Toyota	Direct	161	1984	Aluminum Wheels
Craft Originators	Direct	75	1995	Labels & Emblems
DDM Plastics	Joint	596	1989	Plastic Bumpers
F&P Mtg.	Joint	408	1987	Stampings, Support Beams
Freudenburg-Nok	Joint	140	1991	Gaskets, Fuel System Parts
General Seating	Joint	290	1989	Seating
Intertec Sys	Joint	106	1995	Instrument Panels
Lear Seating	Licence Agr.	2,000	1984	Seat Frames
Manchester Plastics	Licence Agr.	1,230	1995	Door Trim
MSB Plastics	Direct	170	1989	Mould Compnents
Nichirin Inc.	Direct	224	1987	Hosing & Tubing
NTN Bearing	Direct	119	1973	Bearings
Omron Dualtech	Direct	160	1984	Auto Relays
Progressive Moulded Products	Sub-Contract	250	1984	Cooling Fans
Quality Safety Sys.	Joint	668	1987	Seat Belts
Rockwell Int.	Joint	480	1986	Suspension Systems
TS Tech Canada	Joint	100	1995	Seat Assemblies
Vuteq Canada	Direct	238	1989	Window Shields
Waterville TG	Direct	1,343	1986	Weather Strips
Yachiyo of Ontario	Direct	140	1990	Stamping, Welding
	MATERIALS AND MACHINE TOOLS			
Aclo Compounders	Joint	75	1986	Plastic Compound
Canada Mould Technology	Joint	49	1989	Dies
DNN Galvanizing	Joint	100	1993	Galvanized Steel
Monzen Steel	Joint	4	1996	Automotive Steel Coil
Sanyo Canadian Machine	Direct	52	1982	Assembly Line Equipment
Z-Line	Joint	55	1990	Coated Steel

Source: Pacific Automotive Co-operation Inc. (PAC), *JAMA Canada Annual Report, 1997*

began operations in the late 1980s and almost all were located in Ontario (see table 4.4). In 1984 Pacific Automotive Co-operation or PAC was formed to facilitate Japanese investment in the auto parts sector and particularly to assist with the formation of joint ventures between Canadian and Japanese companies.

Investment in Canadian forestry by Japanese companies has a relatively long history, and some important developments occurred after 1985, including the establishment of two pulp mills in northern Alberta. In 1990 Daishowa opened a C$580 million bleached kraft pulp mill near the community of Peace River. The company signed a renewable twenty-year forestry management agreement to harvest an area of more than 24,000 square kilometres. The province spent C$65 million on road and rail access, including some of the costs incurred in building a new bridge to be used only by the mill.[58] The second mill was built by Alberta-Pacific (a joint venture of three primarily Japanese-owned entities, with Mitsubishi Corporation being the dominant interest) between Athabasca and Lac La Biche. Alberta-Pacific had the forestry management rights to a 61,000-square kilometre area in northeast Alberta. It received C$275 million in subordinated debentures from the Alberta government, which also invested about C$75 million in infrastructure costs.[59] Daishowa also purchased High Level Forest Products in Northern Alberta in 1990. Daishowa-Marubeni Ltd. (a joint venture between Daishowa Paper and Marubeni Corporation, a Japanese trading company) announced plans to build a C$900 million coated paper mill in Peace River, Alberta. The mill was scheduled to open in October 2001 and to employ 300 people.[60]

Japanese companies also moved into investments in value-added forest products. The Canadian Chopstick Manufacturing Company (45% owned by Mitsubishi Canada and 55% by Chugoku Pearl and Company) had a chopstick manufacturing operation in Fort Nelson, B.C. (It closed on 1 April 1997.) Mitsui Homes established a prefabricated homes manufacturing plant in Langley, B.C. in 1994. Developments of this sort – Japanese companies working in Canada but exporting back to Japan – gave the impression that Canadian firms were rapidly expanding their trade with Japan. The reality was much simpler: Japanese firms discovered that Canada was a relatively low-wage, high quality base for Japanese production. These were Japanese, not Canadian, initiatives.

While Japan's investment in Canada increased and a number of significant Japanese investments were made, Canada failed to capture a full share of available Japanese foreign direct investment. Canada received US$8.3 billion or 1.78% of Japan's cumulative total overseas investment for the fiscal years 1951-94, while Australia, with a smaller economy than Canada, received almost US$23.9 billion or 5.16% of the cumulative total. In 1992 Canada received US$753 million in Japanese FDI, or 2.2% of all Japanese overseas investments; Australia

Table 4.5   Japan's foreign direct investment, selected countries, 1984–1994
(US$m)

Country	1984	1986	1988	1990	1992	1994	Cumul. (1951– 1994)	Cumul. %
Australia	105	881	2,413	3,669	2,150	1,265	23,932	5.16
Canada	184	276	626	1,064	753	1,265	8,261	1.78
China	114	226	296	349	1,070	2,565	8,729	1.90
Mexico	56	226	87	168	60	613	2,793	0.60
New Zealand	15	93	117	231	67	115	1,376	0.30
S. Korea	107	436	483	284	225	400	5,268	1.14
Singapore	225	302	747	840	670	1154	9,535	2.06
U.S.	3,359	10,165	21,701	26,128	13,819	17,331	194,429	41.94
Total	10,155	22,320	47,022	56,911	34,138	41,051	463,606	

Source: Pacific Basin Economic Council Statistics, 1996 (formerly Pacific Economic Community Statistics, 1988, 1990, 1994)

received $1.9 billion or 6.3% (see table 4.5). As can be seen in table 4.5, in 1994, Australia and Canada received the same amount of investment, due to a sudden drop in Japanese investment in Australia (see chapter 6). Canada generally received about 5% of Japanese investment in North America annually, disproportionately low for its 10% share of the continent's population.

Several factors explained Canada's low share of Japanese FDI. Some reasons were things that the nation could not do anything about – a relatively small population; investor preference for accessing the Canadian market from an American base – but if Canada wished to receive more Japanese investment, it had to do a better job of emphasizing the strengths it did have. According to the author of a 1994 Canadian embassy report on trends in Japanese FDI: "It will be important to continue to stress recent favourable economic developments including the significant drop in cost per unit in Canadian manufacturing and changes in the exchange rate that have moderated the high cost position of a few years ago."[61] The report went on to say: "A key challenge for Canada will be to demonstrate its advantages over the U.S. as a location for JFDI. Decisive factors considered by Japanese investors will be access to technology, improved productivity levels, exchange rates, taxation regimes, and labour climates."[62] The Canadian labour environment, with its frequent strikes and work stoppages, was definitely an area in which Canada could improve. Japanese investors, accustomed to a work world where strikes are rare and when they do occur are often as short as fifteen minutes, were understandably nervous about the labour situation in Canada. However, according to the report, the most important factor for attracting Japanese investment was, and would continue to be, the ability of Canadian industry "to provide Japanese investors with investment opportunities in high growth knowledge-intensive industries."[63] Without the development of those opportunities, Canada was unlikely to see an increase in Japanese FDI.

In September 1996, a Keidanren (Japanese Economic Federation) Business Partnership Mission came to Canada to learn about investment opportunities and to find corporate partners. The mission, instigated in response to an invitation from the Canadian government, was the first to visit Canada since 1989 (around the time of the Canada-U.S. Free Trade Agreement).[64] Meetings were set up with business people in information technology, processed foods, and building products. The goal, however, was as much to collect information on current Canadian conditions as it was to explore possible trade and investment opportunities and technological partnerships. The mission appeared to have been successful, as members were impressed by the vitality of Canada's software companies and by Canada's abilities in biotechnology.[65] (The information technology sector group recommended that a catalogue of Canadian information technology and telecommunications technology companies interested in the Japanese market be compiled.)[66] As the Keidanren mission's report would be well publicized and a significant source of information on Canada for Japanese companies, the fact that the report was positive was important.

The Keidanren mission's key comment, however, was that while their members had learned a great deal about Canada and the Canadian economy during the visit, it was also important for Canadians to be better informed about new economic conditions and changing consumer demands in Japan.[67]

While Canada was largely oblivious to the new opportunities in post-Plaza Japan, the speed with which so may Japanese investments occurred immediately after 1985 reveals that at least some significant Japanese decision-making took place before the accord. The Japanese moved before the yen actually changed in value, in a response to growing western (primarily American) criticism of massive Japanese trade surpluses.[68] In the atmosphere of widespread criticism and the desire of the Japanese government and business community to head off extreme action through voluntary initiatives, Japanese firms were proactive in planning to expand investments to Canada and other countries. To this extent, the Plaza Accord was essentially a turning point in Japanese economic affairs, for it codified processes and

Table 4.6   Canadian exports to Japan, 1984–1998
(US$m)

Year	Value	% of Total Exports
1984	$4,394	4.9
1985	4,222	4.7
1986	4,238	4.7
1987	5,335	5.4
1988	7,085	6.1
1989	7,429	6.2
1990	7,135	5.6
1991	6,190	4.9
1992	6,073	4.6
1993	6,419	4.6
1994	6,857	4.3
1995	8,531	4.5
1996	7,471	3.7
1997	7,250	3.4
1998	4,788	2.3

Source: International Monetary Fund, Direction of Trade Statistics 1990, 1996, and 1999.

understandings that were already in place. In other words, the Japanese were aware of changing international economic conditions, were active in responding to them, and shaped their response to individual countries. Canada was less active across the board.

In 1997, Japan was Canada's second largest trading partner after the United States, and had been in this position since 1973.[69] Approximately 4–6% of Canadian exports went to Japan between 1985 and 1995, although from 1991 on, this percentage steadily declined and reached only 3.4% in 1997 (see table 4.6, which, to provide for greater comparability with New Zealand and Australia, reports the data in American dollars). In contrast, about 82% of Canadian exports went to the United States (and this percentage steadily increased over the same period) and about 1–2% to each of the United Kingdom and South Korea, Canada's third and fourth ranked partners respectively.

In value terms, Canadian exports to Japan grew in the late 1980s, declined, and then peaked in 1995 at slightly under C$12 billion, a 24% increase over the previous year.[70] In 1996, exports dropped approximately 13% to C$10.5 billion, reached C$10.8 billion in 1997, and fell further again in 1998 to C$8.2 billion.[71]

Canadian exports to Japan in 1997 continued to consist largely of resource products (see table 4.7), although sales of machinery and transportation equipment were slowly increasing. Prefabricated build-

Table 4.7   Top ten Canadian exports to Japan, 1997
             (C$,000)

Wood and articles of wood	2,605,188
Mineral fuel (coal)	1,433,438
Oil seed (canola)	1,036,330
Wood pulp	888,655
Fish and seafood	591,074
Ores (copper)	551,569
Meat	462,607
Aluminum	381,072
Cereals (wheat)	325,644
Paper	267,294

Source: Statistics Canada, Exports by Country 1997

ings were the main success story of the mid-1990s, with sales in 1995 increasing to a total of over C$130 million,[72] a jump of almost 140% from the previous year, as Canada "surpassed the United States to become the world's largest supplier to Japan of prefabricated buildings."[73] (While 1995 was an impressive year, the following two years were sluggish for housing starts and Canadian lumber and prefabricated housing companies were affected.) Canada's success here can be attributed, at least in part, to the long-term promotional efforts of the government, including programs like the B.C. Trade and Investment Office's "Canada Comfort Direct,"[74] and the Atlantic Canada Homes Program, both of which aimed to build product demand and awareness.

Canada Comfort Direct began in 1992 under the then B.C. Trade Development Corporation. By 1997, to become a member, companies were vetted by the B.C. government to ensure that they were serious and ready to do business in Japan. Each company agreed to produce promotional material in Japanese, attend at least six trade shows, and pay a $36,000 annual fee. The 1997 program contained three main parts. The first was the Canadian Building Products Showcase, consisting of one big display and two smaller ones, which were displayed all over Japan at trade shows, seminars, and workshops. There was also a permanent building products display in one of the meeting rooms in the B.C. government's Japan office. Member companies were permitted to use these meeting rooms when in Japan on business. The second part was trade promotion seminars and workshops in which member companies would participate. These were highly successful with good attendance and strong interest shown by the Japanese attendees. Third was the incoming buyers' service. The B.C. government organized and arranged itineraries for Japanese buyers to go to Canada. In 1996 there were two or three of these buyers' missions a week.[75]

Canada Comfort Direct also helped Japanese builders through the steps of importing from Canadian manufacturers or consolidators. Direct links were made between Japanese industry and the Canadian companies through the B.C. government. According to Jim Anholt, Japan representative for the government of British Columbia, the program was a major success. Many companies that did not participate were having difficulties in the Japanese market, while those who did were doing well. In 1997-98, there were twenty companies in Canada Comfort Direct, including seventeen from B.C. and one from each of Ontario, Quebec, and Manitoba. Some companies that had been members in previous years now had enough business on their own and no longer needed the program's services.[76]

The B.C. government, pleased with the program, soon invited the other provinces to join in. Each, however, wanted to start its own program. Atlantic Canada Homes began in 1996, and the Quebec Wood Export Bureau, which first appeared in 1991, began full operations in 1996. Quebec felt that participation in Canada Comfort Direct was too expensive and the requirement to participate in a requisite number of trade shows too demanding, so the Quebec Wood Export Bureau differed in these areas.[77]

Canada's 1997 trade profile with Japan (see table 4.7) differed little from its long-standing export list. While Canadian business responded creatively, particularly in the automotive sector, to opportunities in the U.S., it did not do so with Japan. The list of leading exports to Japan – lumber, wood pulp, coal, fish, canola, copper – is scarcely that of a significant industrial power. It is, instead, the market profile of a nineteenth-century, pre-industrial economy, striving to establish a commercial base for itself. For their part, the Japanese found Canada to be a receptive place for selling automobiles into the U.S. and a reliable source of natural resources needed in the Japanese manufacturing process.

CANADIAN RESPONSES TO CHANGES IN THE JAPANESE ECONOMY

In 1997, in one of its periodic statements about Canada's approach to Asia, the Asia Pacific Foundation, a Vancouver-based research and public education agency, concluded:

Ten years ago, Canada lagged well behind other developed countries in paying attention to the rapidly growing Asian economies despite efforts in the late

1970s and early 1980s to increase our focus on Asia. Our preoccupation during this time was with the US market. Top-level negotiations which led to the Canada-US Free Trade Agreement sent a signal to business: look south. Only in the past few years has an awareness of the economic importance and benefits of greater trade and investment ties to Asia spread through the national, and a majority of our provincial governments, as well as parts of the private sector.[78]

In the late 1980s, Peter Campbell, then director of the Japan division of DFAIT, began to notice the changes occurring in the Japanese economy.[79] He recognized that Canada was not in a good position to respond to these changes, and he noted that the country lacked a sense of what it wanted from the relationship with Japan.[80] Officials at the Canadian embassy in Tokyo were also concerned. An embassy report from 1992 noted that Canada did not appear to have paid much attention to the major changes in the Japanese marketplace, and particularly the changes in Japan's import profile. The few Canadian firms exporting industrial machinery and equipment did take advantage of Japan's dramatic increase in imports of these products from 1985 to 1991: Japanese imports of machinery and equipment from Canada rose 233% in this period and reached 4% of total Japanese imports from Canada. Raw materials and resource products remained as the bulk of exports to Japan, however, and the small growth in manufactured products could not offset the decline in the resource sector.[81] As a result, "over the past six years, Canada's overall trade performance in Japan has lagged behind that of all our major competitors (with the exception of the USA)."[82] As another embassy official observed, "Canada's share of Japanese non-oil imports dropped from 5.4 percent in 1985 to 3.9 percent in 1992. In Canadian dollar terms, the failure to hold market share meant a loss of $3.5 billion in export revenue in 1992."[83] The report, which surveyed trade representatives from the U.S., U.K., France, Germany, Australia, and New Zealand, concluded that the higher the proportion of value-added goods in a country's exports to Japan, the better.

All of the countries surveyed (except New Zealand) aimed to take advantage of the new opportunities and increase their exports of manufactured products.[84] Some commonalities existed in their trade strategies. As described in the embassy report, these included:

developing an advocacy approach to persuade competitive firms to pursue the Japanese market seriously and overcome notions about its impenetrability; allowing the duration of Japan-specific trade initiatives to exceed those for other markets in recognition of the time required to establish a foothold in

Japan; encouraging companies to view the Japanese market as a global one (by targeting sales to Japanese subsidiaries abroad, or by pursuing Japanese ODA contracts); enhancing prospects for success by working with Japanese partners, either through distribution arrangements, joint ventures, or by investment in, or acquisition of, Japanese firms.[85]

In the early 1990s the Canadian government realized that it must develop more concrete strategies for coping with the changes in Japan, and in 1993 International Trade Minister Roy MacLaren launched *Canada's Action Plan for Japan*. The plan was developed with a focus on what Canada could do, rather than on its problems in the Japanese market. DFAIT and the embassy wanted the plan to come from Canada, not just the government, and to this end, DFAIT sought to spark industry involvement and leadership.[86] The plan, developed by the private sector and the federal and provincial governments, was intended to "alert industry to the changing market conditions, encourage product adaptation and assist with product promotion,"[87] and a number of sectors where it was thought a strong effort could make a difference were selected. For each sector, an industry lead group was developed. Sometimes this was an industry association; in other cases, a dozen or so of the top companies in the sector were approached to take this role. While DFAIT employees wrote the report (it was initially hoped that the industry groups would write the plan for their respective sectors), they "made sure that what went into the plan represented what our clients wanted, not what we in our ivory tower thought they needed." [88]

The first Action Plan was published in January 1994 (numerous subsequent editions have been published). Its introduction states that it represents "an integrated effort on the part of all federal and provincial governments in support of clearly articulated private-sector strategies for realizing our potential in the high growth sectors."[89] Peter Campbell described the plan as short, to the point, and rather unsophisticated. The goal was to create a plan that the business community "would actually read and use."[90]

The Action Plans were a promising beginning and indicated that Canadian officials were aware of the implications of the changes in the Japanese economy. However, the plans provided only vague guidelines, not clear directions, and offered little real leadership. Much of the booklet consisted of contact names, and it gave few clear indications of what had to be done to capitalize on Japanese opportunities. Representatives from the Japan division of DFAIT argued, however, that contact names were what business people were seeking; they were not interested in the big picture or a strategy but simply in what would help them do business. The problem, then, was that the Action Plan was trying to be two different things: a tool for business people interested in exporting to Japan and a statement of Canada's overall plan of action with regard to Japan.

Nonetheless, the Action Plans articulated a recognition of the importance of Japan as a trading partner for Canada and a desire to improve Canada's sales to Japan, and they defined the sectors through which this improvement should take place. Nine sectors were highlighted in the 1999–2000 Action Plan. Five were identified as priorities (agrifood and fisheries, building products, health industries, information technology, and tourism) and four as emerging markets (environment, aerospace, new energy and electricity, and education). The nine were described as being among Japan's highest growth sectors, but it is not clear if these particular sectors were chosen because of their long-term potential or because they were then doing well. Each edition of the plan has seen some changes to the list of chosen sectors. After two editions, two new sectors were added (consumer products/furniture and health care products/medical devices) and two others (aerospace and auto parts) were "'graduated' from the Plan."[91] The subsequent edition graduated processed food products and added giftware and sporting goods. The word 'graduated' implies that these sectors have realized their potential, but how that was determined is not explained. Discussions with DFAIT employees clarified that placement in the Action Plan carried a guarantee of a certain status of funding: aerospace and auto parts, strong industries with lots of money, were judged not to need the help of the Action Plan. (However, space-related products re-emerged in the 1999–2000 edition.) Clearly, the logic and stability of the Action Plan process was somewhat suspect, and the routine changes in the plan suggest that Canadian priorities were driven as much by political considerations as by an understanding of the Japanese market or a desire to build long-term commercial relationships with Japan.

Only one of the sectors – fish and seafood – overlapped with the list of top ten exports. The sectors chosen ranged from those in which Canada was doing very well (building products, fish and seafood) to those in which Canada showed potential but maintained low market share (health industries and information technologies). Tourism and education fall in the services area and are therefore harder to quantify on a market-share basis.

The Action Plans were successful insofar as their focus on specific fields stimulated growth. Klaus Pringsheim, president of the Canada-Japan Trade Council, attributed a portion of the increase in Canadian processed food sales in Japan to the highlighting of "processed food products as one of Japan's highest growth sectors... There is no doubt that this fact has encouraged Canadian processed food producers to step up their efforts in this area."[92]

Yet, despite the Action Plans, Canada's exports to Japan remained much as they had always been. Forest products, fish, grain, aluminum and, more recently, coal predominated. While progress in diversifying exports and moving toward value-added products was made, the impact was slight. Those years in which the total value of Canadian exports to Japan showed an increase were usually a reflection of temporary price increases for a range of commodities. The handicaps in selling manufactured goods to Asia remained.[93]

"Nowhere is this lack of market penetration in manufactured goods more serious than in Japan. Our dependence on raw material exports to Japan is an Achilles' heel as demand for these products will stagnate or even decline as basic changes that are already underway in the Japanese economy evolve further. The most important of these are the aging of the population, deregulation of the economy and the shift offshore of a large portion of Japan's manufacturing industry."[94] These comments by the Asia Pacific Foundation reflected a concern that Canada's export portfolio was not in the country's best economic interest. The APF was evidently also of the opinion that Asia, and particularly Japan, were significant to Canada's future. Agreement on this, however, was not widespread, and many Canadians, including some in government, were content for Canada to remain primarily an exporter of resources and automotive products to the United States. The continued strength of the American economy during the 1990s buttressed this viewpoint.

The situation on the investment front was similar. Canada had no particular plan for attracting Japanese investment, and it therefore attracted little investment relative to other nations.

Conflicting federal-provincial jurisdiction was mentioned as an investment obstacle in the 1992 *Canada-Japan Forum 2000* report. Since then, the prime minister and the provincial premiers began working to eliminate inter-provincial barriers to trade, investment, and labour mobility.[95] Even more necessary was a national investment strategy to determine the sectors and conditions under which investment would be sought, as well as which sectors needed protecting. In the 1990s Canada protected industries it determined to be culturally significant such as broadcasting; potentially other resource or newly developing industries needed similar protection or assistance.

Canada's collective inattention to opportunities in Japan reflected the combination of a wide variety of factors. The most dominant reason was the most obvious: Canada's continued economic reliance on the United States. With the world's largest economy stretched out along a 3,000-mile, economically permeable border, it made little sense to many Canadians to seek out distant and uncertain markets. That many leading Canadian firms are branch plants or subsidiaries of major American corporations limited their interest in international expansion and their responsiveness to government entreaties. And given the diminished role of government in Canadian life, a legacy of the largely unsuccessful attempts at economic management in the 1970s and 1980s, it was clear that Canadian business generally did not expect the government to provide much leadership. Furthermore, the continuing tensions between federal and provincial governments obstructed creative, collaborative, and consistent economic planning. Even with the rapid growth in the country's Asian-born population, there was reluctance to develop trading opportunities on the other side of the Pacific Ocean. There were other difficulties: a limited culture of entrepreneurship, especially on the international front; a steadfast belief that resource production would fuel prosperity into the distant future; and a limited pool of risk capital in the country, along with a strong pattern of corporate mergers and take-overs that had absorbed large portions of the nation's investment base.

In an era of business-led economic development, when the federal government made only limited attempts at leadership and devoted its efforts to consultation and trade missions, Canada did not participate significantly in the economic transformation of the world's second largest economy. While it is impossible to determine the precise cost of inaction and missed opportunities, it is clear that Canadian businesses did not exploit the opportunities created in post-Plaza Accord Japan and, with only a few exceptions, were not aware of what had been missed.

In the final analysis, this is both a testament to the failure of laissez-faire economics and an indication of the peculiar, parochial tendencies of Canadian business and government. It is worth noting that DFAIT's attempts, through CIBS and the Action Plans, to provide useful assessments of opportunities in Japan were limited by the political reluctance to positively identify target markets and sectors. Whether a more interventionist political regime would have produced better results is impossible to assess with any degree of validity. What is clear is that the Canadian approach to international trade development between 1985 and 1997 failed to capitalize on one of the most significant economic transitions in the past fifty years, and that the country missed out on important, long-term development prospects as a consequence. If nothing else, the experience should raise questions about the legitimacy of a business-driven international trade agenda and about the developing pattern of political acquiescence to the dictates of Canadian business.

Proposing an alternate approach for Canada is limited by the rigidities of the political/constitutional system, the country's ongoing preoccupation with the prospect of Quebec separation, and the North American nature of the Canadian business community. The federal government has the financial resources and, through its embassies and other agencies, the market intelligence necessary to effect a change, but it has lacked the political will. The lingering memories of several decades of failed economic development projects have soured the Canadian public on the idea that the federal government might make careful and judicious investments of long-term national benefit, and continues to spur the movement in favour of smaller government. The response, or lack thereof, to the Japanese economic situation offers a compelling illustration of the potential costs of an economically inactive state and of the relative inability of a government that attempts to lead through consultation to shape a strong, rapid, and consistent economic response.

5 The Kiwis and the Japanese: New Zealand-Japan Commercial Relations 1985–1997

As the global economy develops and interdependence increases, most countries relate to the world on the basis of a strategy, despite varied political, cultural and institutional heritage. That strategy is aimed, with mixed success, at encouraging forex-led growth.[1] It is clear that the development of a strategy is not a recipe in itself for success. But without it, success may be difficult to achieve. Japan and West Germany are countries that have successfully developed strategies and linkages within their economies to provide a competitive focus, with short-term directions always within a constant strategy.[2]

More than any other country, New Zealand typifies the political and economic potency of neo-classical economics. The irony is quite dramatic. For much of the twentieth century, New Zealand had one of the most strongly state-managed economies in the non-communist world. To the delight of social democrats around the world, New Zealand's economy produced a high level of personal prosperity and a stable economic and social system. When the system began to collapse in the early 1970s, advocates of a business-driven economic order came forward with radical prescriptions for the country's reformation. By the early 1990s, New Zealand had been transformed from a closed, highly protected economy to an open, competitive business environment.[3] Based on the leadership provided by the business community, the country was well placed to respond to the opportunities of the globalizing economy. As such, New Zealand provides an excellent test of the efficacy of a free market economy as a means of developing a national economy and capitalizing on opportunities for international trade.

The foundation of New Zealand's protected economy was imperial preference – assured access to the British market – which in turn guaranteed high prices and steady demand for New Zealand's natural products. The country became particularly adept at marketing agricultural products (sheep, beef, and dairy products) to a highly receptive British market. Little effort was made, or was needed, to seek out additional purchasers.

By the 1950s, the steady flow of New Zealand goods to Britain resulted in the country achieving one of the highest per capita incomes in the world. The national wealth encouraged governments, flush with tax revenues and imbued with social democratic fervour, to expand their social welfare programs, thus ensuring that the benefits of New Zealand's prosperity were widely distributed. A government-dominated economy was accepted by New Zealanders as an integral element of national life: as Peter McKinlay states, "New Zealand's experience of government, from the late 19th century, was an interaction of these two main strands: the dominance of central government and the widespread acceptance of the attitude that, given New Zealand's peculiar difficulties, government had an overriding role to intervene in order to bring about outcomes, which, although collectively desired, were seen as unlikely to ensue without government intervention."[4]

However, "historically, the goal of much of New Zealand trade policy was to encourage and subsidize New Zealand exports while protecting its firms at home and targeting particular industries for special favour."[5] The primacy of agricultural and rural society was entrenched through a complex web of farm subsidies and regulations. High tariff barriers and a full slate of state-owned enterprises provided government officials with active tools for the management of the national economy. The creation and protection of New Zealand-based manufacturing, with high tariffs keeping out imports in many key fields, followed logically. As Roger Kerr, executive director of the New Zealand Business Roundtable notes,

Prior to 1984 there was hardly a single area of New Zealand economic policy which could be termed even vaguely orthodox, liberal or outward-looking. Our industrial relations system was notorious for its inefficiency, inflexibility and adversarial nature. Macroeconomic policy was a shambles, and Keynesian demand management an article of faith. We had high personal tax rates, and a welfare state whose generosity was quite out of proportion to our ability to fund it. Capital markets were highly regulated. Anything that moved was licensed, and import protection was fortress-like. Most industries were chronically inefficient, and none more so than those that were delivering what we euphemistically called government 'services.'[6]

New Zealand's closeted economic and social world began to fall apart in the early 1970s. When Britain joined the European Economic Community the imperial preference that had created and protected New Zealand's prosperity was eliminated. The New Zealand government met the gathering economic crisis by rallying to the defense of the existing system. Farm subsidies increased and the government's commitment to protectionism remained in an increasingly desperate attempt to maintain the status quo. Segments of New Zealand's business community, concerned about mounting government debt, campaigned for new approaches to government, initially to little avail.

The New Zealand "revolution" hit in 1984, immediately following the election of the Labour Party in that year. Within an hour of becoming prime minister, David Lange was informed by his predecessor, Robert Muldoon, that the government was in serious financial difficulty. In the crisis-filled atmosphere that followed, a small group within government sought to restructure the New Zealand economy. Within a matter of months, radical measures were implemented, including a major currency devaluation.

The transformation of the New Zealand economy and government was dramatic in scale and impact. In addition to the rapid devaluation of the dollar, the government eliminated most agricultural subsidies, turned government departments and statutory corporations into state-owned enterprises for gradual privatization, reduced government regulations, and substantially decreased the size and authority of the civil service.[7] New Zealand changed, with stunning speed and depth, from a government-controlled, centrally managed economy to a free market, limited-government business environment. By the early 1990s, scarcely half a decade after the beginning of the changes, most vestiges of state management had been eliminated. There was a complete retreat from the belief that government intervention is either necessary or recommended for economic success. As Peter McKinlay wrote, "Instead, almost as a 'swing of the pendulum' effect, the perceived failures of the policies of intervention of successive New Zealand governments have seen a growing concern that government intervention is to be avoided if at all possible."[8] Economic commentator Brian Easton went even further, saying that "'Commercialisation' defined as the application of business principles to the public sector ... became an all-encompassing application to all public sector activity, whether or not there was a problem."[9]

Business groups, particularly the influential New Zealand Business Roundtable, urged the government to complete the revolution. Undertaken by the National Party after the 1990 election, this included a preoccupation with eliminating the deficit and the international debt burden (the latter was completed in 1996), further reductions in tariffs and regulations, user-pay approaches to government services, and the application of business principles to government operations. Advocates argued, successfully in the main, that the internationalization of trade and New Zealand's growing reliance on export markets required that business be left substantially unregulated in the management of market opportunities. As Rick Christie, former CEO of the New Zealand Trade Development Board, said, "for the first time in decades, we are seeing exports driven by the fundamentals of our comparative and competitive advantages, rather than by historical/political relationships or centrally-driven subsidies and other economic distortions."[10]

While it is hardly surprising that New Zealand's business community would back a free market approach, the positive response of the government sector was in some ways unexpected. Many civil servants not only adapted to the new national situation but strongly supported it, having advocated a need to move in this direction for years. Peter McKinlay writes, "It is clear, for example, that Treasury was advocating major reforms to the structures of both trading and non-trading activities of government well before the 1984 election."[11]

Civil servants were aided in accepting this stance by substantial reductions in the government payroll, staff reorganization, the sale of state enterprises to private owners, and the seeming success of the business model in reversing New Zealand's fortunes. Nonetheless, it is surprising that government officials, the very ones charged with managing the transformation of the New Zealand economy, now accepted as a matter of faith that government was to have only a minimal economic role. It is particularly striking that this acceptance of a much smaller government role remained after the transformation was complete.[12]

New Zealand realized that functioning in the world of the 1980s required more efficiency, more drive, and more awareness of the global marketplace. Nonetheless, in the late 1980s, New Zealand was caught up in its own domestic turmoil and was too preoccupied at home to be paying much attention to economic changes occurring in Japan. This was understandable, but what is less clear is why New Zealand continued to delay responding to its second most important trading partner. As Japan quickly escalated its imports of manufactured products, New Zealand remained an exporter of primary products. As of 1998, the composition of New Zealand's exports had not changed dramatically, and the civil service and industry associations had not made a systematic attempt to create a new trading relationship with Japan or anyone else.

NEW ZEALAND'S TRADE POLICY

New Zealand is a unitary state. There are twelve regional councils, but their power is limited and accorded to them by the national government. During the time period of the case study, two government bodies dealt with New Zealand's international affairs: the Ministry of Foreign Affairs and Trade (MFAT)[13] and the Trade Development Board (also known as Tradenz). MFAT conducted the government's business with other governments and international organizations and was the principal agent for trade policy strategy and negotiations,[14] and was supported in these areas by other government departments such as Treasury, the Ministry of Commerce, and the Ministry of Fisheries. It also worked closely with Tradenz, a Crown entity created in 1988 with a mandate to develop and expand New Zealand's foreign exchange earnings.[15] Responsibility for the direction and activities of Tradenz devolved to an independent board of directors, whose members came primarily from private enterprise.[16]

Responsibility for investment rested with a Foreign Direct Investment Advisory Group, established in December 1991. The FDIAG was chaired by the prime minister and composed of private sector members and representatives from MFAT, Tradenz, and the Ministry of Commerce.[17] The Secretariat was housed in Tradenz along with the Tradenz Investment Services Group, whose help desk answered inquiries about investing in New Zealand. MFAT broadly promoted investment in New Zealand ("the green and pleasant land" approach, as one official described it)[18] while Tradenz focused on the sectoral and individual company level,[19] particularly by matching the interests of offshore investors with New Zealand investment opportunities.[20]

MFAT and Tradenz both came into their 1990s existence as part of the public sector reforms. The previous Department of Trade and Industry split off into three segments: the Trade Commissioner Service, which merged with the Market Development Board and became the New Zealand Market Development Board, the forerunner to Tradenz; the Ministry of Commerce, which focuses on domestic issues; and the trade policy and negotiations section, which merged with the Ministry of Foreign Affairs to become MFAT.

The MFAT trade policy function, which was complemented by Tradenz's "programmes to promote foreign exchange earnings,"[21] was to research and analyse international events and developments, provide advice on issues relevant to New Zealand's international and trade interests, and liaise with the New Zealand government's international counterparts.[22]

The Ministry negotiated with other governments on market access and trading regulations, managed New Zealand's relationships with other nations, and managed government programs such as Official Development Assistance and Asia 2000.[23] (Asia 2000 began in 1989 as a government initiative to encourage the business sector to think about Asia and has since attracted considerable corporate sponsorship.) In 1993 MFAT had slightly over 600 staff, about one-third of whom served overseas in forty-five embassies, high commissions, or consulates. The Ministry was divided into seven regional divisions (Americas, Australia, Europe, Middle East and Africa, North Asia, South Pacific, and South/South East Asia) and four functional divisions (Development Cooperation, Economic, Environment, and Multilateral Trade).[24] Tokyo, Washington, and Canberra were MFAT's largest overseas offices. The secretary of Foreign Affairs and Trade was the Ministry's chief executive.

In 1993 MFAT published *New Zealand Trade Policy: Implementation and Directions*, a detailed look at New Zealand's trade policy options and objective: "to promote New Zealand's economic growth through trade and thus improve the living standards of New Zealanders on a sustainable basis."[25] The four policy tracks for pursuing this goal were domestic policy (ensuring that economic policies promoted efficiency and improved export performance), the GATT (working with other countries for a successful conclusion to the Uruguay Round), regional economic groupings (the Closer Economic Relations, APEC, closer trading relationships with other trading partners), and bilateral negotiations. Within the field of bilateral negotiations, and keeping in mind New Zealand's four main markets of Australia, the European Community, the United States, and Japan, priorities were determined: "Too strict a segmentation of the world is a misleading approach for setting New Zealand trade policy objectives. But with six out of ten top export markets in the rapidly growing Asian region, Asia is clearly the priority area. Our strategy can be summed up as 'Asia first, but not Asia first and last'."[26]

In keeping with these policy tracks, the New Zealand government played active roles in APEC and in GATT, particularly through the Cairns group on agriculture.[27]

The idea for both Tradenz and its predecessor the Market Development Board developed from a 1984 private sector steering committee recommendation that the work of offshore trade commissioners needed to be supported and enhanced by a New Zealand-based business-led organization.[28] Tradenz began by setting a goal as to the amount of foreign exchange New Zealand needed to obtain to increase the country's GDP per capita levels and thereby its standard of living. In 1955 New Zealanders had ranked eighth in the world for standard of living, but by 1987 had fallen to twenty-third.[29] Tradenz's 1990 vision document "Ten by 2010: A Goal for New Zealand" described the goal of a top ten standard of living ranking by the year 2000. To achieve this, New Zealand's foreign exchange earnings had to increase from $18 billion in 1990 to $32 billion by the year 2000.[30] Increased foreign exchange earnings occur by making products to sell overseas and by encouraging foreigners to spend money in New Zealand either as tourists or as investors.

The Trade Development Board brought together the private and public sectors. As many of the Board's directors were business people, the Board acted as a link and adviser from business to government. (The same mechanism could also spread information and ideas from government to the business sector; in practice, the consultation flowed from business to government.) Feedback from the business sector was strongly supportive of having a government organization that was involved in export development without hindering the development of private sector services and initiatives.[31] Joint Action Groups (JAGs) were set up as a forum for discussion on strategic issues, sector priorities, and implementation programs.[32] The first Joint Action Group, the Food and Beverage Export Council, was established under the Department of Trade and Industry, prior to the formation of Tradenz. Its purpose then was to give the government advice on trade promotion. JAGs evolved after that time to helping industry members develop their international market development strategy.

The JAGs, which included such groups as the New Zealand Wine Guild, the New Zealand Software Association, and Constructive Solutions (the building industry group), decided on products, markets, and promotional strategies. As of 1996, there were thirty JAGs[33] with approximately 1,100 exporters participating, a sizable proportion of the 1,650 significant exporters in New Zealand.[34] Tradenz actively assisted in the formation of JAGs, but once the JAG was formed, the participants took over and Tradenz staff attended meetings as observers only. Each JAG determined its membership criteria, goals, and projects. Shared market research and generic product promotion were examples of common JAG activities.[35] As of the late 1990s, JAGs had not moved into the area of product research and development. Tradenz provided limited funding for the JAGs, available competitively; the rest of the funding was supplied by the participant firms.

The JAGs worked out sectoral goals and then, with Tradenz assistance, determined target countries. JAG members would visit a country first to get a feel for the market and learn a little about how things were done there. On the second visit, they might meet potential customers or agents, and by the third visit were possibly ready to attend trade shows or more specific meetings. Tradenz's focus was on 'capabilities': on determining what New Zealand companies could produce and matching those products with an appropriate market. Eugene Bowen, senior trade commissioner (Japan), noted that in 1997 Tradenz began to look more specifically at markets and sectors in which they saw potential, and to encourage the formation of JAGS in those areas.[36]

In 1996, Tradenz had slightly more than 300 people on staff; over half of these were based offshore. Most of the overseas staff were local employees, including New Zealanders hired while abroad. Thirty-three offices overseas were centred on seven regional hubs: Singapore, Tokyo, Sydney, Hamburg, Los Angeles, Dubai, and Santiago.[37] According to the 1994 report of the review committee on Tradenz, East Asia, particularly China, had been the primary focus of Tradenz's initiatives since 1990.[38]

From 1992 through 1995, Tradenz published three documents[39] in which it described New Zealand's economic position and outlined an export strategy designed to achieve the targeted progress in terms of foreign exchange earnings and address the issues standing in the way of improved export performance. The documents were a valuable national exercise and a first attempt to identify potential markets.[40] While the three publications discussed the broad outlines of a strategic plan, Rick Christie, then CEO of Tradenz, stated in 1992 that responsibility for a strategic plan for New Zealand lay elsewhere: "While it is not the role of Tradenz to develop a strategic plan for New Zealand, from our work with companies in the export sector we have concluded that an export strategy for New Zealand would not be out of place. It would certainly be very relevant if New Zealand is to succeed in deploying its scarce resources effectively and profitably."[41] Where responsibility for a national strategy lay remained unclear (although one Tradenz official suggested the Treasury department might logically take the lead).[42]

In 1997 Tradenz produced the final document of this series, in which it discussed some of the forces and changes likely to shape market opportunities in the coming decades. Its aim was to encourage New Zealand companies to consider these changes and the implications for their business activities.[43]

While the Tradenz documents were a useful point of departure for discussion of a New Zealand trade policy, they illustrated the underlying lack of national direction in this area. In a government wedded to the idea that economic leadership came first and foremost from the business community, it was hardly surprising that government agencies did not rush to take responsibility for the formulation of a "national" plan; such a government-initiated, centralizing initiative would run counter to declared government policy. Tradenz, therefore, was limited to providing vague guidelines and, more commonly, export assistance at the request of business. It did not have and did not take responsibility for carving out an international trade agenda.

Tradenz was been greatly influenced by the work of Michael Porter, a professor of economics at Harvard University, on national competitive advantage. His 1990 book, *The Competitive Advantage of Nations*, was the culmination of a five-year research project based on the study of competitive advantage in ten countries.[44] Porter identified four main determinants of competitive advantage in international trade: factor conditions (for example, natural resources, location, climate); home demand conditions; related and supporting industries; and firm strategy, structure, and rivalry. He analysed each of these determinants and discussed their implications for company strategy and government policy. Porter concluded that governments must strive to stimulate the continual upgrading of the economy by shaping and influencing "the *context* and *institutional structure* surrounding firms, as well as the *inputs* they draw upon."[45] His examples include "stimulating early demand, confronting industries with the need for frontier technology through symbolic cooperative projects, establishing prizes to highlight and reward quality, encouraging rivalry" and other policies to keep upgrading and innovation on track.

In 1990 a group of New Zealanders led by academic Graham Crocombe examined New Zealand's economy based on Porter's methodology and findings and produced a report often referred to as the Porter Report.[46] It indicated New Zealand's weaknesses: "The Porter Report showed that our exports can be broadly categorized as lower margin commodities sold into lower growth market segments. Our production tends to be based in primary industries that have low barriers to competitors' entry and are politically vulnerable as other governments protect and support their domestic producers and markets."[47]

The final chapter, 'Implications for New Zealand,' discussed clear suggestions for government policy on areas ranging from upgrading New Zealand's human resources to stimulating domestic competition; upgrading the technological base, transportation and communication infrastructure, and local demand conditions; and stimulating cluster and new business development. The chapter ended by urging the formation of a new business/government relationship:

The New Zealand government should move forcefully to embrace a new role, one that focuses on creating an environment in which New Zealand firms can prosper. Government must put in place the institutions and policies that provide the pressures, incentives and opportunities for New Zealand firms to improve and upgrade. This is a very different role from, and a far more subtle one than either heavy intervention or a strictly hands-off policy. This new role will also require a change in mindset in both government and a business community that too often sees government as both the source of and solution to its problems.[48]

Tradenz responded to a number of the Porter Report recommendations, particularly those that focused on the areas in which government should *not* be involved. The government started a number of initiatives to stimulate the development of industry clusters, including the film industry in Wellington, forestry and forest engineering in the Rotorua area, and the marine industry in Auckland. Other recommendations, including educational and technological upgrading, symbolic cooperative research projects, and government white papers signaling possible directions for the private sector, were not adopted immediately. Initiatives like Asia 2000[49] and Focus Latin America (a 1996–97 program to highlight the market potential of Latin America through the media and governmental announcements) and the formation of the Joint Action Groups were along the line of Porter's recommendations.

Porter's work assumed importance within New Zealand but, according to a senior Foreign Affairs official, Tradenz responded more directly to the report than did the country's diplomatic corps.[50] The New Zealand government, and the people who worked for it, had a laissez-faire approach, but it seemed that more discussion on the appropriate role for government could still occur. As Douglas Myers, former chair of the New Zealand Business Roundtable, stated, "The relevant debate is not about big government or small government, do-everything government or do-nothing government. It is about what constitutes good or efficient government: governments doing the right kind of things – the things that only governments can do – and doing them well."[51]

Debate about "the right kinds of things" government could do, along the lines that Porter discussed – the organization of cooperative research projects, signaling, high profile awards, long-term planning – was useful. Myers also argued that "the ingredients of good government today are now widely understood around the world,"[52] but this was not completely true. There might have been agreement, at least in most of the western world, that private entrepreneurs and not government created wealth, and that government's role was to get the infra-structure and setting right to allow business to produce and sell goods and services. Definitions of "getting the setting right," however, varied considerably.

In New Zealand, a residue of the old, interventionist order remained in place, and government retained an active role (particu-larly when compared internationally) in the provision of basic social services, welfare, health care, and education. Where government policy was more consistent with neo-classical models was the accep-tance of a limited role in the ownership and management of the national economy. Under the National Party, New Zealand pursued an active policy of "getting the fundamentals right"[53] and provided an open, competitive, and favourable environment for business.

New Zealand Trade Policy: Implementation and Direction stated an inten-tion to improve market access and trading regulations and to strengthen diplomatic and trading relationships, whether multilater-ally, regionally, or bilaterally. MFAT's *Corporate Plan 1995–96* identified a number of key economic and political objectives. These included pursuing and enhancing an open, international trading system, improving upon key economic relationships, asserting a greater role for New Zealand in the wider Asia-Pacific region, building New Zealand's reputation as a responsible international citizen and acting internationally in support of the environment and sustainable devel-opment, and promoting New Zealand's Antarctic interests. The only specific trade-related priority was the second one – moving key eco-nomic relations to a new level. As part of this objective, the ministry noted that it planned to continue discussions with ASEAN on possible links between CER and the ASEAN Free Trade Area, to conclude a Trans-Tasman Mutual Recognition Agreement, and to continue discussing with Chile the possibility of a free trade agreement.[54]

These major policy statements on New Zealand's international trade priorities represented the public manifestation of a complex consulta-tive process. Under their new approach to managing the national economy, the government worked closely with the business commu-nity in developing national priorities and identifying future opportu-nities. To a substantial degree, the economic sections of the nation's foreign service agencies saw their function as working alongside New Zealand business in the cultivation of markets. New Zealand had an advantage in the small size of its civil service. Inter-agency and field-headquarters liaison was generally quite open and supportive. Whereas larger states generally develop policy within agency or depart-mental limits, bringing more fully formed statements forward for general discussion, New Zealand was able to cultivate contacts, share ideas, and prepare more consultative plans with other government and business groups and individuals.

NEW ZEALAND-JAPAN INVESTMENT AND TRADE TO 1997

New Zealand defines foreign direct investment as investments by non-residents that are equal to or greater than 25% of a corporation's voting share capital. This is seen as the minimum ownership which gives the investor some "control over the management and activities of the business."[55] After 1985, with the exception of investments in broadcasting, commercial fishing within the Economic Exclusion Zone, and rural land, investments below NZ$10 million did not require government consent. Those over NZ$10 million required approval by the Overseas Investment Commission. However, very few applications were turned down.[56] While the government saw foreign investment as vital to New Zealand's economic future (former Prime Minister Jim Bolger said that in order to maintain current levels of development $10 billion in new investment was needed annually),[57] the general public was not convinced and quickly became wary of announcements of investments from overseas, particularly from Asia. Roger Peren summed it up well when he wrote in 1992 that "Though most New Zealanders seem to be broadly in agreement about the benefits of foreign investment, and prepared to acknowledge the historical importance of British, Australian and American capital in our own development, there is still quite frequent criticism of particular new projects or of sales which might lead to 'foreign ownership.'"[58]

One of the election platforms in 1996 of the New Zealand First Party (subsequently part of the ruling coalition government) was a strong stand against "too much" foreign ownership and immigration. A 1994 National Research Bureau survey found that "the predominant position of New Zealanders with regards to Asian investment is that they have mixed feelings about it (46%) with a near balance among those who think it is good for New Zealand (25%) and those who think it is bad (18%)."[59]

Through the 1990s, Australia, the United States, the United Kingdom, Japan, and Germany accounted for over 90% of foreign direct investment in New Zealand, with Australia as the largest cumulative foreign investor, followed by the others in the order listed. The majority of investment by all these nations took place after 1985 when New Zealand began to liberalize its trade and financial sectors.[60] Brian Easton argues that "independence of the New Zealand government was bought at the price of surrendering the ownership of New Zealand business to overseas concerns, for they covered the gap in the shortage of local savings. Today over half of the members of the New Zealand Business Roundtable (a private sector sponsored think tank which contributes extensively to public discussion on New Zealand's economy) run firms which are largely overseas-owned. The New Establishment has become hostage to foreign investors."[61] There was growing recognition that foreign ownership of New Zealand exacted a price. The increase in foreign ownership of major Kiwi companies and the retirement of a generation of business leaders prompted an April 1998 article in the *New Zealand Sunday Star Times* to ask, "Who is left to lead Corporate New Zealand?"[62] Including unlisted companies and state-owned enterprises, over half of the largest fifty companies in New Zealand were either completely foreign owned or controlled. Some of the biggest of these included Telecom (78% foreign ownership), Carter Holt Harvey (80%), Fletcher Energy (58%), Fletcher Paper (55%), Fletcher Forests (65%), Wilson & Horton (99%), and Lion Nathan (now about 75% following the May 1998 investment by Kirin Breweries.)[63]

Japan invested in New Zealand through the 1980s at a slow but relatively steady rate. During the period of Japan's dramatic increase in overseas foreign investment from 1985 to 1989, however, New Zealand received nowhere near the levels of investment that Japan made in other countries.[64] (This applies however the investment relationship is assessed, as a total sum or on a per capita basis.) Not only did countries like the United States and the United Kingdom receive large sums of Japanese investment but so did the Netherlands, Singapore, Hong Kong, and Australia. As of 1985 New Zealand had received only 0.3% of all Japanese offshore investments and the percentage was probably lower in the following years. Japanese investment in New Zealand represented a tiny portion of Japan's total overseas FDI, and it was also a small portion of total FDI in New Zealand. It was stated in 1996 that, with the exception of 1990, "Japanese investment has never exceeded 3% of total net FDI flows into New Zealand."[65]

Until the late 1980s, there were no policies or government-directed activities to attract investment into New Zealand from anywhere, including Japan. Around this time, concern began to be expressed by the Japan/New Zealand Business Council about New Zealand's small share of Japanese investment and the relatively low number of investments occurring outside the real estate, tourism, and transportation sectors. Although the general public and many leading politicians remained nervous about encouraging overseas investment, Cabinet ministers began taking trips to Japan to promote investment in New

Zealand, and an investment counsellor was attached to the embassy in Tokyo from 1992 to 1994 to spark interest in Japanese investment into New Zealand. The government's commitment to the development of investment leads and business opportunities was limited to stimulating initial private sector interest. The government's strategy was to open the office in Tokyo, demonstrate the opportunities, and then remove the Japan-based position, and this is exactly what occurred.[66]

In 1990 the Japan/New Zealand Business Council published a report on Japanese foreign direct investment in New Zealand. The report was initiated by the council's perception "that investment between Japan and New Zealand is inadequate relative to the growth in Japanese global investment, as a proportion of the growing trade between the two countries and relative to other countries which welcome investment."[67] Along with a synopsis of the current investment situation, the council explained its views on the problems of attracting Japanese investment and made recommendations on how to address these shortcomings. A number of the problems, such as competitiveness, policy stability, and internal cost structures, became a focus of the government in the 1990s and improvements were made. Others required changing a Japanese perception (for example, that New Zealand was too small and too far from other markets to warrant investment). The final group of problems were those of lack, or perceived lack, of commitment, coordination, or strategy.

Japanese investment into New Zealand increased in 1990 and 1991 but fell again as the glow of New Zealand's economic restructuring and privatization began to fade (see table 4.5). Even at its peak, however, Japanese investment in New Zealand did not represent more than 0.6% of Japan's total foreign investment, putting New Zealand on par with Bermuda.[68] While visiting at the New Zealand Institute of Economic Research in 1991–92, Professor Masahiko Ebashi completed a study of Japanese companies in New Zealand and discovered that "as far as Japan is concerned trade is directly linked with investment. The 43 of 59 major Japanese companies operating here who responded to his survey accounted for more than 44% of all New Zealand exports to Japan in 1990–91."[69] This data suggests that little of New Zealand's trade with Japan was the result of Kiwi initiative; as in other areas of the New Zealand-Japan relationship, Japan and the Japanese companies made the first move. This conclusion was also backed by the results of a New Zealand Institute of Economic Research survey that found that "In terms of innovation, the most common source of new product ideas was the Japanese participant, rather than the New Zealand manufacturer."[70]

The diversity of Japanese investment in New Zealand increased in

Table 5.1   Major investments in New Zealand by Japanese companies, 1986–1996

Japanese Company	Company Purchased	Product	Ownership	Year
*Shiseido (NZ) Ltd	Shiseido Co. Ltd	Cosmetics, Manufacturing		1960s
Brother Japan	Brother Distributors	Building products	100%	1987
Mitsubishi Motors	Todd Motors	Motor vehicles	100%	1988
Honda Motor Corporation	NZ Motor Corporation	Motor vehicles	100%	1988
*International Pacific College		Education	100%	1989
Okazake	Oliver Corporation	Farm	100%	1989
Sumitomo	Nelson Pine Forests	Forestry	100%	1989
Canon Electronics	DRG Business Equipment	Business equipment	100%	1990
Orix Corporation	Budget Lease	Motor vehicle leasing	100%	1990
Tachikawa Forest Products Ltd	New Plant	Forestry	100%	1990
Suntory Japan	Cerebos Gregg New Zealand Ltd	Food	100%	1990
Nissho Iwai/Juken Sangyo Co. Ltd	Northern Pulp and Forests Ltd	Forestry	100%	1991
Juken Nissho	Carterton Forestry	Forestry	100%	1991
Asahi Chemical Industry & Co. Ltd	Watties Prepared Foods	Food	Joint Venture	1991
Itoham Foods	Five Star Beef Ltd	Beef	Joint Venture	1991
Innosho Woods/ National House Industrial	New Plant	Wood Processing	100%	1992
Oji Paper Co. and Co. Itoh	Southland Plantation Co. of New Zealand	Forestry and Pulp Processing	Joint Venture	1992
Sumitomo Forestry Company Ltd	Nelson Pine Industries Ltd	Forestry	100%	1992
Shiseido Company Ltd	Plant Expansion	Cosmetics	100%	1992
Sumitomo Corp.	Summit Wool Spinners	Carpet Yarn Mill	100%	1992
Mitsui Osk Kogyokaisha	Greenhouse Park Flowers	Flowers	100%	1992
Southland Plantation Forest Company of New Zealand Ltd	Takitimu District Block	Forestry	100%	1994
Kirin Brewery Co	Lion Nathan Ltd	Beer	75%	1998

Source: Bancrop Holdings Ltd. 1990–94 *Review of Operations and Economic Commentary*.
*R.D. Cremer and B. Ramasamy, *Tigers in New Zealand? The Role of Asian Investment in the Economy* (Institute of Policy Studies, Wellington, 1996), 67.

Table 5.2   Major New Zealand hotel and resort properties purchased by Japanese
investors, 1988–1993

Company	Property Purchased/Developed	Year
Eiichi Ishii & Kohei Yamashita	Millbrook Resort (50%)	1988
Tokyu Corporation	Pan Pacific Hotel	1988
Okabe Enterprises	White Heron Hotel	1989
EIE Corporation	Finance Centre	1989
Pasco Corporation	Telecom House	1989
Pan Pacific	New Hotel Auckland	
Otaka Holdings Ltd	Hotel du Vin	1990
Otaka Holdings Ltd	Hyatt Kingsgate Hotel	1990
Hotel Shuzan	Maruia Springs Motor Inn	1991
Japan Golf Systems (since purchased back by NZ firm)	Wairakei Golf Course	1991
Victoria Group	Mt. Hutt Ski field	1991
Hando	CBD Property	1991
Convelle Enterprises	Walter Peak Tours	1991
Nakano Corporation	Peat Marwick House	1992
NZ Plan International	Coutts Island	1992
Hirai Family	NZ Plan International Resort (50%)	1992
Masafumi Fukumoto	NZ Golf Systems Ltd	1993
Tokyu Tourist Corp & Tokyu	Pan Pacific Properties	1993

Source: Bancrop Holdings Ltd 1994, Review of Operations and Economic Commentary, 28–33.
Ownership is 100% unless otherwise indicated.

the late 1980s through the early 1990s (see table 5.1). Forestry
(timber and pulp) and auto production were major areas of manufacturing investment, while interest in New Zealand's agricultural sector
grew, particularly in the production of venison and beef, pumpkin,
and wasabi (Japanese horseradish).[71]

During the late 1980s and early 1990s, investment in hotel and
resort properties increased dramatically (see table 5.2.) Japanese interest in the real estate sector was sparked by the growing travel industry
(as Japanese began increasingly to travel abroad, Japanese companies
capitalized on the opportunity to cater to them) and by international
investors' desire to move into stable property investments.[72]

The final section of the Japan/New Zealand Business Council report
spoke of a need for New Zealand to show more professionalism and
coordinate its approach among both public and private sector organizations when marketing investment opportunities to Japanese
investors. As one observer commented, "We (New Zealanders) were
not good at attracting investment, even when we were keen to get it.
We had to learn to put together attractive projects."[73] The council saw
a role for government in determining priority areas for investment

("Government has a responsibility to inform the investment markets of sectors of investment which meet the economic, social and regional objectives of New Zealand")[74] and developing a larger sense of purpose and direction for the nation. As the report's authors observed, "It is critical that New Zealand determines the vision for its economy over the next decade and communicates this vision to those who are in a position to assist with its implementation, by means of future investment. This process requires leadership from Government with formulation shared equally between Government and the private sector."[75]

A 1996 Institute of Policy Studies publication also supported the concept of selecting priority sectors for FDI: "prioritizing certain sectors to attract more FDI may not necessarily be a bad thing. Given the small size of the domestic market, New Zealand could, for example, prioritise export-oriented industries for foreign investment. Foreign investment could thus be used to develop a competitive advantage."[76]

The government of the 1990s was now firmly committed to attracting foreign investment from anywhere. In 1997 Tradenz published three booklets for potential investors, painting a broad picture of New Zealand's social and economic climate and describing the opportunities available in New Zealand's main business sectors (food, resources, manufacturing, and services). These sectors were broken down further into five sub-headings,[77] each describing the various regions of New Zealand and their infrastructure, work force, current business activities, and potential opportunities.[78] These publications represented the first step in addressing the concerns raised by the Japan/New Zealand Business Council and the Institute of Policy Studies.

In 1997 Japan was New Zealand's second largest export destination, after Australia. The United States, United Kingdom, and South Korea were third, fourth, and fifth ranked export markets respectively. In 1995/96, 16.3% of New Zealand's NZ$20 billion-worth of exports went to Japan; Australia received 19.7%.[79] (See table 5.3, which, to provide for greater comparability with Canadian and Australian tables, reports the trade data in American dollars.)

New Zealand's exports to Japan consisted primarily of resource and agricultural products. Wool had ceased to be as important an export item, being replaced by aluminum, forest products, dairy products, fish, fruits, and vegetables.

New Zealand's trade profile with Japan was very similar to Canada's, involving exports to Japan of sizable quantities of raw and partially processed materials and imports of highly processed and manufactured items from Japan. Like Canada, New Zealand was content to let

Table 5.3   New Zealand exports to Japan, 1984–1998 (US$m)

Year	Value	% of Total Exports
1984	$ 817	15.2
1985	828	14.5
1986	863	14.6
1987	1,168	16.2
1988	1,562	· 17.7
1989	1,538	17.4
1990	1,493	15.8
1991	1,523	15.9
1992	1,463	15.6
1993	1,531	14.7
1994	1,873	15.7
1995	2,225	16.2
1996	2,207	15.4
1997	2,013	14.4
1998	1,528	13.3

Source: International Monetary Fund, Direction of Trade Statistics 1990, 1996, and 1997.

Japan determine the shape and contour of its international trading relationship and did little to develop new markets in line with the evolution of the Japanese domestic market. On a gross national level, this meant that absolute values of New Zealand exports to Japan remained high, and even grew, giving the impression that the country was doing well in maintaining and extending its economic relationship with its second largest trading partner (see table 5.3). As the list of the leading exports in 1996 reveals (see table 5.4), New Zealand made few inroads into Japan's consumer markets, save for the sale of agricultural products. As well, despite substantial increases in Japanese imports generally, New Zealand was unable to significantly change Japan's presence in its national trade picture. Trade to Japan represented over 17% of New Zealand's total trade in 1989 and accounted for slightly more than 15% in 1996. The country's businesses had not, in the first decade after the Plaza Accord, made significant inroads into the Japanese marketplace.

RESPONSES TO CHANGES IN THE JAPANESE ECONOMY

New Zealand's response to the major economic changes occurring in its second largest trading partner was, as of 1998, minimal. Japan's dramatic import profile shift toward manufactured products did not

Table 5.4   Top ten New Zealand exports to Japan, 1996 (NZ$, 000)

Aluminum, unwrought	$ 458,843
Wood in the rough	250,038
Cheese and curd	157,188
Fish, frozen	132,797
Casein	112,376
Acyclic alcohols	109,678
Fruit, fresh	104,222
Fibreboard of wood	100,018
Wood pulp	97,751
Wood sawn or chipped lengthwise	90,277

Source: Ministry of Foreign Affairs and Trade, *New Zealand External Trade Statistics June Year Ending 1996*

appear to have been noticed, let alone to have caused concern. When in 1996 a New Zealand embassy official in Tokyo was asked about this change and the impact it could have on a resource-based economy like New Zealand's, the response was that "New Zealand will never sell anything to Japan that it doesn't grow."[80] The previously mentioned Canadian embassy survey of trade representatives from six nations reported that New Zealand was the only nation surveyed that did not have plans to take advantage of Japan's import change and increase exports of manufactured products.[81] As in other areas of national trade policy, this approach indicated New Zealand's willingness to leave the initiative to the private sector.

As of 1997, there were fifteen staff in New Zealand's Tokyo embassy and two staff in the Osaka consulate. In the view of the general manager of Tradenz's strategic development unit, such a number of people and the accompanying resources meant that New Zealand was already putting into Japan "a level of effort over and above what the market warrants,"[82] an opinion not shared by all Tradenz staff, including John Jenner, the deputy chief executive officer. Tradenz staff helped individual companies decide whether or not to enter the Japanese market, but Japan was not promoted in any general sense. There was some encouragement of specific industries that might do well in Japan or any other geographic market, but the returns were minimal.

New Zealand's trade with Japan had continued largely unchanged for decades. Wool sales declined and logs, wood panels, and aluminum exports increased, but otherwise cheese, casein, meat, fish, and vegetables remained primary export items. With the important exception of Eugene Bowen, Tradenz's senior trade commissioner (Japan), no officials were overly concerned about whether or not it changed. For most other New Zealand government officials, while there was a desire to add more value to agricultural products, there was no strong belief about the importance of diversifying away from agriculture or primary products.

Most New Zealanders had a deep faith in their ability as an extremely efficient producer of agricultural products and believed, therefore, that the country's economic future was secure. In some sectors, such as dairy, New Zealand was perhaps the most efficient producer in the world. While many countries could no longer compete efficiently or economically in agriculture, the argument went, New Zealand was one of the few countries that should keep producing what it was producing. In the world of comparative advantage, New Zealand's lay in agriculture. And, as people will always need to eat, there would always be a need for what New Zealand produced.

While this argument has some validity, it falls short in a couple of areas. Primary products are vulnerable to competition from others and to rapid changes in price. This makes for a shaky foundation on which to rest a nation's economic future. In addition, technological changes were having an impact on agriculture and the number of people that sector could likely employ in the future. Economists like Jeremy Rifkin believe that the "technology revolution is changing the nature of modern agriculture and, in the process, raising serious questions about the future of farm labor."[83] William Knoke illustrated this brilliantly in his 1996 description of recent changes in carrot harvesting in California, "where society has taken another step in the march toward zero-labor agriculture. A gigantic self-propelled 'Bolthouse Harvester' rambles along speedily, enabling only three workers to pick seventy-five tons of carrots an hour. Nonexistent ten years ago, two dozen harvesters supply over half the US carrot market today, revolutionizing the industry and throwing thousands of laborers out of work."[84]

Eugene Bowen recognized challenges ahead for New Zealand's participation in the Japanese fruit and vegetable market. He said that both New Zealand's absolute costs, "due to the strength of the New Zealand dollar, very high sea-and-air-freight rates, a high cost structure including land prices, and high price expectations among suppliers," and relative costs were high "as lower priced suppliers such as Chile, Mexico and China provide cheaper alternative product. This factor will cost us market share and depress exports." New southern hemisphere suppliers like Chile and Tasmania were becoming an additional threat as they reduced New Zealand's off-season supply advantage.[85]

Japanese consumers had also changed and were no longer prepared to pay high prices for excellent quality (for example, perfectly shaped fruit), which was a niche market for New Zealand with sales of fruit for the gift market. Bowen said that "the price-quality compromise has impacted heavily on New Zealand." Importers, distributors, and retailers reported a certain degree of dissatisfaction with New Zealand due to rising prices and a perceived recent decline in quality, particularly in asparagus, beans, melons, and paprika. These two complaints were probably linked: "as higher prices become increasingly difficult to command, this is interpreted by some traders as a reduction in quality."[86]

On top of these factors, while people will always need to eat, what they eat changes. The number of vegetarians increased exponentially in the last two decades of the twentieth century. Within this group, an increasing number became vegans and stopped eating all animal products, including eggs, milk, cheese, yogourt, and ice cream. Questions began to be raised, including within the medical community, about the health implications of ingesting dairy products. The Japanese, perhaps more than peoples of other nations, are subject to fads or changes in group thinking. Mad cow disease and a 1997 e-coli outbreak made the Japanese particularly concerned about food safety. Despite the often-heard Kiwi remark that there would always be a market for dairy, it seemed that the reality of this was beginning to change. As Klaus Pringsheim of the Canada-Japan Trade Council pointed out with regard to the agri-food market, "The Japanese consumer's tastes and proclivities are constantly changing in response to domestic and international perceptions in regard to food safety, nutritional considerations, pricing, and various fads which suddenly affect the popularity of one or another food product."[87]

New Zealand's other prime commercial areas – tourism, fish, and aluminum – were also in strongly competitive fields. The emergence of new competitors – Russia in timber, for example – could undercut New Zealand's current markets. This vulnerability was exacerbated by Japan's tendency to cultivate numerous suppliers of particular items and not to allow itself to be caught without options. As journalist Colin James identified in 1992, "the lambs-for-cars economic base of the prosperity consensus is not an option. To do better than stand still economically – a state which caused serious social damage over the past half-decade – New Zealand will have to find investment and innovation that improves the diversity of and return from its products."[88]

While the mid to late 1990s saw Tradenz make a concerted effort in fresh horticultural produce, Bowen believed that New Zealand had done as much as it could to promote the nation's horticultural products in Japan. There were a large number of trade missions and extensive commissioned research, but increased competition meant that volumes of New Zealand fruit and vegetable exports to Japan were "unlikely to grow significantly, and returns, especially expressed in dollar terms, are likely to gradually decline."[89]

Opportunities for New Zealand in Japan in agriculture rested in two main areas: organic produce (as part of a concerted campaign emphasizing New Zealand's record for food safety) and processed food products. Organic products were rapidly increasing in popularity and were likely to remain an important growth area. A major hurdle, however, was the automatic fumigation of imported produce that "effectively robs the product of its pesticide-free status. For this reason some supermarkets are handling only domestic organic product while others are labeling the product 'organically grown.'"[90] In response to this emerging market opportunity, Tradenz encouraged the formation of a separate organics Joint Action Group.

Japanese consumers were purchasing more frozen, prepared, and processed food products. Busy lives and family members who increasingly eat separately saw consumer demand for individual portions, boil-in-the-bag meals, and more user friendly forms of all foods. Fruit juices instead of fresh fruit and frozen sliced vegetables instead of fresh vegetables were trends in future Japanese consumption.

In the processed food area, Bowen also said that Tradenz in Japan had been active in finding customers for potential new products and giving New Zealand companies the specifications of the required product. Over NZ$50 million in new processed food business had been generated this way and Japanese clients were approaching Tradenz directly with their requests. Tradenz passed these requests to companies.[91] According to Bowen, other sectors in Japan with potential for New Zealand companies included telecommunications, software, products for the aged, including health products and barrier-free buildings, furniture, and garden products; Tradenz began to encourage the formation of JAGs in a number of these sectors. New Zealand was striving, however, to enter markets several years behind major competitors (North American companies in telecommunications and health care and software, European companies in furniture), some of whom had already made sizeable inroads into the Japanese market.

While MFAT and part of the business community saw New Zealand's future substantially in Asia, there was no certainty on how important Japan would be. Government officials said that Japan was of enormous significance, but followed up with the argument that Japan was a tough market and that while it was New Zealand's second largest market, it might not always be so; if it was easier to sell in China, Korea, or Southeast Asia, then companies would sell there. While this made sense, it emphasized the sporadic and limited nature of New Zealand's commitment to trade promotion and missed the continuity that is essential to the development of long-term trade relations with Asian partners, including Japan.

Speaking in 1997, Bowen believed it would be difficult for New Zealand to sustain its level of trade with Japan, and he stated that New Zealand wanted balanced trade and did not want to become too dependent on one market the way the Australians were on Japan. While there was no intention of discouraging trade with Japan, Japan's own internal restructuring and the recent economic surges of various other Asian nations made it a good time to let things in Japan settle and get a foothold in China.[92]

John Jenner, deputy chief executive officer of Tradenz, pointed out that for the small to medium new exporters of 1996, the second most prominent market was Japan. First time New Zealand exporters entered the Japanese market with products ranging from a sports drink to live ferrets to prefabricated houses and were successful (defined as having made at least one sale).[93]

Surprisingly, despite the small size of the New Zealand government bureaucracy, there appeared at times to be little communication between officials at MFAT and those at Tradenz. As documented earlier, the opinions expressed by Eugene Bowen at Tradenz in Tokyo concerning future developments in Japanese trade were very different than those held by the leading trade officials in Wellington. Summarizing, therefore, what constituted the New Zealand government's view on various aspects of the New Zealand-Japan relationship is somewhat difficult. If Bowen's arguments were followed, a more government-directed, proactive approach would be taken to cultivating opportunities in Japan. And from his base in Tokyo, Bowen was able to take a more direct role in encouraging business development. But Bowen's position was not shared by key personnel in the national administration, nor did they appear to have discussed their views on this important theme. The more proactive approach advocated by the individual in most direct contact with the Japanese situation was unlikely to become effective national policy.

As discussed in this chapter's introduction, a coincidence of timing meant that New Zealand was in the process of its own radical transformation just as Japan's economy was restructuring. This meant it did not pay as much attention to Japan's changes as it would have otherwise done. Nonetheless, as New Zealand is of less importance to its trading partners than they are to New Zealand, it had a special need to nurture its trading relationships. Proper nurturing implies paying attention to developments in other countries and adjusting exports to meet needs. As Roger Peren, director of the New Zealand Centre for Japanese Studies, observed, "Adjusting exports is a matter of practical-ities (and calculations of profit and loss) as well as policy – or strategy. Many in this country and elsewhere insist that 'relying on business' is the only way; 'governments are bound to get it wrong!' they say."[94] Relying on business to make these adjustments without government guidance or leadership was not necessarily proving to be effective either, particularly as a long-term strategy.

Commercial links with Japan provided an important benchmark because the change in Japan's import mix should have been heralded as an exciting opportunity for New Zealand business. Japan was now beginning to import the very products that an economy hoping to be strong in the future should produce. As Michael Porter said, speaking at an Auckland Trade Development Board function in April 1997, "It is not just cranking out butter more efficiently or simply adding value to goods. It's the value per day of work that we are worried about. You want to produce products that can command high value per day worked so that you can always keep raising your salary and the nation's."[95]

New Zealand's willingness to base its future on the sale of primary products and to ignore changes in major trading partners that foretell future loss of market share had a potentially enormous price tag. For a country and a government bureaucracy that had managed to trans-form certain sectors so comprehensively and generally successfully to stand back from tackling this vital international challenge seemed incomprehensible. Michael Porter summed it up best when he explained that the challenge now was "whether New Zealand enjoys this moment of brief prosperity and lapses back, or if you are going to continue going forward."[96]

New Zealand, like Canada, prospered for many years on the basis of its endowment of natural resources. An economy based largely on agri-culture and the international trade in raw materials provided the country with an enviable standard of living and considerable long-term stability. For New Zealand to reorient its economic system repre-sented a substantial challenge, for it required the restructuring of political, business, and social relationships that sit at the heart of national culture. New Zealand's determined support for its agricul-tural sector, after all, had striking parallels in most countries, includ-ing Japan. There was, moreover, little sense of urgency surrounding the need to develop new commercial relationships, and the successful restructuring of the economy generated considerable confidence in the value and sustainability of the "New Zealand model." If the country does not see a compelling reason to change, does not feel that a major economic reorientation is essential, and maintains its strong faith in traditional economic enterprise, there is little pressure on public officials to change. And if that same country, and its government, count on the business community to identify opportunities and to make productive use of the nation's natural and commercial endowments, there is little chance that a government-led initiative will find much favour. To summarize, few individuals involved with New Zealand business, government, or Japan relations saw a compelling reason to question current policies, and as long as economic stability and general prosperity were maintained there were few if any demands to develop new approaches to international trade. For better or worse, by 1997 it seemed that New Zealand had decided to proceed on the assumption that a laissez-faire approach to economic management was in the country's best interests.

6 Waltzing with the Japanese: Australia-Japan Commercial Relations 1985–1997

A country with a strong Labour Party tradition and with a deep commitment to social welfare programs, Australia has nonetheless joined with other western nations in downsizing its governments, restricting the power of trade unions, and otherwise limiting the role and authority of the state. At the same time, however, Australia has made a concerted effort to re-position itself economically, to lessen dependency on traditional trading relationships with Britain and the United States, and to embrace the idea of being an Asian nation. Improving its trade connections with Japan gives Australia the opportunity to achieve several of its objectives. The goals of expanding trade with Asian countries, diversifying the country's export base, and developing a more internationally competitive economy emerged, as in Canada, at a time when the government spoke openly about limiting the role of the state and liberating the nation's entrepreneurial energies. Along with many countries, Australia has been wrestling with the seemingly contradictory objectives of providing a new direction for the national economy while reducing the influence of government in the marketplace.

Japan has been of great importance to Australia since early in this century and has been Australia's most important trading partner for a number of decades. Australia has, therefore, been more committed to the Japanese market than has either Canada or New Zealand. During the years after the Plaza Accord, Australia paid attention to the economic changes taking place in Japan and attempted a variety of strategies to try to better position Australia to respond to these new realities.

These strategies were directed at diversifying Australia's exports to Japan toward more value-added products, in recognition that Japan's import needs were changing and that Australia was too dependent on mineral, energy resource, and agricultural exports. Australia's efforts at investment promotion in Japan came both because Japan had dramatically increased its investments abroad and because Australia hoped to attract the manufacturing investment that would allow it to increase its exports of manufactured products to Japan and to other countries.

From the end of World War II until 1983, Australia deliberately focused on a manufacturing sector designed primarily to serve the domestic market. According to Ian Marsh, "The idea was to increase population and to build a 'modern' society. This policy was adopted in full recognition that economies of scale would probably not be realized and that continuing protection would be required. The price was willingly accepted as the cost of enhanced defense capability and a richer citizenry."[1] However, increasing current account deficits and resultant higher unemployment gradually made it clear that Australia needed to make its manufacturing sector internationally competitive if it wanted to ensure a decent standard of living for its citizens. Moreover, commodity and resource prices had been fluctuating, but primarily declining, for decades, a situation well summed up in the following description: "In 1981, Japan had to export 500 cars to buy one shipload of Australian coal. In 1991, 200 cars were enough. By the year 2001, only 100 cars will have to be sold to pay for a shipload of Australian coal."[2] Although Australia had a relatively small public sector in comparison to other OECD countries, it had a reasonably interventionist government that saw a role for itself in charting the nation's destiny.

Much of this changed in the 1980s. The groundwork for economic and public sector reform was developed during the Liberal government of Prime Minister Malcolm Fraser (1975–March 1983),[3] but the reforms themselves were implemented by the Labour government under prime ministers Bob Hawke and Paul Keating, in power from 1983 to 1996, demonstrating the bipartisan support for a changed role for government and for initiatives that would make Australian industry more internationally competitive.

Prime Minister Paul Keating, though attempting to hold onto Labour's traditional political support, recognized the need for sweeping economic and administrative changes. In particular, he argued that the nation's economic future lay in developing greater ties with Asian countries and with modernizing and adapting the Australian system. Keating was not, however, able to prevent the gathering power of the right-wing Liberal-National Party coalition, and in 1996, John Howard led the coalition into office and took immediate steps to challenge the long-standing power of Australia's trade unions, reduce government spending, and limit administrative interventions in the economy and society. Starting with the Keating administration and accelerating with the Howard government, Australia found itself closer to the ideological and political models already in place in New Zealand and Canada, and very much a part of the neo-classical revolution that had taken root throughout the western world.

AUSTRALIA'S TRADE POLICY

Australia is a federal parliamentary state comprised of six states and two territories. The federal government has primary responsibility for immigration, defense, foreign policy, customs and excise, the national economy and Reserve Bank, and the postal system. The states generally look after justice, education, health, transportation, and housing. This division of jurisdictions is outlined in Australia's constitution of 1901, drafted when the Commonwealth of Australia was first proclaimed.

Responsibility for the government's foreign investment policy during the period of the case study lay with the Treasury Department. The Foreign Investment Review Board, a unit of Treasury, acted as an adviser on foreign investment issues generally, examining foreign investment proposals and making recommendations to the government. Generally, Australia encouraged foreign investment and recognized the benefits FDI brings to the country, though a number of investment types and sectors required government approval. Under the Foreign Acquisitions and Takeovers Act (1975), proposed investments in rural properties, agriculture, forestry, fishing, resource processing, oil and gas, mining, manufacturing, non-bank financial institutions, insurance, sharebroking, tourism (hotels and resorts), and most other services all needed government approval.[4] In addition, all proposals valued over certain thresholds (A$3 million for rural property, $5 million for the purchase of an existing business, $10 million for new businesses, $20 million for offshore takeovers and all tourism facilities that include accommodation) required approval.[5]

The Department of Foreign Affairs and Trade (created when the Department of Trade and the Department of Foreign Affairs were merged in 1987) dealt with the broad issues of international relations, including ensuring Australia's security, encouraging global cooperation, and promoting Australia's standing as a member of the international community. The first objective of DFAT, however, was "to increase Australia's economic prosperity through trade and investment flows."[6]

While Treasury was in charge of Australia's foreign investment policy, responsibility for promoting foreign direct investment into Australia rested elsewhere. In 1987 the Investment Promotion and Facilitation Program (IPFP) was established to "encourage foreign direct investment (FDI) in Australia."[7] The program was a partnership between the Australian Trade Commission (Austrade), whose Investment Australia unit had primary operational responsibility, and the Department of Industry, Science, and Technology.[8] Investment commissioners were located overseas and assisted by Austrade's trade commissioners in additional locations and by staff in Australia itself.

Austrade was established in 1986 and soon became part of the DFAT portfolio, reporting to the minister for trade as Australia's "export and investment facilitation agency."[9] Its mandate was to assist Australian exporters sell their products and services offshore and to encourage and promote direct investment into Australia from overseas investors. Austrade worked on a fee-for-service basis and employees had strict performance standards. Austrade worked closely with companies through to the culmination of a deal.

Austrade had a flat organizational structure. Ten executive general managers reported to the managing director, who reported to a Board of Directors drawn largely from the private sector. Six of the executive general managers were based overseas in the regions they managed. In 1995 Japan and South Korea were designated as a single region.[10] Austrade had main offices in Tokyo and Osaka and smaller offices in Nagoya, Fukuoka, Sendai, and Sapporo.[11]

Austrade began creating Joint Action Groups (JAGs) in 1992. JAGs began as government initiatives but evolved to become industry-funded. The need or opportunity for a JAG was identified and an industry audit undertaken. Market and product priorities were selected and then the JAG developed its own marketing strategy and business plan. Gradually, responsibility for the JAG moved from Austrade to the industry. Austrade's contribution was, on average, 400 hundred hours of work.

The advantages of the JAGs were joint promotional activities in overseas markets and access to government funding that would not otherwise have been available. As of 1997, funds for promotional activities were cut (other than the Export Market Development Grant Scheme, an incurred expense rebate program also available to independent companies). When JAGs had to pay for themselves and coordinate the sharing of information without government support, companies lost interest in forming them.[12]

Table 6.1   Joint Action Groups 1997

Joint Action Group	Year Established	# of Companies	Estimated/Projected export impact 5 years from establishment (A$m)
Hay	1992	8	$ 165
China	1992	35	200
Wood	1993	7	90
Peppermint	1993	11	20
Teatree*	1994	15	25
Horses	1994	20	100
Fellmongery**	1995	6	50
Seeds	1996	7	75
Furniture	1996	120	150
Internet	1997	30	100+
Geoscience	1997	20	300+

Source: Peter Harrison, manager, Austrade Export Network Centre in Melbourne. Powerpoint presentation material, June 1998.
*Teatree is an Australian tree that produces a sap with antiseptic properties.
**Fellmongery is the process of separating the wool from skins in the tanning process. This JAG supplied high quality Australian merino sheepskin leather to garment producing countries.

Australia's experience with the JAGs demonstrates one of the limitations of the restricted government approach to economic management. The concept underpinning the JAGs made sense: the government would establish the joint action groups, assist them in developing a presence, and provide initial funding. Once started, successful JAGs would continue, financed by private sector interests who would see the demonstrated merit in this approach to market improvement. In reality, the JAGs that remained in operation generally represented a continuation of industry associations or groups that were functioning before the government initiative started. The initiative did help introduce some companies to opportunities for commercial development, but the effort lost momentum after the government reduced its support. Businesses operate within a narrow frame of self-interest; convincing commercial firms to devote time and resources to initiatives of more national or collective benefit (or to an activity that might strengthen a competitor or require the sharing of sensitive information) is a difficult task that many companies and sectors were unwilling to undertake. In Australia, the challenge inherent in the government's decision to set up and then withdraw funding from the JAGs was not one the private sector appeared prepared to accept.

Although the transition to industry-led JAGs was difficult, Australia's

Joint Action Groups did have an impact on exports. Table 6.1 lists the main JAGS that were in operation in 1997 and the estimated increase in exports each created. The furniture JAG had the greatest number of companies, while the geoscience JAG had the strongest export impact in financial terms.

In *Trade Outcomes and Objectives Statement 1997*, the Australian government set out its mission statement and described the five fundamental objectives of its national trade policy. The mission statement read: "Australia's trade policy aims to create jobs and increase living standards by raising the sustainable rate of economic growth. The central task is to secure the best possible conditions and opportunities, especially market access, for Australian firms and industries trading and investing overseas, as well as supporting measures which increase the competitiveness of the Australian economy."[13]

The five objectives were to raise Australia's international competitiveness; to secure better market access for Australian goods, services, and investment overseas; to promote Australia as a destination for inward foreign investment (including as a destination for regional corporate headquarters); to develop markets and promote Australian business and exports overseas; and to defend and advance Australia's commercial interests through stronger and fairer trade and investment rules.[14] Australia's trade policies were direct and specific. Clear priorities like the promotion of Australia as a foreign investment destination put the onus on the government to be an active player in changing the country's destiny.

CONTOURS OF AUSTRALIA-JAPAN INVESTMENT AND TRADE TO 1997

In the 1980s, Australia began to recognize the necessity of moving away from an overdependence on resource and agricultural products. As Foreign Affairs Minister Bill Hayden said in his speech at the ninth Australia-Japan ministerial committee in early 1987,

The Australian economy has depended for decades on its exports of mineral and energy resources and agricultural products. Indeed they still constitute 80 percent of all our exports. Economic circumstances dictate that this must all change. Our major exports face a near term trend of falling prices and-or massive subsidization. Our terms of trade have fallen so precipitously that we have had to produce almost 3 per cent more since 1984 just to cover lost purchasing power of our exports. The present Australian government has resolutely and innovatively sought to shift the orientation of our industry to promote a modern, outward looking industrial structure.[15]

Politicians were not the only ones concerned. The Australian Manufacturing Council (AMC) also expressed its fears about Australia's over-dependence on raw material exports in a time when the value of resources was decreasing as a percentage of total world trade. The council hired a consulting firm to analyse "the issues and impediments to growth, with the objective of initiating positive responses from all those groups and individuals who must contribute to a reversal of the trend."[16] One of the study's three main conclusions was that "Australia needs to take a more strategic approach to assisting industrial development. This will entail an approach that is built around an understanding of our own competitive position and the recognition of the actions and reactions of countries in this area. Finally, it requires us to have broadly agreed national objectives to which we are committed, and a clear sense of how we can best achieve these."[17] The AMC decided that more work needed to be done to build on the conclusions of the study, and commissioned three Australian Graduate School of Management professors to look at, among other things, the "policy changes required to maximize the benefits of the process of internationalization for Australia."[18] The resulting report, published in 1992, produced mixed conclusions.[19] Although eleven manufacturing sectors with export potential were identified and general agreement on the main focus of industrial policy was reached, the authors did not agree on the best approaches for government. Two of the authors supported a more interventionist approach, while the third did not. The review was not important enough to alter government policy, nor did it offer a sufficiently strong conclusion to compel the government to respond to its recommendations in any direct or meaningful way.

On the investment front, Japanese FDI represented over 7.5% of total direct investment in Australia in 1984. While Japan continued to rank behind the United Kingdom and the U.S. as a source of Australian investment capital, 7.5% was a dramatic leap from the 3% that Japanese investment had constituted a decade earlier.[20] Japanese investment continued to increase through the 1990s, and by mid-1995, Japanese investment constituted 14% of the total FDI stock in Australia and was valued at A$18.7 billion.[21]

The rapid growth in Japanese investment in 1990 and 1991 (as seen in table 6.2) was due partly to the second surge in Japanese investment abroad discussed in chapter 3 and partly to the concerted efforts by the Australians to bring Japanese investment to their country. Britain and the United States retained their positions as the leading sources of Australian direct foreign investment, but Japan emerged in the post-Plaza Accord era as a major player in the Australian investment scene.

Table 6.2   Direct investment in Australia by Japan, the United States, and the United Kingdom, 1984–1991 (US$m)

	Japan			United States			United Kingdom			
Year	%	US$	Base 1984	%	US$	Base 1984	%	US$	Base 1984	Total
1984	7.5	2,159	100	36.1	10,405	100	31.0	8,914	100	28,790
1986	10.2	2,892	134	33.3	9,431	91	30.3	8,590	96	28,335
1990	14.3	9,929	460	27.0	18,764	180	28.7	19,978	242	69,582
1991	16.2	12,397	574	26.9	20,568	198	25.2	19,271	216	76,421

Source: Stephen Nicholas, David Merrett, Greg Whitwell, William Purcell, with Sue Kimberley, *Japanese FDI in Australia in the 1990s: Manufacturing, Financial Services and Tourism,* Australia-Japan Research Centre, Pacific Economic Papers, No. 256, June 1996

The effort to attract Japanese investment began in the early 1980s, particularly in the manufacturing sector. With only a small number of large corporations and a relatively low domestic savings rate, Australia lacked significant investment capital, and the government hoped for increased Japanese investment in the manufacturing and processing sectors. An investment mission to Japan took place in November 1986 to discuss the impact of the increased value of the Japanese yen and the economic adjustments Japan was looking at making, as well as the benefits for both parties if Japan were to invest in Australian manufacturing. As the minister for industry, technology, and commerce at the time explained,

A major objective of the mission, therefore, was to demonstrate the capabilities of Australian industry, particularly in the following areas: the further processing of food, wool, metal and mineral resources; areas where Australia has world class scientific skills and technical capabilities such as computer software, biotechnology and telecommunications; and the automotive components industry where existing links with Japanese industry provide the base for competitive manufacture of components in Australia both for export and for domestic use. The other major objective was to outline the structural changes that have occurred in the Australian economy recently and which provide the base for industry's improved competitive position.[22]

A large Japanese investment mission then came to Australia in February 1987. The resulting Japanese report was mixed, but generally indicated that Australia had work to do before the Japanese would be prepared to invest significant sums. Australia recognized that it was not seen by the Japanese as a natural location for manufacturing, having neither low-priced labour like some of the Asian countries, nor access to a large domestic market as Canada does with the United States.[23]

Australia responded to the various mission reports with the Investment and Promotion Facilitation Program, and an investment commissioner was assigned to the Tokyo embassy. Initially, the program took a facilitatory role by running seminars and producing brochures, but this had so little impact that the program was changed. The investment commissioner's position was reorganized to become part of a new Investment Promotion Section within Austrade and by 1996 there were three investment commissioners assigned to Tokyo.[24] The parameters of the job also shifted from a focus on generic investment promotion to the promotion of particular projects (preferably in manufacturing or processing of products of interest in Japan) with specific investors.[25] The investment commissioners, whose numbers increased to four in 1997, all came from industry and were in their positions for a maximum of four years. They were responsible for getting results, measured through specific targets for the amount of investment capital and employment, or they were not kept on. The government's approach was pragmatic: if the investment was not going to add value or create jobs, agents were not to pursue it.[26]

The investment commissioners dealt with manufacturing and service investments but not with real estate. They had a targeted list of sectors (including forestry and wood-based products, food processing, mineral processing, and high tech) but generally focused on what they thought was possible to accomplish. Since most, if not all, of the easy deals were done by the private sector, those worked on by the IPFP were already considered "too hard": private companies would not be interested. Private companies usually work on a fee-for-service basis and would not start without that initial fee. The IPFP commissioners, therefore, took on those investment possibilities that would take more work.[27]

The IPFP was strict about performance and verified its results annually through a survey of each of the companies that invested in Australia. Companies were specifically asked if they would have invested had the program not been in place. Table 6.3 lists those companies from 1994 to 1997 that answered that they would not have invested without the program. On an annual basis, the four investment commissioners carried about 100 projects, generating an average of A$200 million in investment from Japan and about 250 jobs in Australia.[28] Other investment counsellors were based in London, New York, Frankfurt, Singapore, and China.

Table 6.3   Direct results of the Investment Promotion and Facilitation Program, Tokyo, 1994–1997

Company	Business Area	Investment Location	Investment Capital (A$m)
Sakata Beika	Food processing	Victoria	6
Hino Motors	Automotive	New South Wales	8
Stehr Group	Fishery	South Australia	1.6
Bao Shan	Mineral trading	Western Australia	0.6
Hokushin Co. Ltd	Forestry value-added	Tasmania	90
Enya Systems Ltd	High technology	Queensland	1.3
Enya Systems Ltd	High technology	ACT	0.7
Konaka Corporation	High technology	New South Wales	0.6
Asahi Industries	Hay	Victoria	2
Meiji Milk Ltd	Milk powder man.	Victoria	49
Shin-Etsu Chemical	Mineral processing	Western Australia	67
Mitsui Company – Nippon Paper	Forestry	Western Australia/ Victoria	200
Dowa Mining	Mining	Tasmania	Depends on deposits identified
Japan Petroleum Exploration	Petroleum exploration	Western Australia	10 (+ 20% of all additional costs incurred)
Nozaki & Co. Ltd	Food retail	New South Wales	0.7
ANA Trading Co.	Retail	New South Wales/ Queensland	0.7
Nichiyu Giken Kogyo	High technology	New South Wales	0.5
Asahi Chemical Industry Co. Ltd	Beverage manufacturer	South Australia	not available
Nittetsu Mining Co.	Mining	New South Wales	60
Work Vision Co.	Media service sector	Queensland	0.7
SBR	Software	Victoria	0.5
Woodland	Software	Queensland	0.2
TOTAL			523.2

Source: Austrade Tokyo, IPFP Tokyo Successes since February 1994, unpublished paper

The IPFP was evaluated for its effectiveness in 1995 by the Bureau of Industry Economics (BIE). The resulting report discussed whether or not this kind of government intervention was warranted and whether or not it had been successful, and to determine this, the evaluation took into account "an economy-wide view of the effects of any additional activity induced by the IPFP which assumes that such activity will largely displace domestic activity in the long run,"[29] for example by competing against domestic companies or driving up labour costs.

The BIE confirmed that many potential foreign investors were unaware of investment opportunities in Australia or held negative views of Australia's potential as an investment location. It concluded that "Private markets do not always provide the incentive and expertise to fully address these deficiencies....The BIE is satisfied that the IPFP is an appropriate intervention to deliver promotion and facilitation services and has successfully done so."[30] The report continued by saying that the BIE was "satisfied that the IPFP has been successful at the margin in attracting additional foreign direct investment (FDI) to Australia. The BIE estimates that around A$235 million a year on average has probably been directly invested in Australia by foreign companies as a result of the IPFP's activities over the three financial years."[31] A large part of these additional investments were made by the Japanese, including, for example, Hokushin's new fibreboard plant in Tasmania, Meiji Milk's milk powder manufacturing plant, and Hino Motors' automotive plant[32] (see table 6.3).

Other government initiatives to encourage investment included visits to Australia by members of the Japanese media to ensure they were accurately informed, a newsletter, trade and investment seminars in both Australia and Japan, and regular visits to each country by people from industry and government.[33]

The Partnership for Development and Fixed Term Arrangements programs, developed in the late 1980s, were designed to encourage international companies in the information technology industry "to expand their strategic global activities in Australia and to actively seek out Australian products, services and skills with international prospects and mutually beneficial returns."[34] In exchange for access to federal government supply contracts, the government attempted to extract a commitment to Australia from the international information technology company in question, and sought to ensure that the company maintained agreed-upon levels of exports and of research and development. Companies who signed a memorandum of understanding with the government were encouraged to have a strategic plan for their business future in Australia, including entering into "strategic alliances with local firms and institutions where commercially viable and appropriate to do so."[35] The partnership agreements were not legally enforceable but appeared to be designed to let participating international companies know that the Australian government was paying attention and hoping for future benefits to accrue to Australia.

Investment statistics reveal that Australia's promotion activities in Japan had a positive impact. From 1988 to 1992 Australia received approximately 5–7% of total Japanese foreign direct investment, a

Table 6.4   Japanese direct investment in Australia by sector, 1984–1990 (US$m)

	1984		1986		1988		1990	
	$	%	$	%	$	%	$	%
Manufacturing	29	27.6	123	14.0	211	8.7	360	9.8
Mining and agriculture	5	4.8	195	22.2	186	7.7	769	20.0
Banking and insurance	9	8.6	92	10.5	363	15.0	200	5.5
Real estate	6	5.7	127	14.5	1,270	52.6	1,333	36.4
Commerce	27	25.7	77	8.8	92	3.8	326	8.9
Other services	31	29.5	265	30.2	292	12.1	679	18.5
TOTAL	107		881		2,414		3,667	

Source: Peter Drysdale, *Japanese Direct Foreign Investment in Australia in Comparative Perspective*, Pacific Economic Papers No. 223, Australia-Japan Research Centre, September 1993

sizeable percentage for a reasonably small population and substantially more than Canada and most of the APEC countries (see table 4.5). This relative share of Japanese investment monies continued until 1992 and then decreased slightly in 1993 and even more in 1994. In 1995, however, there was a dramatic increase in Japanese direct investments into Australia to a value of US$2.6 billion, representing 5.2% of total Japanese FDI.[36] This made Australia the fourth highest Japanese FDI recipient, after the United States, China, and the United Kingdom. 1996 saw another dramatic change when Australia's share fell suddenly to only 1.6%.[37] The sudden drop was partially the result of circumstances: for example, following the usual pattern of large investments followed by minimal investments, no investment took place in the automotive sector in 1996 as there had been a significant investment the previous year. Australian observers hoped this would be an aberration.[38] The Australian government's program of investment promotion, designed to link Australian needs with Japanese investors, represented a substantial effort to move beyond a simple reliance on the marketplace. Using a strongly commercial model of investment promotions – officials responsible for an area worked to substantial investment targets – the Australian government developed specific leads and opportunities and, over a three-year period, was able to claim significant achievements (see table 6.3)

While the increased value of Japanese investments in Australia was important, even more striking was the change in composition of these investments. Australia began to attract Japanese direct investment into manufacturing industries, which, combined with Japanese divest-

Table 6.5   Japanese direct investment in Australia by sector, 1992–1995
(US$m)

Sector	1992	1993	1994	1995
Food	$ 34	$ 619	$ 58	$ 25
Textiles	0	0	4	0
Wood/pulp	0	0	0	75
Chemicals	0	7	0	6
Metals	131	42	18	281
General machinery	36	9	4	6
Electrical machinery	22	4	3	0
Transport machinery	2	27	18	383
Other	0	4	1	24
Total manufactures	224	712	629	800
Agri/forestry	16	9	6	26
Fisheries	1	1	0	2
Mining	206	292	117	364
Construction	15	12	0	22
Commerce	187	173	54	321
Finance	63	38	120	129
Services	164	106	196	218
Transport	2	8	0	5
Real estate	1,272	540	143	744
Total non-manufacturing	1,925	1,179	636	1,83
Branch/Expansion	0	13	0	4
Grand total	2,150	1,904	1,265	2,635

Source: Australia Foreign Affairs and Trade, Country Economic Brief – Japan, May
1997, 36 and Australia-Japan Economic Institute, Economic Bulletin 4, no. 6 (June
1996), 2

ments of real estate and business services, saw manufacturing assume
a much larger percentage of total Japanese FDI in Australia. This
increase, however, was not just relative to other industries. As tables
6.4 and 6.5 indicate, Japanese investment in manufacturing increased
enormously from 1984, when it was US$29 million, to 1995, when it
was US$800 million, a twenty-six-fold increase in Japanese manufac-
turing FDI in dollar terms. This increase, though dramatic, represented only a relatively small addition to Australia in total foreign
manufacturing investment.

The manufacturing sectors that saw the most Japanese investment
through this time period were transport equipment, processed food,
and metals. Toyota and Mitsubishi dramatically increased their investments in the late 1980s. Toyota Motors Australia was formed as a joint

venture with Toyota and United Australian Automotive Industries (UAMI), itself a joint venture between Toyota and General Motors,[39] while Mitsubishi Motors took over Chrysler's Australian operations and improved their plants. In 1995, Mitsubishi Motors began to manufacture six-cylinder engines and Daimante vehicles, an investment valued at A$525 million.[40] The foodstuffs sector saw Japanese companies establish yogourt, infant formula, sake, and rice cracker operations, among others.[41] The mining and metals sector had always attracted Japanese interest due to their demand for Australian resources from coal to non-ferrous metallic ores.[42]

In 1995 there was a particularly noticeable increase in Japanese FDI in the metal and transport machinery sectors. In addition, in 1997 MFAT reported that "research by Austrade's investment promotion office in Tokyo also points to continuing interest among Japanese companies in the areas of food processing, timber processing, mineral processing and oil and gas exploration. Growth in Japanese investment into Australia is likely to occur in these areas."[43]

The pattern of Japanese direct investment in Australia (table 6.4) illustrates the changing nature of post-Plaza Accord Japanese business activity. In the period from 1984 to 1990, for example, Japanese manufacturing investment in Australia declined from over 27% of the total to less than 10%. Real estate investment, perhaps the most high profile outlet for the cash-rich Japanese, soared from US$6 million in 1984 to over US$1.3 billion six years later. The influx of Japanese money, much of it to the tourist regions of Queensland, sparked considerable local backlash and concern about the high level of Japanese ownership. After the first flush of post-Plaza prosperity, Japanese investments shifted back closer to the traditional pattern of long-term commitments to resource development and local manufacturing. Japanese investment in Australian manufacturing increased four-fold between 1992 and 1995, with the greatest advance coming in the transport machinery fields. In other sectors, Japanese firms continued their high level of investment in Australian mining, reduced their commitments in real estate, and added significantly to Japanese holdings in the finance and service sectors.

Two of the more interesting events in the Australia-Japan relationship were the Silver Columbia Plan and the Multifunctionpolis proposal. The Silver Columbia Plan was a Japanese MITI idea to send large groups of Japanese retirees overseas to live out their remaining years in sunnier and less polluted climates – but still in Japanese communities. The two countries most seriously considered to receive these Japanese senior citizens were Australia and Spain. The Japanese bureaucrats who designed the plan "had expected that it would be welcomed as a token of closer cooperation that Japan was being asked for, since the overseas settlement of Japanese elderly people might be expected to stimulate various service industries in the host country to cope with their needs."[44] Public reaction in Australia was strongly opposed, however, and the plan went nowhere. It is interesting to note, though, that in Spain a slightly altered version did indeed occur. This version has Japanese technicians who are still working "sent to the Barcelona area to train people as skilled technicians and then settle there for their old age."[45]

The Multifunctionpolis or MFP was also originally a Japanese idea. It was proposed in early 1987 by the Japanese minister for international trade. When the Australians expressed interest in receiving more detail, a MITI planning group completed a more comprehensive plan. Gavan McCormack explains the proposal:

At the core of the project was the notion of constructing somewhere in Australia a new city (to cost around $1 billion), a prototype twenty-first century city in which residence, work, leisure, health and education needs for a population of about 100,000 people would be met in a single, integrated physical location. As the MITI report expressed it: 'the MFP would be a fusion of high-tech industries destined to comprise core industries in the 21st century and high-touch oriented industries which support creative human people accompanied by their families.' Computer and information technology, biotechnology and health sciences, new and rare materials technology were identified as strategic industries whose development should be fostered on the 'high-tech' side, while 'high-touch' implied the growth of a 'Convention Services' industry, based on resorts, sports and tourism.[46]

The MFP plan would therefore have seen Australian and Japanese business and government working together on an unprecedented scale. As a beginning, eighty companies from each country contributed a $10,000 annual fee. This money was matched by the two governments and used to fund a Joint Secretariat and a Joint Steering Committee.[47] Despite this good start, however, it quickly became apparent that the two countries had different visions and priorities: "The question of priorities almost immediately divided the two sides. While the Japanese were anxious for a site to be quickly designated and the character and components to be settled thereafter, the Australian side wanted first to decide on what the 'multi-functions' might be before turning to the location of the 'polis.' And the Australian side was notably slow to warm to the 'high-touch' and 'resort' elements of the Japanese vision."[48]

These differences continued, and although the Japanese began to play less of a role and the MFP began to become more of an "intense effort to

Table 6.6   Australian exports to Japan, 1984–1998 (US$m)

Year	Value	% of Total Exports
1984	$ 6,150	25.8
1985	6,295	27.8
1986	6,065	26.9
1987	6,791	25.6
1988	8,881	27.1
1989	9,761	26.4
1990	10,232	26.3
1991	11,496	27.5
1992	10,737	25.3
1993	10,466	24.6
1994	11,613	24.5
1995	12,184	23.0
1996	12,019	19.7
1997	12,438	19.7
1998	10,909	19.5

Source: International Monetary Fund, *Direction of Trade Statistics Yearbook 1996* and *1997*

Table 6.7

Commodities for which Japan was Australia's biggest market, 1995 (%)		Commodities for which Australia was Japan's biggest supplier, 1995 (%)	
Cotton	22.3	Wool	54.9
Woodchips	99.0	Iron ore	48.8
Iron ore	44.2	Lead ore	36.3
Copper ore	54.9	Zinc ore	55.6
Lead ore	44.6	Aluminum ore	49.7
Zinc ore	41.5	Titanium ore	63.5
Coking coal	41.3	Salt	49.0
Steaming coal	55.7	Coking coal	50.0
LNG	97.0	Steaming coal	55.1

Source: Australia-Japan Economic Institute, *Economic Bulletin* 4, no. 8 (August 1996)

secure Japanese involvement in and commitment to Australia,"[49] Australian public and media opinion of the proposal was hostile and suspicious. In 1990 Australia settled on the site for the project as Adelaide rather than the Gold Coast as the Japanese had hoped. The Japanese gradually lost interest and the project never materialized.

In terms of trade, Japan had been by far Australia's largest export market since 1970. Japan accounted for over A$15 billion (or 20 %)

Table 6.8   Top ten Australian exports to Japan, 1996 (A$m)

Coal, coke, and briquettes	$ 3,556
Combined confidential items of trade and commodities	2,858
Metalliferous ores and metal scrap	1,935
Meat and meat preparations	1,252
Non-ferrous metals	911
Cork and wood	552
Textile fibres and their waste	490
Petroleum and petroleum products	464
Gold, non-monetary	466
Fish and seafood	411

Source: Australian Bureau of Statistics, *International Merchandise Trade December Quarter 1996*

of Australia's total exports in 1996.[50] Australia's next largest markets were South Korea (9.5%), New Zealand (7.3%), and the United States (6.4%). While the total value of Australian exports remained fairly stable, Japan's percentage of Australia's total exports declined from over 25% in the late 1980s to approximately 20% in 1996. In this pattern, Australia closely paralleled the experience of other resource-dependent countries, like Canada and New Zealand. And as with the other two countries, Australia adhered to a similar pattern of exporting raw and partially processed trade goods.

In 1997, Japan remained a critical market for many of Australia's agricultural and resource industries. It was the most important market for beef, cheese, animal feeds, seafood, iron ore, natural gas, copper ore, coal, lead ore, zinc ore, aluminum, and petroleum and one of the largest for sugar, wheat, and wool.[51] Not only was Japan Australia's biggest market for these traditional commodities but Australia was also Japan's most important supplier for an equally large number of products (see table 6.7). In 1995 Australia sold a smaller percentage of its wool, cotton, iron ore, copper, zinc ore, liquified natural gas, and a variety of other products to Japan than it had done five years previously.[52] This was probably due to the relocation of Japanese firms to other countries in Asia such as Indonesia and Malaysia that supply some of the raw materials themselves.

Japan remained Australia's most important market for crude materials and mineral fuels, but while worldwide exports grew in the later 1990s, Japan's share declined. Other Asian markets, China and South Korea particularly, increased in importance.[54]

AUSTRALIAN RESPONSES TO CHANGES
IN THE ECONOMY

Australia's trading relationship with Japan began to change prior to the Plaza Accord, with the election of the Hawke Labour government in 1983. The previous Liberal-Country Party government had made little effort to direct or monitor this relationship, and as a result, Australia found itself dependent on a declining Japanese need for its resources. The Hawke government recognized that raw and barely processed primary products composed the vast majority of Australian exports to Japan, and that many of these products were in Japanese import sectors in which there was little or no growth. Australian exports to Japan as a proportion of total Japanese imports had been gradually declining over the previous decade.[55] As Hawke said in a speech to the Australian-Japan Cooperation Committee soon after his election,

Important structural changes have taken place, however, in the Japanese economy. We must recognize and adjust to the implications for Australia. Lower, though, still significant growth rates in Japan, and a re-alignment of Japanese energy and industry policies are of particular importance to Australia. Most importantly, the growth prospects for Australian raw material exports to Japan, are diminished. Alternative, supplementary markets must be sought and, with Japan, new growth sectors we can profitably supply identified.[56]

Australia, therefore, began in 1983 to develop concrete strategies for diversifying Australian exports to Japan away from resources and barely processed goods in the low growth sectors of the Japanese economy to higher value-added products in high growth sectors. In early 1984 the government commissioned two Japanese consulting companies, Nomura Research Institute and Seibu Marketing Information Services, to put together a report "on what Australian companies have to do to effectively enter the Japanese market,"[57] and seminars were subsequently held around Australia to disseminate the results to Australian companies.

As another part of the market strategy for Japan, an Australian senior trade mission visited Japan in July 1984 and a Japanese mission came to Australia later that same year. These missions identified products with good potential for growth in the Japanese market (examples included computer software, medical equipment and instruments, aluminum products, and wine). The Australian mission recommended that promotional missions take place in Japan throughout 1985, which did occur.[58]

The report from the Japanese mission outlined ways to promote Australian products in Japan and tips on the quality Japanese consumers demanded. It specifically emphasized the benefits of joint ventures with Japanese companies:

Australian exporters are advised to make a thorough study of just where they have an advantage over Japanese companies, and then go into partnership with Japanese firms in order that they may provide complementary assistance as required. Rather than undertaking the total manufacturing process right through to packaging in Australia, depending on the circumstances, Australian companies may be better off employing a flexible policy whereby the degree of processing prior to export is decided by the particular characteristics of individual products.[59]

Even more directly, the report suggested that a good public relations campaign might help improve the 'Made in Australia' image and "make up for the somewhat high prices and less-than-perfect quality of some manufactured products from Australia."[60]

The early 1980s also saw the Australian and Japanese governments agree to establish the Australia-Japan Business Forum, made up of senior business leaders from both countries. The forum created an opportunity for discussion on ways that Australian goods and services could be better promoted in Japan.[61] From 1986 to 1991, in cooperation with Austrade, the AJBF "conducted no fewer than seven survey missions to Japan to investigate marketing opportunities for Australian exporters in areas as diverse as ferrous castings and forgings (1987), building materials (1988), marinas (1989), giftware (1989), processed food (1991) and automotive parts (1991)."[62]

In June 1987 the AJBF conducted an Economic Survey Mission to Japan in order to "develop an Australian business perspective of the structural changes taking place in the Japanese economy (and) as a result to identify the implications for Australian industry."[63] The subsequent report mentioned Japan's need for deregulation and its growing focus on high technology and domestic demand, and went into some detail on the implications of Japan's increase in overseas investment and on the adjustments in Japan's import mix. Regarding overseas investment, the report stated, "Substantial movement offshore of resource intensive production is also occurring, either to tap lower costs of production, for example in the N.I.C.s, or to invest behind emerging protectionist barriers in major markets such as the United States and Europe. This movement will have major implications for Australia, as a major supplier of primary commodities.[64] As more labour-intensive manufacturing moves offshore, "some of the manufacturing industry which moves from Japan will go to countries that are themselves resource rich (for example, Brazil). Most will go to countries remote from Australia (in particular North America), where we will face strong competition from suppliers such as South Africa, Brazil and Columbia."[65] While the outlook in the area of resources was not so positive, the report pointed out that "there are some positive signs in parts of the manufacturing and service sectors...Australia will need to adapt its attitude and approach if it is to capitalize on these opportunities – including development of links with Japanese companies."[66] Clearly then, Australia was aware of what was happening in Japan and what would be required of Australia to take advantage of this transformation.

From 1986, the Japan market strategy initiatives were taken over by the newly created Austrade. The government continued to work to expand Australia's range of exports, particularly processed or manufactured exports. Most of these efforts consisted of trade promotion events, the provision of research and other business services, and general encouragement and assistance to Australian companies considering the Japanese market.[67]

The most extensive of these promotions, and the largest Australia had ever undertaken anywhere,[68] was 'Celebrate Australia,' which took place in November 1993. Celebrate Australia was a month of events ranging from "exchanges and seminars in business, education, science and technology" to ballet performances and street theatre to department store and restaurant promotions.[69] A desire to convey a strong positive image of Australia's export potential, particularly of manufactured products, and to highlight Australia as an investment location underlay many of the Celebrate Australia events.[70] The government's goal was to present Australia "as a centre of high quality educational services, cutting-edge scientific and medical research, outstanding food and wines, dynamic business activity and cultural achievement."[71]

The Australian government began to realize the high costs and difficulty for small and medium companies to enter the Japanese market, particularly through Tokyo or Osaka. The 1991 McKinsey Review of Austrade's operations therefore "recommended a major reallocation of Austrade's resources to the Asia Pacific region. In response to the review, the Federal Government announced a 40 percent boost in Austrade resources over the following three years to strengthen its presence in Asia."[72] Japan was the focus of a considerable portion of the new funds, which bought increased resources for Australian exporters interested in entering the Japanese market. In January 1991 a new consulate and Austrade office were opened in Fukuoka, and additional consulates with Austrade representation opened in 1992 in Sendai, Nagoya, and Sapporo. In conjunction with the Australian Chamber of Manufactures, the Ministry of Small Business, Construction, and Customs opened the Australian Business Office in Osaka in December 1992. The main purpose of this office was to assist smaller Australian companies by matching them with Japanese business partners.[73]

The Australian Business Centre opened in Tokyo in May 1995. Its purpose was to bring together in one place all of the Australian governmental organizations involved in the promotion of trade, investment and tourism with Japan, and to thereby create "a united Australian presence in Tokyo."[74] The member organizations could also keep costs down by sharing everything from meeting rooms and receptionists to promotional efforts and market research. This small, low-profile move was indicative of the Australian government's attempts to address the practical requirements of Australian firms seeking to do business in Japan. While there was little that was proactive in the initiative, and it did not offer leadership or direction, the Business Centre was a pragmatic effort to help national businesses overcome the high cost of doing business in Japan.

These initiatives, reports, and speeches show that Australian government and industry were well aware of the changes in the Japanese economy and formulated steps to address the impact of these changes on Australia. Unfortunately, as we have seen, these initiatives, while not unsuccessful, appear not to have been dramatic enough to affect Australian exports to Japan in any meaningful way.

The action taken in pursuit of Japanese investment, particularly into the manufacturing sector, has been described. The 1996 evaluation of the IPFP concluded that the program was successful, bringing investment to Australia that would otherwise have not occurred. Australia had a larger share of Japanese investment per capita than most other nations and many of the recent investments were in manufacturing. However, as far as adjusting Australia's export profile to Japan to one that contained more processed and manufactured goods, the Australian government was less successful.

In the final analysis, not a great deal changed between the early 1980s and the late 1990s. Because the Australian government left the fundamental decisions to the business community – a cornerstone of the neo-classical approach to the economy – Australia remained economically dependent on the extraction and export of resource products. While there were minor gains in value-added and manufactured items (more the former than the latter), Australia, like Canada and

New Zealand, remained predominantly wedded to a nineteenth-century economic foundation based on resource production. Australia's recent history illustrates that governments can, even in a neoclassical framework, influence trading and investment patterns and redirect elements of the domestic economy to respond to international opportunities, but it also reveals that there are significant limits on what can be accomplished when governments lack direct influence and control over key levers of economic decision-making.

7 Comparisons and Analysis

Numerous political conditions influence international trade and affect a country's capacity and ability to manage its economic affairs. (The cultural, economic, and industrial factors that also shape the manner in which a country responds to changing international circumstances are not the subject of this study.) This comparison of Australia, Canada, and New Zealand begins with five key variables: political structure, the nature of internal economic changes, economic and political preoccupation with a major trading partner, the centrality of Japan to each nation's plans for long-term economic development, and governmental awareness of the post-Plaza Accord changes in Japan's economy (see the summary in table 7.1). These political and administrative influences on trade help illustrate the similarities and differences in the responses of the three countries to the changing Japanese economy and indicate the manner in which they implemented their neo-classical economic ideas in their export policies.

POLITICAL CONTEXT

Political structure

A nation's political arrangements exert a significant influence on the development and implementation of government policy. The nature of decision-making, division of powers, the relative strength of regional governments, and a variety of other factors can determine a

Table 7.1 Influences on trade and investment policy with Japan

	Canada	Australia	New Zealand
Political structure	federal/provincial	federal/state	unitary
Internal changes	privatization	export promotion	market liberalization
Major partner	U.S.	Japan	Australia
Centrality of Japan	secondary	key nation	limited priority
Administrative awareness of changes in Japan's economy	delayed awareness	aware	relatively unaware

country's ability to respond on a national level and therefore the government's capacity to manage the economy.

In Canada, the existence of and competition between ten provincial, three territorial (two during the period under study), and a national government make understanding Canadian governance extremely difficult for Canadians, let alone foreign importers or investors. Although the federal government is responsible for international trade, a number of the provinces have ministries of international business and some have trade offices abroad. As Michael Porter wrote, "The combination of federal and provincial trade promotion programs and trade office abroad can cause confusion for prospective exporters and creates the impression of a highly fragmented national export promotion effort."[1] Provinces often appear to be (and are) selling competing products. For a company hoping to invest in Canada or buy its products, this confusion is an unnecessary burden.

Australia's combination of federal and state governments poses similar though less severe problems. The eight states have been known to fight among themselves either to attract investment to Australia or to entice projects to go to one state rather than to another.[2] According to Michael Pusey, sociologist from the University of New South Wales, however, the federal government "has enjoyed a considerable authority and prestige which has in many respects overshadowed the other two tiers of government – the states and local government respectively."[3] This has meant that, compared with Canada, the national government exercises considerable control, is better able to establish and implement a nation-wide agenda, and is seen in the country at large as the legitimate locus of major decision-making authority (although states like Queensland and Western Australia routinely challenge this assertion). The Australian government's reorientation of the national economy toward Asia is a strong example of national influence and leadership.

New Zealand's unitary system of government is of great advantage in the international arena. It allows the country to present a unified front to the outside world and helps limit the number of competing visions of the country. The national government can speak for the country knowing that no significant dissenting or contradictory voices will be heard from its constituent parts. Other nations are clear on the rules and who they should deal with.

The unitary system has additional benefits on the domestic front. One level of government means that decisions can be made more quickly – even complete changes of direction can take place rapidly. (Some New Zealanders would argue that this can also be a liability. Many felt that the events of the mid-1980s were far too dramatic and rapid and subsequently voted for a new electoral system [Mixed Member Proportional] that would likely ensure coalition governments and slower decision-making.) The business community has greater access to government and government to business, opening the opportunity for more coordinated decision-making and greater inter-action generally.

Internal changes from the mid-1980s through the 1990s

All three countries went through similar philosophic and economic shifts in the mid-1980s. The prevailing ideology in the Anglo-American world supported the free market and limited the role of government. The newly elected 1984 Progressive Conservative (Canada), Labour (New Zealand), and Labour (Australia) governments all embraced this philosophy and spent much of their terms in office restricting government and facilitating industrial leadership.

In Canada, Brian Mulroney's Conservative government cut government spending and privatized many government-owned enterprises. Their purpose was to do more than simply save money: they sought to significantly curtail the government's management of the Canadian economy and society, and they capitalized on the widely recognized budgetary crisis to begin the process. The election of the Liberal Party in 1993 did not change government priorities. The end of the twentieth century, therefore, saw severe restrictions on the ability and willingness of the Canadian government to intervene in the economy, with the one exception of macroeconomic management. The Canadian government largely adopted the neo-classical approach to business management.

The mid-1980s were a time of political change for Australia also.

The government had traditionally seen itself as leading Australia and had not hesitated to intervene in seeking to chart the nation's destiny. This began to change with the Hawke Labour government, which built on the groundwork for economic and public sector reforms established by previous Liberal governments. The election of John Howard's Conservatives in 1996 (subsequently re-elected in 1998 and 2001) saw government become even more "hands off." Howard cut government spending, challenged the power of the unions, and limited intervention in the economy to an even greater extent. These changes were less dramatic and far reaching than those that occurred in New Zealand or even in Canada, but the general trends were the same. At this time, Australia also decided to make its manufacturing sector internationally competitive, a radical change from its previous focus on a manufacturing sector designed to primarily serve the domestic market.

For New Zealand, the latter half of the 1980s was a time of radical political, social, and economic change. What became known as the New Zealand 'revolution' began in 1984, immediately following the election of the Labour government. Serious financial difficulties forced the government to restructure the economy: within a matter of months, radical measures were implemented, including a major currency devaluation, the elimination of agricultural subsidies, the transformation of government departments and statutory corporations into state-owned enterprises (later privatized), reduced government regulations, and a substantial decrease in the size and authority of the civil service.[4] By the late 1990s, New Zealand had changed from a government-controlled, centrally managed economy to a free market, limited-government business environment. A complete retreat from the belief that government intervention is either necessary or recommended for economic success had occurred, ironically led by the government itself.

Preoccupation with major partner

National preoccupation with a particular trading partner (usually its most important) has the potential to blind a country to economic possibilities with other nations. In some cases, as in New Zealand's pre-1980 dependence on Great Britain, a concentrated focus can have disastrous consequences when conditions change. An assessment of the trading emphases of Canada, Australia, and New Zealand illustrates the degree to which each nation has, at different times, been fixated on a major partner and the effect this has had on economic development.

Despite Canadian government rhetoric that "Canada ranks as one of the world's leading trading nations"[5] and that "in relative or per capita terms, Canada is far more deeply involved in international commerce than is the U.S.,"[6] the reality is that in the 1990s Canada became increasingly continental in its trade. As of 1997, over 82% of Canadian exports were destined for the United States and almost 68% of imports originated from there.[7] The emphasis on North American trade carried significant costs. As stated in a 1997 report on Canada's economic relationship with Asia, prepared by the Asia Pacific Foundation of Canada, "dependence on one market, no matter how big, has its drawbacks. This is all the more so because of the integration of the U.S. and Canadian economies, which necessarily follow much the same business cycle. When the U.S. economy slows, ours inevitably follows, and export growth dries up."[8] Another important cost of Canada's over-emphasis on the U.S. is the limits continentalism places on Canada's view of Asia. The APF report goes on to say that "During the early 1990s, it seemed as if Canadian companies that were not already selling overseas decided that the obstacles in Asia were too great to overcome."[9] Further, "In Canada there is often a need to explain, 'why Asia' to hesitant export-ready companies."[10]

Canada has traditionally found it easier to take the path of least resistance. For Canadians at the end of the 1990s, it simply required less effort to export to the United States than to Japan or anywhere else. That this resulted in Canada becoming an economic satellite of the United States seemed to cause little concern. A Canadian embassy official in Tokyo, when asked about Canada's over-dependence on the U.S. market, said, "Exports are exports. It doesn't matter where they go."[11] As Japan's market was commonly considered to require more time, money, knowledge, and effort to enter than almost any other market, it was natural that many potential exporters shied away. Canadian officials and the Canadian business community generally took a short-term outlook on economic and political developments. The national government operated with a view to the next election (generally held every three to four years) and was loathe to gamble on policies or initiatives with a long-term return. Canadian companies had a similarly narrow time perspective, operating with a close eye to quarterly returns and with less attention to the longer view.

For Australia, Japan had been the largest trading partner since the 1960s, purchasing large quantities of Australian wool, minerals, energy, and foodstuffs. While Australia was well aware of Japan's importance, Japan did not assume a position of economic dominance in Australia. Government and industry encouraged Japanese tourism and investment and the education sector worked hard to educate

Australians about Japan and provide opportunities to learn Japanese. As the manufacturing sector began to look beyond the domestic market, though, Japan was not the only country on its mind. Many Australian manufacturers saw the Japanese market as too difficult and immediately turned their attention to other markets in Asia or North America. This decision was not made on the basis of careful cost-benefit calculation but rather on the general assumption that investment in Japan is difficult, costly, and with uncertain returns.

In 1960, only about 4% of New Zealand's exports went to Australia. By the 1990s, this had risen to almost 20% as Australia became New Zealand's most important trading partner. A Closer Economic Relations (CER) agreement was signed between the two countries in 1983 and revisited in 1988 and 1992.[12] New Zealand's trading relationship with Australia is important and most tariff, subsidy, and restriction issues have been resolved over the last decade or so. Negotiations tended to focus on the harmonization of standards across both countries.[13] The relationship was made more interesting by the fact that in numerous sectors (e.g. beef and wool), Australia was New Zealand's main competitor. Due to this and to New Zealand's past experience with relying too heavily on the British market, New Zealand recognized Australia's importance but did not let Australia dominate its trade planning. There was also talk of expanding the CER to include other countries, particularly those in the South Pacific and Southeast Asia, as a way to further Australian/New Zealand interests in the Asia Pacific region.[14]

Centrality of Japan

Japan continued to be an important trading partner for each of the three countries through the 1990s. In 1997, Japan was Canada's second most important trading partner, and often touted publicly as such, but it was such a distant second to the United States (3-5% of exports as compared with over 82%) that, outside of British Columbia, it was often overlooked. Japan's primary importance to Canada was the opportunity it offered to diversify both geographically away from its over-dependence on the U.S., and sectorally away from resource products and toward the value-added products the Japanese were now buying.

For Australia, Japan was of the utmost importance. It was Australia's largest trading partner and took about 20% of Australia's exports, over double the next largest export market, South Korea. Japan was, therefore, likely to continue to be Australia's most vital export market for the foreseeable future. Australia had also been positioning itself, both to the international community and to its domestic audience, as part of Asia, and was attempting to carve a role for itself in that part of the world. Its political and diplomatic relations with Japan were of paramount importance.

Japan was New Zealand's second largest trading partner, buying about 16% of New Zealand exports. While Japan was seen as important, there was concern that New Zealand not be too dependent on one market (one government official suggested that New Zealand wanted to avoid the kind of dependence that Australia had on Japan). From this thinking came the view that New Zealand trade should be diversified. While trade with Japan was certainly not discouraged, there was no specific focus on Japan either.

Awareness of the changes in Japan's economy

Recognizing the importance of trade with Japan did not of necessity mean that Japanese developments were followed carefully. The importance that each country attached to Japan at the time was crucial in determining how much attention was paid to the post-Plaza Accord changes occurring in the Japanese economy, and whether any systematic or creative policy or economic response was deemed necessary or appropriate. Moreover, the level of knowledge and insight possessed by each nation into the internal dynamics of the Japanese economy contributed significantly to their ability to respond to and capitalize upon the changing circumstances.

From the mid-1980s through to the early 1990s, Canada was preoccupied with negotiations for the Canada-U.S. Free Trade Agreement and later the North American Free Trade Agreement. This meant that for the best part of the decade, both government and business were looking south, focused on the American market. However, about 1989, government officials at the Canadian embassy in Tokyo and the Japan Division of the Department of Foreign Affairs and International Trade in Ottawa began to comment on the changes in the Japanese economy and point out the implications of a lack of action on Canada's part. Within the next few years, the government began developing its response.

The Australian government and business community were aware of the changes occurring in the Japanese economy almost as they were happening. As early as 1983, Prime Minister Hawke, in a speech to the Australian-Japan Cooperation Committee, noted that structural changes were taking place in the Japanese economy and that these, particularly the decline in growth prospects for raw material exports, had implications for Australia.[15] A report from the Australia-Japan

Business Forum's 1987 Economic Survey Mission to Japan explained in great detail the economic changes happening in Japan and their importance for Australia. Government reports and speeches make it clear that the Australian government was particularly aware of Japan's increasing overseas investment and its shifting import profile and that it wanted to capitalize on these changed circumstances.

New Zealand did not pay serious attention to the changes occurring in Japan. Few government publications mentioned much about what was happening in Japan or the implications for New Zealand. This can be partially explained by the fact that, for much of this time period, New Zealand was engulfed in its own economic transformation and was too busy with domestic matters to focus on Japan. This also reflects New Zealand's more casual attitude toward Japan as its trading partner relative to Australia and Canada.

The four countries covered in this study have approached the matter of trade and investment promotion from a variety of angles and perspectives. For the most part, Australia, Canada, and New Zealand relied on business initiatives to stimulate international trade and viewed government as a comparatively passive partner in identifying opportunities and encouraging new commercial initiatives. Japan, conversely, operated on the basis of a more interactive relationship between business and government, and attempted (not always with success) to develop strategies that suited the nation's long-term interests. When compared, striking differences emerge between the policies adopted by the four countries.

In the twentieth century, the spectrum of national economic policies in so-called free market countries ranged widely, from state ownership and centralized control (the New Zealand model), to mixed economies that sought a balance between government control and the private sector (the Canadian model), to countries that emphasized trade and market liberalization but often used protectionist measures to safeguard domestic industry (like the U.S.). The rush to market liberalization removed many of the old levers of economic control. Few countries see state ownership as a viable tool for economic management, and widespread domestic and international pressures mitigate against the use of protective tariffs, subsidies, or substantial government investment in private sector initiatives. This has caused considerable difficulty for political parties of the left (the New Democratic Party in Canada and the Labour Party in Australia and New Zealand) as they have struggled to develop economic platforms that draw together their parties' historical beliefs and actions with contemporary sentiment against major government intervention. The "New Labour" strategy of the British Labour Party attracted significant interest in all

Table 7.2   Government responsibility for trade and investment promotion, 1970s

Minimal Responsibility		Full Responsibility
Canada	Japan	
Australia		
New Zealand		

Table 7.3   Government responsibility for trade and investment promotion, 1990s

Minimal Responsibility		Full Responsibility
Canada	Japan	
Australia		
New Zealand		

three countries, but only at the cost of considerable dissension within the individual parties.

Demonstrated graphically (see tables 7.2 and 7.3), the political spectrum shifted dramatically from the 1970s, when governments in Australia, Canada, and New Zealand operated on the assumption that government would play a major role in economic planning and development.

Global and national forces clearly eroded the authority and flexibility of the state on matters of economic management, and the influence of the arguments in favour of market liberalization was observable in all four countries. Canada, Australia, and particularly New Zealand, however, generally accepted the idea that governments play a relatively small, supportive role in the cultivation of international trade and investment opportunities. In Japan, in contrast, and even in the wake of a lengthy period of political and economic upheaval, the belief in the efficacy of government involvement in economic planning and trade development remained strong. Even the Keidanren (Federation of Economic Organizations), while arguing for deregulation, supported a role for government in long-term planning and strategy. Given the widespread agreement in political and business circles that national governments did not have primary or even major responsibility for the promotion of international trade and investment, it was hardly surprising that Australia, Canada, and New Zealand did not respond as nations to the changing conditions in Japan. There was also substantial evidence, and this is a telling point, that the business communities in these three countries also did not react with innovation and creativity to new Japanese economic realities.

GOVERNMENT AND THE MANAGEMENT
OF INTERNATIONAL TRADE:
THE JAPANESE EXAMPLE

The analysis of the reaction by Australia, Canada, and New Zealand to Japan's changing economic realities reflects the implicit assumption that national governments had options available to them, even in an age of widespread laissez-faire capitalism and expanding globalization. Politicians and civil servants in all three countries have argued, supported by business leaders, that the changing realities of global economics effectively tied their hands and limited the program options available. Although observers have argued strongly against the "myth of government impotence," to use Canadian Linda McQuaig's phrase, the idea that governments can do little to direct or manage national economies has become widely accepted.

But not in Japan. Analysing the actions adopted by the Japanese government from the 1970s through the 1990s to promote international trade is a useful counterbalance to the assessment of actions taken in Australia, Canada, and New Zealand, and provides a view from the opposite end of their trading relationships. More importantly, the Japanese experience with international trade promotion provides a useful test of the main argument that governments can play a significant role in the management of international trading relationships and can do so without upsetting the basic competitive structure of the modern market economy.

When most people think of Japan and industrial policy, they focus on many of the methods Japan used in the early stages of industrial expansion. These included promoting selected industries and changing this focus as economic conditions changed; setting out economic objectives in five-year plans; controlling foreign exchange and the licensing of new technology; avoiding the creation of monopolies and encouraging competition by ensuring that two or more companies received similar technology but trying to avoid "excessive" competition; encouraging the merger of weaker companies with stronger ones; using tax strategies to encourage industries with good growth prospects; attempting to steer companies into the most productive lines of activity; and helping companies in declining industries to diversify.[16] The Ministry of International Trade and Industry (MITI) and the Ministry of Finance (MOF), the primary players in executing Japan's industrial policy, adjusted their strategies and activities as times and conditions changed. In the 1980s and 1990s, adjustments followed a variety of factors: a nation-wide push toward deregulation of the economy, increased conflict between the nation's business community and its bureaucrats, Japan's position at the leading edge of manufacturing technology and on the world scene economically, and international pressure to avoid industrial subsidies.

Japan's industrial policy at the end of the twentieth century focused much more on "signaling" areas of potential development, encouraging specialized research and development targeted at international markets, and using government procurement to support industry. Through massive government investments in research and development and organized encouragement of private sector investment,[17] far beyond anything attempted by Australia, Canada, or New Zealand, and through cooperative initiatives between government, universities and the private sector, the Japanese government identified areas of crucial development. As one study observed, "Japan does not pick winners. It picks teachers, key technologies such as microchips, whose brains will spread most diffusely through the economy. Japanese culture has a logic of community that asks: 'Which are the technologies whose contribution to other technologies, to people in general, and to the economic infrastructure as a whole, will do most to develop these?'"[18]

The Japanese government clearly believed that strength in certain industrial sectors (eg. industrial robots, semiconductors, microchips, and consumer electronics) were the key to the nation's future and did not hesitate to support those industries accordingly. As historian and Japan specialist Thomas Huber observes, Japan believes in the production of "high technology, high value-added manufactured goods, in quantities beyond what is domestically consumed so that they can be easily converted to capital flows or goods flows abroad. Production of a surplus of tradeable goods, especially high technology tradeable goods, is of strategic value because it can be easily converted to political influence."[19] From the 1970s, Japan's economic development strategies were firmly focused on international objectives and on expanding the country's overseas trade and investment position.

As described in chapter 3, in the 1990s, Japan opted for production of high value-added, technologically demanding products. Although large amounts of Japanese FDI went overseas in the last fifteen years of the twentieth century, the most expensive and technologically demanding products continued to be produced in Japan. The Japanese government specifically emphasized manufacturing, especially high tech manufacturing, and communicated this to the nation's business leaders. The bureaucracy focused on what was in the best interests of Japan and made decisions accordingly; those who know Japan best know that to get permission in Japan to do something, one must first demonstrate how the granting of that permission will benefit Japan. Unlike in Australia, Canada, and New Zealand, the government of Japan decided that a coordinated approach between business and government was crucial to the nation's success and widely communicated this expectation of cooperation in the national interest. The result was the establishment of a formidable international trading nation with extensive overseas investments.

The Japanese government rewarded and promoted excellence, believing that to do so would ensure the domestic success of Japanese industry and maintain the attractiveness and competitiveness of Japanese products internationally. Consumers (government, industry, and individual) were encouraged to be demanding and particular, and firms were in turn pushed to satisfy this demand. For government purchases or government-assisted industry purchases, consumers expected the most up-to-date products or the next generation's systems rather than that which was currently acceptable. Companies vied for the Deming Prize, which highlights excellence in productivity and quality control. Consumers and employees continually looked for ways to make both products and services better, expected excellence, and were willing to pay for it. The result, in terms of international trade, was to establish an effective Japanese 'brand' that equated Japanese-made products with technological excellence and commercial creativity.

The Japanese government's management of the international trading environment was not an unblemished success. International pressure to liberalize Japan's domestic marketplace resulted in sanctions and resistance directed at Japanese exports and foreign direct investment. There was in the U.S. an ever-present threat to restrict Japanese imports and to demand greater reciprocity in the trading relationship. Moreover, the widespread acceptance of the 'limited government' approach to economic development had raised concerns in many countries about the tight bonds between government and industry in Japan. The country itself underwent significant internal changes. The recession of the late 1990s, although not as severe as many western analysts assumed, lessened public support for the constant interventions of MOF and MITI. Domestic political turmoil, particularly the decline of the once vaunted Liberal Democratic Party and a series of bewildering scandals in the financial sector, also lessened public confidence in government and business. In addition, according to many observers, Japan's bureaucrats remained locked in a regulatory mindset and were not fully enthusiastic about the shift in their role from direct management to indirect guidance of the national economy. [20] Combined with widespread trade liberalization and the emergence of powerful international financial organizations like the World Trade Organization, expectations grew that Japan would have to compete internationally largely on western terms.

But, while acknowledging the shortcomings of the Japanese system of industrial policy and international trade promotion, it is also important to recognize the country's notable successes. Faced with significant internal changes – the rise in the value of the yen, demographic pressures, soaring domestic labour and infrastructure costs – and a globalizing world economy, the Japanese government worked closely with industry in developing a coherent and nationally relevant industrial and international trade and investment strategy. The pattern is well known: the shifting of manufacturing capacity to low-wage countries, development of overseas plants to capitalize on markets within regional trading blocs and protected national economies, efforts to maintain the value of the yen at a level tenable for exporters, a lessening (but not abandonment) of domestic barriers to imports and foreign direct investment, industrial specialization in key, high-return sectors (particularly relating to computers and robotics). The result was the maintenance of an exceptionally high level of international trade, a massive trade surplus with the U.S., and the continued refinement of the country's industrial plant to focus on new and emerging technologies and key, high-value industrial products.

The Japanese model is not readily transportable to Australia, Canada, or New Zealand (although, interestingly, some aspects of Japanese business practices have been introduced and widely adopted in all three countries); political and administrative conditions and national cultures in the three countries differ profoundly from those in Japan. But Japan's experience is nonetheless relevant and salutary, for it demonstrates that, in international market conditions similar to those faced in Australia, Canada, and New Zealand, government agencies could and did intervene in economic management and did assist industry and business in responding to rapidly changing international realities. Japan's economy remains competitive, internationally and domestically, and operates on standard free market principles. Government intervention has not forced the Japanese economy onto a path of subsidies, overt protectionism, or state ownership. The message from Japan is that government can play a formidable role in the management of national economies and the cultivation of international trade.

GENERAL TRADE AND INVESTMENT PROMOTION AND DIVERSIFICATION INITIATIVES

Between 1985 and 1997, Canada, New Zealand, and Australia all undertook major reforms of their approaches to trade promotion and development. These were discussed in detail in chapters 4, 5, and 6 and are summarized below in table 7.4.

Table 7.4   Summary of general trade and investment promotion initiatives

	Major Initiative
Canada	• Canada's International Business Strategy • Team Canada • National Sector Teams
Australia	• Formation of Austrade • Joint Action Groups • IPFP
New Zealand	• Formation of Tradenz • Joint Action Groups

Prior to 1990, Canada's international business planning was coordinated through a system of annual reporting from Canada's embassies and consulates abroad. Canada's International Business Strategy developed out of a desire to more fully represent all of the government efforts to promote international trade and not just those of the one international trade department. By 1995 CIBS formed the core of Team Canada initiatives – the new name for a variety of efforts designed to increase Canadian exports. (Team Canada trade missions to Asia [1996] and Mexico and South America [1998] were the most high profile of these initiatives and the ones of which the general public is most aware.) The purpose of CIBS was to develop the federal government's long-term plans for international business development strategies through a consultative process with provincial governments, various federal departments, industry associations, and private companies. Representatives from these groups met in National Sector Teams (matched with sectors that the government quietly determined as priorities) to develop sector strategies and promotional plans. CIBS and the National Sector Teams were a concerted effort to streamline government involvement and focus Canada's international business activities, although the desire to avoid political problems stopped the government from publicly stating priorities for either industry sectors or countries. Following the 1985 Investment Canada Act, Canada openly encouraged foreign investment with restrictions in only a minimal number of areas.

The Australian Trade Commission (Austrade) was formed in 1986 as part of the Department of Foreign Affairs and Trade. The Austrade mandate was to assist Australian exporters to sell their products and services offshore and to promote foreign direct investment into Australia. Austrade worked closely with companies on a fee-for-service basis. It started creating Joint Action Groups in 1992. These JAGs, industry groupings that came together to develop international market development strategies, began as government initiatives but gradually became industry led and funded. JAGs determined their own membership criteria, goals, and plans. They worked out sectoral goals and selected target countries.

The Foreign Acquisitions and Takeovers Act of 1975 outlined a variety of investment types and sectors that required government approval. Efforts at promoting foreign investment into Australia began in 1987 with the establishment of the Investment Promotion and Facilitation Program (IPFP).

This program promoted Australia as an investment destination by ensuring that foreign investors received as much information as necessary about Australia and by locating investment commissioners in various overseas locations. Initially, investment commissioners focused on generic investment promotion (e.g. running seminars and producing brochures), but this did not generate results. Later, investment commissioners promoted specific projects and had clear targets for the amount of investment capital and/or future employment the procured investment generated.

As part of New Zealand's public sector reforms, the Trade Development Board (also known as Tradenz) was created in 1988. The idea for Tradenz developed from a steering committee recommendation that there was a need for a New Zealand-based business-led organization to support the work of trade commissioners overseas. Tradenz had an independent Board of Directors whose members came primarily from private companies, and its mandate was to develop and expand New Zealand's foreign exchange earnings. Between 1992 and 1995, Tradenz published three documents that outlined the basics of an export strategy for New Zealand and set target goals in terms of foreign exchange earnings. Tradenz, however, did not feel that responsibility for developing an export strategy fell within its purview and discussions with various government officials did not indicate a consensus on who had responsibility for this.

Tradenz encouraged the development of Joint Action Groups, which were similar to those of Australia, and assisted in their formation. Once a JAG was formed, the industry participants took over and Tradenz stepped back.

On the investment front, New Zealand became much more open. After 1985, investments of less than NZ$10 million no longer needed approval, with the exception of those in broadcasting, commercial fishing, and rural land. The government saw foreign investment as vital to the country's economic well-being and actively encouraged investment from everywhere.

JAPAN-SPECIFIC TRADE AND INVESTMENT PROMOTION INITIATIVES

As well as changing their general trade promotion, Canada, Australia, and New Zealand began various initiatives to promote trade specifically with Japan. Again, these were explained in detail in chapters 4, 5, and 6 and are summarized below.

Canada's most specific Japan-related trade initiative was its launch of the annual *Canada's Action Plan for Japan*. Coordinated by DFAIT, the federal and provincial governments worked with industry representatives to put together this report, which identified seven high-growth sectors with potential for Canada. The primary strengths of the Action Plans were the clear identifications of Japan's importance to Canada as a trading partner, of the need and desire to improve Canadian sales to Japan, and of sectors through which this could be done.

Other successful initiatives were provincial programs for manufacturers of prefabricated homes and their components (for example, windows and doors). The British Columbia Trade Development Corporation (now B.C. Trade and Investment Corporation) launched Canada Comfort Direct in 1992. Companies paid an annual fee and their representatives could participate in trade promotion seminars and workshops, have their products displayed as part of the Canadian Building Products Showcase, and were linked directly with Japanese builders looking to import from Canada. This increased sales significantly for participating firms, and the Quebec Wood Export Bureau and Atlantic Canada Homes (comprised of the four Atlantic provinces) began similar initiatives. (All the provinces were invited to join Canada Comfort Direct, but Quebec and the Atlantic provinces started their own programs in an unfortunately typical example of provincial rivalry.) Disappointingly, Canada Comfort Direct was scaled back, despite its evident success.

As mentioned earlier, Australia was both aware and concerned about the economic changes occurring in Japan very early on. A large number of small initiatives took place in response. These ranged from trade promotion events – the most involved of which was Celebrate Australia, a month of events highlighting Australia to Japan – to increased provision of business services (Austrade offices were set up in several Japanese cities) to economic missions to general encouragement of Australian companies to consider the Japanese market. As part of diversifying Australian exports to Japan away from primary products toward more value-added goods, the government sought to promote Japanese investment in manufacturing or processing industries in Australia, with the idea that the products these companies produced in Australia would, in all likelihood, be sold back to Japan. Under the Investment Promotion and Facilitation Program, four investment commissioners were assigned to Tokyo in 1997, and they generated approximately A$200 million in investment annually.[21] They promoted specific projects (usually investment opportunities in manufacturing or processing of products) to specific investors and were judged on the results they obtained. The IPFP was generally, and in particular for Japan, judged to be a success by the Australian government.

New Zealand undertook little in the way of Japan-targeted initiatives, programs, or publications. Tradenz in Japan (in the person of Eugene Bowen, senior trade commissioner Japan and regional director), however, was active in encouraging the formation of JAGs in sectors in which it saw potential for New Zealand and in seeking customers for New Zealand products. In the late 1980s, the Japan/New Zealand Business Council noted New Zealand's small share of Japan's skyrocketing overseas investment and urged that the situation be addressed. Cabinet ministers began visiting Japan to promote investment and an investment counsellor was attached to the embassy in Tokyo from 1992 to 1994.

COMPARISON OF TRADE WITH JAPAN: VALUE, VOLUME, AND COMMODITY COMPOSITION

The degree of Japan's importance as a trading partner for the three countries ranged from Australia, which sent 20% of its exports to Japan, to Canada, which sent slightly over 4%; New Zealand fell somewhere in the middle, with Japan receiving just over 16% of its exports. In 1996, Australian exports to Japan were worth about US$12 billion (after bouncing around the US$10–11 billion range throughout the early 1990s), Canadian exports to Japan were approximately US$7.5 billion, and New Zealand exports to Japan around US$2.3 billion. Trade volumes remained relatively stable over the period in question, with the annual fluctuations revealing the inevitable variability of international trade, including exchange rates, short-term shifts in markets, commodities' prices, and localized matters.

In the period of this study, Canadian exports to Japan did not substantially increase in value, with the exception of 1995. In 1989 they were US$7,429 million, and in 1996 they were US$7,471 million. As a percentage of total exports, exports to Japan declined from 6.2% in 1989 to 3.7% in 1996 (see table 4.6).

Australian exports increased in value between 1989 when they were US$9,761 million and 1996 when they were US$12,019 million. As a percentage of total Australian exports, they declined from 26.4% in 1989 to 19.7% in 1996 (see table 6.6).

New Zealand exports to Japan increased in value between 1989 when they were US$1,538 million to 1996 when they were US$2,207 million. As a percentage of total New Zealand exports, exports to Japan declined from 17.4 % in 1989 to 15.4% in 1996. Worried about becoming overly dependent upon Japan, New Zealand made an effort to diversify its trade and did relatively little to expand its economic relationship with Japan.

Earlier chapters have described the dependence of Canada, Australia, and New Zealand on their rich national endowments. As Michael Porter wrote, "Canada, Australia and New Zealand, with national advantages primarily in resource industries, have a similar problem. In a sense, a nation without abundant natural factors has a sort of advantage in economic development. It avoids the temptation of relying too much on natural advantages."[22]

As discussed in previous chapters, the three countries were all primarily resource and agricultural exporters, particularly when it came to Japan. As might be expected, there was some overlap in those products that were the most important Japanese exports for each of these countries. The one product category that fell in the top ten exports to Japan for all three countries was fish and seafood. Given the importance of the fisheries in these countries and Japan's position as the world's largest market for imported fish and seafood, this was hardly surprising.

Otherwise, the most important Australian and New Zealand exports to Japan did not coincide. Australia's main exports were in the minerals and energy sectors while New Zealand's tended toward agricultural products. Canada and Australia were both major exporters of coal to Japan. (The further development of coal extraction in both countries was instigated by the Japanese after the 1970s oil shocks. A desire to diversify away from oil and to guarantee multiple sources of supply sent Japanese steel producers abroad. Once the Japanese had signed long-term agreements with multiple suppliers, they began to bargain down the price.) Canada and New Zealand both exported sizeable quantities of aluminum and forest products (wood pulp, sawn wood, lumber) to Japan. Competition in forest products appeared likely to increase as New Zealand discovered ways to improve the tightness of its wood's grain. New Zealand trees grow too quickly for the wood to develop an adequately tight grain to make it strong enough for use in construction. Companies have been working on a processing plant to make lamstock (small wood strips laminated with glue) to overcome this problem. In 1997 New Zealand

Table 7.5   Commodity composition: Japanese imports from Canada, 1985 and 1997
(% of total trade)

Commodity	1985 (%)	1997 (%)	% Change
Live animals	.04	.01	-75
Food, feed, beverages, and tobacco	17.7	16.8	-5
Crude materials, inedible*	50.1	28.8	-43
Fabricated materials, inedible**	28.8	44.0	53
End products, inedible***	3.3	9.9	200

  *Grains, ore, pulp, and natural gas
 **Leather, lumber, pulp, wood products, metals, organic and inorganic chemicals
***Machinery, transportation and communication equipment, personal and household goods, mis-
    cellaneous end products
Source: Statistics Canada, *Exports-Merchandise*, various editions, Catalogue 65-202 Annual, and the
Canada Japan Trade Council Newsletter, January–February 1998

Table 7.6   Commodity composition: Japanese imports from Australia, 1985 and 1997
(% of total trade)

Commodity	1985 (%)	1997 (%)	% Change
Food and live animals	15.6	17.4	10
Beverages and tobacco	<.1	0.2	50-75
Crude materials, inedible	29.3	21.6	-26
Mineral fuels	34.3	27.5	-20
Animal and vegetable oils	0.1	0.1	0
Chemical and related products	0.3	1.1	73
Manufactured goods, classified by material	7.1	8.8	21
Machinery and transport equipment	0.8	2.7	70
Misc. manufactured articles	0.3	0.9	67
Commodities and transactions (includes confidential items of trade)	12.2	19.6	38

Source: Australian Bureau of Statistics, International Merchandise Trade Catalogue 5422, March,
June, September, and December 1985 quarterly reports, and December 1997 report

wood was used mainly for packaging, which was not as highly valued
as construction materials.

The emphasis of all three countries on resource and agricultural
exports caused varying levels of concern nationally. The Australian
government expressed many times its concerns about the country's
dependence on exports of barely processed products. New Zealand
was much less worried: government officials often stated the belief that
people would always have to eat and therefore New Zealand's food
exports would always find a market. Declining fish stocks on both the
Atlantic and the Pacific coasts, combined with shrinking markets for

British Columbia lumber, forced Canadians to realize that a resource-based economy might not guarantee a prosperous long-term future. At the same time, economists and political analysts of all shades of opinion agreed that "for developing and developed economies alike, for Canada and Australia as well as for Brazil and the OPEC nations, natural resources are no longer the key to wealth."[23] As Australian industry policy analyst Jenny Stewart wrote, "Countries exchanging commodities for manufactured goods are fighting a losing battle. The only way they can maintain their incomes is by selling higher volumes at the world price."[24] Faced with the prospect of declining living standards in the future, Canada and Australia began to recognize that diversifying the composition of their exports to Japan was very important. This became a critical goal, particularly for Australia, during the period of this study. Tables 7.5, 7.6, and 7.7 compare the commodity composition of each country's exports to Japan in 1985 and in 1997. The key category is the final one, as this contains manufactured products. Canada's success at diversifying its exports away from primary and partially processed goods toward manufactured products is reflected in the increase in the percentage of its exports contained in this category. As table 7.5 reveals, from 1985 to 1997 the percentage of Canadian exports to Japan in the "end products, inedible" category increased 200%, but from a low base of 3.3%.

In Australia's case, it is important to note that this commodity breakdown can be misleading with regard to manufactured products. The category entitled 'Manufactured goods, classified by material' comprises various basically transformed materials. The sub-categories are leather and leather manufactures, rubber manufactures, cork and wood manufactures, paper and paperboard, textile yarn, non-metallic mineral manufactures, iron and steel, non-ferrous metals and manufactures of metals. In 1997 80% of total exports to Japan in this category were non-ferrous metals and an additional 9% were non-metallic mineral manufactures. In 1985, the percentages were 85 and 6 respectively. In fact, the increase from 7.1% to 8.8% shown in the table does not indicate a diversification of exports but simply an increase in the value of non-ferrous metal exports.

In the 'Machinery and transport equipment' category, the total value of Australia's exports rose 600% from about A$72 million in 1985 to A$459 million in 1997.[25] As table 7.6 shows, this category grew as a percentage of total exports to 2.7%, a definite improvement over 1985's 0.8%. In 1985 road vehicles constituted over 50% of this category at a value of about A$39 million. By 1997, they were worth A$87 million but had decreased as a percentage of total exports in this category to 19%. Exports of office machines and automatic data

Table 7.7   Commodity composition: Japanese imports from New Zealand, 1989* and 1997 (% of total trade)

Commodity	1989 (%)	1997 (%)	% Change
Food and live animals	41.9	39.3	-6
(HS2 categories 1-11, 16-21, 23)			
Beverages and tobacco	0.1	0.2	50
(HS2 categories 22, 24)			
Crude materials, inedible	21.4	25.1	15
(HS2 categories 12, 25, 26, 31, 41, 43, 44, 45, 47, 51)			
Mineral fuels	2.5	1.4	-44
(HS2 category 27)			
Animal and vegetable oils	1.5	1.6	6
(HS2 category 15)			
Chemical and related products	5.4	11.1	51
(HS2 categories 29, 30, 32, 32, 33, 35, 38, 39)			
Manufactured goods, classified by material	25.9	19.0	-27
(HS2 categories 40, 42, 46, 48, 49, 52, 54-9, 63, 68, 72-4, 76, 78, 81-3)			
Machinery and transport equipment	0.7	1.3	46
(HS2 categories 84-9)			
Misc. manufactured articles	0.4	1.0	60
(HS2 categories 34, 37, 61, 62, 64-6, 69, 70, 71, 90-7)			

*Figures for 1985 are not available.
Source: Statistics New Zealand, Overseas Trade Exports, Country of Destination by HS2 Chapters, For the Calendar Year 1989.

processing systems skyrocketed from slightly over A$7 million of exports in 1985 to A$148 million in 1997, constituting 32% of exports in this category. 'Power generating machinery and equipment' also experienced a large increase in sales, from barely A$6 million in 1985 to A$89 million in 1997.[26]

Statistics New Zealand supplied the export information in HS2 commodity breakdowns, and these have been adjusted to fit the same categories as those in table 7.6. The same caveat, therefore, applies to the 'Manufactured goods, classified by materials' category. For New Zealand, the vast majority of this category is aluminum, which made up a full 95% of the category in 1989. By 1997, this had decreased to 88%, but the difference was made up by exports of iron and steel, which were 9% of the category total.

There were clear increases in the percentage of exports in the two categories that contain manufactured goods. In 'Machinery and transport equipment,' increases occurred in the sub-categories of nuclear reactors, boilers, and machinery, and mechanical appliances, electrical machinery, and equipment and vehicles. In 'Miscellaneous manufactured articles,' exports of optical equipment, furniture, soaps, and apparel all increased substantially. New Zealand did increase the proportion of manufactured exports it sent to Japan. The increase, however, was small, and as the starting point was itself a tiny portion of overall exports, little changed.

Despite general agreement that this dependence on resource exports is unwise, neither New Zealand nor Australia succeeded in changing the situation much, at least with regard to exports to Japan in this time period. Although slightly less than 10% of Canadian exports to Japan in 1997 were manufactured, this was a substantial improvement over 3% a little over a decade before. Government literature in both Canada and Australia spoke of an increase in manufactured and processed exports to Japan, but the real increase has been slight in Australia's case and moderate in Canada's.

It is interesting to note that the governments of Canada, New Zealand, and Australia all saw similar products as being key future exports to Japan. Government officials in each country mentioned that sectors with potential for Japan included processed foods, health care and medical products (particularly products for the aging population), building products, and software and information technology. The software market in Japan in 1995 was worth more than US$6 billion and the increase in the use of computers in Japan was likely to continue, particularly as the Japanese Ministry of Education pledged to equip all schools with computers. For Australia and New Zealand organic foods had significant potential and Canada and New Zealand shared an interest in adding value to their wood products by increasing their exports of furniture.

COMPARISON OF INVESTMENT FROM JAPAN

Japan was the third most important investor in Canada and Australia and the fourth for New Zealand in the 1990s. Japanese investment made up 4% of the total investment in Canada, about 14% of Australia's total, and less than 3% in New Zealand, in a direct reaction to the rapid appreciation in the value of the yen. Japanese automobile and forestry companies increased investments in Canada, Australia, and New Zealand to take advantage of lower relative labour costs (and in Canada's case, to capitalize on the free trade agreement with the United States) and to circumvent growing protectionist feelings. In Canada and Australia, major investments also took place in metals and minerals. New Zealand received investments in agriculture (particularly meat processing) and Australia received major Japanese investments in a range of food processing areas.

Table 7.8   Japan's foreign direct investment, selected countries, 1984–1994 (US$m)

	1984	1986	1988	1990	1992	1994	Cumul. (1951– 1994)	Cumul. Total Japan FDI %
Australia	105	881	2,413	3,669	2,150	1,265	23,932	7.4
Canada	184	276	626	1,064	753	1,265	8,261	2.6
China	114	226	296	349	1,070	2,565	8,729	1.9
Mexico	56	226	87	168	60	613	2,793	0.9
New Zealand	15	93	117	231	67	115	1,376	0.4
South Korea	107	436	483	284	225	400	5,268	1.6
Singapore	225	302	747	840	670	1154	9,535	3.0
U.S.	3,359	10,165	21,701	26,128	13,819	17,331	194,429	60.4
Total	10,155	22,320	47,022	56,911	34,138	41,051	463,606	

Source: *Pacific Basin Economic Council Statistics*, 1996, *Pacific Economic Community Statistics*, 1988, 1990, 1994

In dollar terms, Australia received the largest share of Japanese investment of the three countries studied. Cumulatively to 1994, Australia had received US$23,932 million of Japanese investment compared with US$8,261 million for Canada and US$1,376 million for New Zealand. Throughout the late 1980s and the 1990s, Australia's efforts to attract Japanese investment were successful and resulted in dramatic increases. Although geographically and demographically Australia is much smaller than Canada, Australia received a much greater proportion of Japanese foreign direct investment than did Canada. In 1988, when Canada received US$626 million in Japanese FDI, Australia received four times as much at US$2.4 billion. Over the next few years, Australia's comparative success at attracting Japanese investment continued (see table 6.2). While Australia was less successful at attracting Japanese investment in 1994 and 1996 than in previous years, in 1995 Australia attracted US$2.6 billion of investment, over 5% of total Japanese overseas FDI.

Australia was also successful with its attempts at diversifying the range of sectors into which it attracted investment and, in particular, at attracting investment into manufacturing industries. Japanese MOF reports show that notifications of investments in Australia's manufacturing sector were 30% of total Japanese investment in Australia between March 1994 and March 1996, compared with 8% between 1987 and 1990.[27]

In summary, in dollar value terms, Australian and New Zealand exports to Japan increased while Canada's stayed constant (with the exception of 1995) within the 1985 to 1997 period. As a percentage of total exports, exports to Japan for all three countries declined. Canada was reasonably successful at diversifying its export mix to Japan, although 90% of its exports remained raw materials or barely processed goods. New Zealand made little effort to diversify the exports sent to Japan and its export profile did not change at all. The Australian government was very concerned about its over-dependence on resource exports and spoke publicly about the need for a more balanced export profile, but its 1997 export commodity breakdown was little different from that of 1985.

As for attracting investment, while New Zealand and Canada signaled an increased openness to investment in all sectors, they did little to directly solicit investment from Japan or to set guidelines for what kind of investment they wanted to get or how they would get it. Japanese investment in New Zealand and Canada was seldom a result of anything these countries did but more a Japanese response to outside factors, such as looking for access to the U.S. market (in Canada's case), or having a need for timber or a hotel or resort property. The Australian government, on the other hand, targeted Japanese investors specifically and worked to match them with projects in need of investment. The Australian focus was on investment in manufacturing and processing industries. Australia was successful both in receiving Japanese investment and in obtaining it in the sectors it had targeted.

The neo-classical approach to improving trade and investment between Japan and Canada, Australia, and New Zealand achieved limited results. The three governments attempted to varying degrees to increase Japanese investment in their countries, increase exports, and diversify their export profiles to include a higher percentage of manufactured goods, within neo-classical constraints. While Japanese investment in all three countries increased, much of that increase was due to the desire of Japanese corporations to circumvent the rapidly escalating yen and growing protectionist sentiment. Australia is the exception of the three countries here, as its government's carefully orchestrated Investment Promotion and Facilitation Program was directly responsible for orchestrating $532 million in Japanese investments into Australia betwen 1994 and 1997. On the trade front, change for all three countries was limited. Although the total value of exports to Japan increased for New Zealand and Australia, they did not increase as a percentage of total exports, and exports from Canada to Japan did not increase at all. As far as diversification of exports into more processed and manufactured goods, Canada was somewhat successful but Australia and New Zealand were not.

Changing a nation's export profile or investment procurement within the bounds of neo-classical philosophy, then, appears unlikely. Despite various efforts by government to encourage the business sector, and though responsibility for change was left largely in the hands of the business community, little occurred in any of the three nations under consideration here. In a period where considerable economic change took place in the Japanese market, neither business nor government in any of the three countries responded with much creativity or innovation to the post-Plaza Accord realities. Canada, Australia, and New Zealand opted to continue along proven pathways, even when faced with considerable evidence that such an approach limited their commercial opportunities in Japan. The reasons for this reluctance to innovate varied from country to country, and regionally within each nation. The Australian government committed much of the nation's economic future to developing trade with Asia, and it is not surprising that this country was the most proactive of the three nations. At the same time, as with Australia's response to the Multifunctionpolis, cultural limits and nationalistic considerations slowed economic adaptation. In New Zealand, in contrast, the country's wholehearted commitment to business-led economic development convinced the government that national leadership in the field of international trade cultivation was not necessary. Canada continued to wrestle with the delicate balance between federal and provincial responsibilities and lacked the national will and central control necessary to mount a truly coherent response to the changing Japanese economy.

Canada, Australia, and New Zealand ended the first twelve years after the Plaza Accord in much the same economic relationship with Japan as they had in 1985. The impetus for trade relations remained largely with the Japanese; Japanese corporations set the agenda for expanding trade and investment activities. And each of the three countries continued to rely on natural resources to hold Japanese interest and to maintain a share of the rich and expanding Japanese market. Absolute and relative increases in the value of Canadian, Australian, and New Zealand trade with Japan, due largely to the high prices available in the Japanese market, gave each of the nations the misleading impression that they were capitalizing on Japanese opportunities to prepare their countries for future expansion in Japan. That the fundamentals of the Japanese marketplace had changed, and that the country's import/export profile had shifted dramatically largely escaped the notice of the Canadian, Australian, and New Zealand business communities. Most tellingly, none of the three national governments saw it as their mandate to provide determined and systematic economic leadership.

8 Conclusions and Future Prospects

Liberal states are primarily those of the English-speaking world: Britain and the settler societies of the United States, Australia, Canada and New Zealand. They can be usefully distinguished by their regulatory goals and by their state-society relations, in particular the government-business relationship and the state's role in the economy. With a state tradition built on the primacy of individual over collective rights, the suspicion of state power and the celebration of free markets as the key to prosperity, liberal states have long approached their economic role, and the interventions that must perforce be carried out from time to time, as something to be tolerated, however momentarily, rather than improved and perfected.[1]

The world's economy experienced dramatic transitions in the last quarter of the twentieth century. The circumstances faced by the governments of Canada, New Zealand, and Australia were part and parcel of a broad international reconfiguration of the global economy spurred by such central political events as the collapse of the Soviet Union and such diffuse phenomenon as the profound impact of technological innovation. The difficulties that these three countries faced in attempting to capitalize on opportunities in the Japanese economy between 1985 and 1997 are but a small piece of a complex global puzzle. The issues investigated here, particularly the administrative and commercial transitions associated with the shift from state intervention toward a neo-classical economic philosophy, have implications that both affect the specific countries and trade relationships under investigation and extend beyond them.

While this study has emphasized the international influence of neo-classical ideology, other factors also affected government decision-making and the formation of national policies that contributed to the pattern of comparative inaction and reliance on business-led initiatives displayed by the three countries. Political and policy-making consider-ations weighed heavily on government leaders and, in many cases, opened the door to market liberalization.

It is important to remember, for example, that mounting national debts and deficits had, by the early 1980s, effectively tied the hands of governments. This was particularly the case in New Zealand, where unwise expenditures by the Muldoon administration had brought the country to the edge of bankruptcy. Australia and Canada were in only marginally better fiscal shape, having lived through two decades of intense state intervention in social and economic affairs and having produced massive national debts as a consequence. The rise to power of the Progressive Conservatives in Canada and the attempts by Paul Keating to reorient the Labour Party of Australia around a less inter-ventionist economic strategy originated in the realization that their governments had little financial flexibility. The financial difficulties also created considerable doubt among the electorate about the ability of governments to make decisions and investments in the long-term interests of the nation. Adoption of the laissez-faire model, then, came at least in part by default, due to the absence of a suitable, viable, and politically acceptable plan for national economic leadership.

Further, in each of the three countries, pressing domestic matters distracted attention away from matters of international commerce and investment; in neither Australia, Canada, nor New Zealand was there a groundswell of public interest in patterns of international trade or in the nation's international economic performance. Canadian politi-cians devoted far more time, for example, to the ongoing debate about Quebec independence and to discussions on First Nations' treaty rights than they did to international trade concerns. New Zealanders argued at length about the current and future role of their vaunted welfare state and about the need to respond to the country's legal and moral obligations to the Maori. Australia addressed similar concerns about Aboriginal rights, and faced a debate similar to that in New Zealand about the future of state intervention and support. In Australia and Canada, long-standing conflicts over the division of powers between the national government and state/provincial admin-istrations made it difficult to develop a coherent national policy in any field, including international trade. The financial pressures described above also generated intense national debate about the future of state-owned utilities, resources, and service providers (especially in the health care sector), many of which were the focus of considerable public sentiment.

As well, national governments sought to reassure electorates reeling from years of economic turmoil that they were protecting the nation's well-being by strengthening existing trade connections, rather than by trying to convince the business community and the public at large to take bold steps toward comparatively unknown markets. Canada, for example, used its political resources to negotiate a free trade agreement with the United States (later expanded to include Mexico), a process that engulfed the country in dramatic political debate. Australia and New Zealand likewise expanded trade connections between themselves, adding to what was already a very strong economic relationship. Following this line, and given that Japan was, before 1985, already Australia's largest trading partner, it is not surprising that the Australian government was able and willing to do more than Canada or New Zealand to extend commercial relations with that country. In all three countries, pursuing the familiar was easier and politically more acceptable than chasing after new markets.

The argument that governments had but a minimal role to play in business development and in the direction of the national economy found adherents in many places, including political parties of the right and the left and among leading civil servants. But the pattern of inactivity in the promotion of international trade and investment with Japan reflected more than the extension of a political ideology: in each case, neo-classical policies suited the countries, providing an appropriate model for international business development that fit with the nation's fiscal and administrative resources and that meshed with the political preoccupation with domestic affairs.

UNDERSTANDING OF JAPAN

Part of international business development is a good understanding, at both the government and corporate level, of the countries with which one is doing business. Too much of what Canadians, Australians, and New Zealanders know about the Japanese economy is gleaned from secondhand sources, translated materials, or official Japanese representatives. Australia is the only one of the three countries to have a permanent newspaper or magazine correspondent stationed in Japan. While programs like those run by New Zealand's Asia 2000 Foundation and Canada's Asia Pacific Foundation sponsor journalists to go to Asia for a period of time, this is a poor substitute for the long-term Japan-based correspondent. By the same token, while the number of Canadians, Australians, and New Zealanders living in

Japan has increased over the last decade, few stay for extended periods or devote that time to developing a deep understanding of the Japanese economy and political situation. In telling contrast, Toyota Motor Corporation's Tokyo office alone devotes most of the resources of a twenty-member department to simply monitoring relevant international political and economic events, particularly those in the United States. When long-time Japan-based financial journalist Eamonn Fingleton spoke in Tokyo in November 1997 on the future of the Japanese economy, no Canadian, Australian, or New Zealander attended. A March 1998 talk in Vancouver by Canadian embassy official John Sloan about recent events in the Japanese financial system, the impact of the Asian currency crisis on Japan, and what this meant for Canada attracted only a couple of dozen people, mostly local Japan experts.

In other words, few Canadian, Australian, or New Zealand individuals or companies are well informed about what occurs in Japan. The cartelization of the Japanese media and Japan's desire to paint itself a certain way to the outside (and even inside) world makes it difficult to know the truth, so Japan is a challenge even for those who truly make an effort. Those who do not try hard to know what is really happening in Japan see only what the Japanese government wants them to see. A nation that is not well informed cannot accurately analyse events or trends or reach well-reasoned conclusions.

For the most part then, the changes between 1985 and 1997 in the Japanese economy that were most noticed in Australia, Canada, and New Zealand were those that appeared on the surface and were well covered in the daily media. After the mid-1980s, when the prevailing theme was that Japan was buying up the world, the media emphasized the fall-out from the bursting of the bubble economy and lower Japanese growth rates. North Americans and others in the Anglo-American world easily accepted the proposition that Japan and Asia were in decline; doing so backed up the dogma that government intervention in the economy (at least in a different way than the critics were familiar with) was economically unsound, and it restored confidence in Anglo-American laissez-faire policy. As this was what many people wanted to hear, few looked much further.

While there is no question that Japan's financial system was in considerable turmoil and that substantial debt from the aftermath of the bubble economy continues, what this meant for Japan and what it means over the longer term is far from clear. As was described in chapter 3, some serious analysts of Japan have argued that much of the bubble economy and its subsequent burst were carefully engineered by the government to move capital from the hands of consumers and small businesses into corporate coffers.[2] This is a radical departure from the perception that errors in judgment allowed the financial sector to go wildly out of control only to be eventually roped in by a desperate government. As the result was the addition to Japan's GNP an amount equivalent to the GNP of France, fully competitive industries at ¥110 to the dollar, and dominance of most key industries,[3] one is forced to contemplate the idea that the Japanese government did indeed know what it was doing.

This is true also of the second stage of the financial crisis, which occurred in late 1997 when a number of blue-chip financial institutions, including Sanyo Securities Corporation, Hokkaido Takushoku Bank, and, most startlingly, Yamaichi Securities (one of Japan's big four brokerage houses), declared bankruptcy. In addition, Yamaichi and some other institutions were indicted for corporate malfeasance, including bribing government officials, paying gangsters not to disturb annual general meetings, and compensating special corporate clients for trading losses. While much was reported about these events, most coverage was a simple description of what took place or a lament on the seriousness of Japan's economic crisis. Few people, foreign or Japanese, asked the most pertinent questions. The Japanese government could easily have bailed out Yamaichi Securities – why did it decide not to do so? Companies have been paying gangsters not to disturb annual general meetings for years. The practice is so well known that it is described in introductory books about Japan. What made the government suddenly decide to crack down on Yamaichi? There are several possible answers to these questions, and it will probably be difficult to discover which is correct. What matters, though, is that countries like Canada, Australia, and New Zealand need commentators to ask questions, and not accept what appears on the surface to be the full story. Each country has a distinct national interest in operating in Japan; it follows, therefore, that each country should have its own independent economic and political intelligence about the country.

Critics spoke of the early 1990s as a time of Japanese recession, yet in the first seven years of the 1990s, Japan's per capita GDP (measured by market exchange rates) rose 56% and Japan's current account surpluses increased 300-fold from the same period in the 1980s. The emphasis on Japan's financial woes masked, for most observers, the fact that Japan was continuing to make powerful inroads into critical high technology areas. Japan retained its emphasis on a manufacturing-based economy and did not follow the west in assuming that a service-based economy would provide a sustainable high national standard of living. Japan's rosy future is not guaranteed, but the land of the rising sun should not be lightly dismissed. Many Canadian, New Zealand, and Australian officials and companies, however, were happy to buy the idea that Japan was in decline or that the market was too difficult to warrant the necessary effort. Officials at all three embassies reported frustration at how new exporters from their countries were all too ready to bypass Japan for what were perceived as more promising markets elsewhere in Asia. The lack of understanding of Japan, then, had – and still has – the potential to exact a heavy economic price in missed opportunities to develop new export markets and, in the process, to diversify national economies away from a heavy reliance on natural resources and primary products.

BEYOND THE FREE MARKET MODEL – DO GOVERNMENTS MATTER?

In different ways, our three countries began to alter their approach to government involvement in international business development over the period of study. New Zealand went through its dramatic shift away from a government-dominated socialist economic model toward a free trade business-led model. The Canadian and Australian governments began to worry about their over-dependence on resource exports and, looking for ways to develop alternate exports, experimented with numerous proactive approaches on the international business front; these initiatives, however, remained within the limited band of options acceptable to a neo-classical mindset. As we have seen, the success of some of the Australian and Canadian approaches produced only minimal changes and results. In none of these countries was there much serious discussion of forming a national industrial policy, targeting specific sectors, promoting more strongly directionist government-business policies, or of anything less than a policy of international free trade. Other options were seen as being either economic heresy or as extending outside the role of government. Government wished to take its cue from business, but the corporate sector was not concerned with national economic planning. Not surprisingly, forestry or mining companies, for example, were too busy with their own work and with the future of their industry to be wondering if the nation should be developing a computer industry.

Some broad conclusions can be proposed from the results of this study. First, without some form of leadership (whether supplied by government or by industry), dramatic intentional changes in a country's export profile are unlikely to occur. In areas where the Canadian, New Zealand, and Australian governments did nothing to change their trade or investment relations with Japan, nothing changed that Japan did not initiate.

Second, while even simple leadership – for example, governments pointing out certain recommended directions through speeches or signed agreements – builds awareness in the business community and has some impact, bold and clear initiatives are required if significant change is desired. Australia did a lot of talking about the need to diversify its trade with Japan, but the initiatives it actually undertook were small and had little impact.

Third, if Canada, Australia, or New Zealand want more out of Japanese investments, then it is up to them to make that clear. Japan forms its overseas investment policies according to what is best for Japan and assumes that the recipient countries will look out for their own interests. While many of the Asian nations now receiving most of the manufacturing investment apply conditions on investment (e.g. only in certain sectors or only as joint ventures) to protect their own economies or nurture their own industries, western countries are often reluctant to do so. In fact, as described in chapter 1, inter-state or provincial rivalries or a desire for political advantage have led to situations where the federal and/or provincial or state governments not only did not apply conditions but actually offered far more in the way of inducements than the investing company anticipated or needed. The result is that investments are made as a series of individual decisions, with no overarching sense of what is economically and socially best for the nation as a whole.

Fourth, the initiatives that governments undertake can either operate on a private sector model, as with Australia's Investment Promotion and Facilitation Program; they can be government-led; or they can be government-started but industry-led. Canada's National Sector Teams and Australia and New Zealand's Joint Action Groups are good examples of the latter, and representatives from all three countries extolled the virtues of these industry-government collaborations. It is important that the initiatives be well thought-out and coordinated, that there is industry participation, and that there be some guidelines by which success can be monitored.

Fifth, governments will not get everything right; neither does the public sector. But if change is needed and governments do nothing, very little will occur. Governments need to see the national picture and determine if the country is on the right path toward the future. If adjustments are needed, it is up to government to put them in motion or ensure that someone else will. If a national government is going to be peripheral to international business development, then it needs to be sure that the country has a proactive and innovative business sector willing to take risks and display leadership. It is far from clear that such a business sector exists in Canada, Australia, or New Zealand.

Analysts from as broad a spectrum as Kenichi Ohmae, Michael Porter, and Jenny Stewart all agree that it is folly for a country in the twenty-first century to stake its economic future on the sale of its natural resources. Increased competition in the resource sector, along with the decreased value of commodity exports, means that more value-added exports are needed to underpin an export economy. The passion with which this is felt by the general public naturally varies depending on recent events; desperation in British Columbia's forestry industry in early 1998 rekindled sentiments about the dangers of relying on a resource-based economy.[4] Yet despite the recognition by analysts and members of government, little changed in the export profile of two of the three countries with Japan, Canadian exports remained at 90% resources or partially processed goods, and no manufactured products made the list of top ten exports from any of the three countries to Japan, despite the overall rise in Japan's manufactured imports. It is incumbent on the governments of Canada, New Zealand, and Australia to ensure that their populations have something beyond resources to sell, but depending on industry to lead this change, when the captains of industry are busy keeping their own companies afloat, makes no sense.

Canada, New Zealand, and Australia must also recognize that the neo-classical approach is not followed in many other places in the world. Analysts have begun to identify the flaws and tensions inherent in neo-classical approaches to the management of national economies. The preoccupation with free market economics at the expense of social agendas has not brought uniform prosperity, nor has it brought widespread public acceptance of the new approach to governance. As Jenny Stewart wrote about Australia,

If history teaches us anything it is that nations whose ruling elites hold to beliefs inappropriate to their circumstances will, at the very least, fall behind those with a more realistic view of the world. Australia's governing elite has been held in thrall by the dogma of the level playing field: the belief that the path to prosperity lies in exposing our industries to the cleansing power of market forces. Somehow, an assumption made for analytical and expository purposes in a single academic discipline – economics – has become the mainstay of public policy.[5]

Can governments operating in a neo-classical framework have an impact on national economic development? The answer is yes, but only if they view their neo-classical bounds as being somewhat elastic.

Canada was able to adjust its exports to Japan to include more manu-factured products and Australia was able to attract a disproportionate share of Japan's FDI through programs that were government-led but used private sector methods and ensured industry buy-in. Otherwise, these governments produced little in the way of concrete change, and less than they might have had they tried. The belief that it is up to busi-ness to lead the way and that government is to facilitate what business wants has proved constraining. Tight reins on government may not be the answer when more dramatic change is needed. Perhaps, then, the idea of a more direct role for government in national economies in need of re-direction will gain greater public and business acceptance.

INTERNATIONAL TRADE AND MARKET LIBERALIZATION: THEORETICAL IMPLICATIONS

In recent years, scholars in a variety of academic disciplines have debated the contemporary and future impact of economic globaliza-tion and the widespread acceptance of neo-classical concepts of the state's role in economic management. At one extreme, analysts argue that the age of the nation-state is essentially over, and that interna-tional forces and organizations have effectively eviscerated the author-ity of national governments. Others contend that the general aban-donment of government intervention as an economic strategy has left individual countries vulnerable to international market pressures and to the decisions of multinational corporations. Overriding the debate is a growing sensitivity to the fundamental reality of an interconnected global economic system that limits the ability of national governments to manage their economies in isolation from international pressures and events. The free market system invariably implies that there will be winners and losers: some countries will benefit from the shift to glob-alization and to interconnected international markets, and others will suffer economically in the more open-ended competition.

The private sectors of Canada, Australia, and New Zealand, even with reduced barriers and hindrances imposed by governments, did not react in a positive manner to the changing dynamics of one of the world's largest economies and did not shift their production, market-ing, or investment activity in a strategic fashion to capitalize on new opportunities. (There were internal reasons for this relative inaction. Canadian and Australian businesses are effectively locked into a pre-1980s mindset of reliance on exports of raw materials. As well, in New Zealand and Canada – and, to a substantial extent, Australia as well – many of the major corporations are foreign-owned, and they have tended to use Canada and New Zealand not as bases for innovation or economic transformation but as sources of traditional products and manufactures.)

The inability of Australia, Canada, and New Zealand to respond to major changes in the Japanese market suggests that the three countries will have difficulty adapting to the opportunities and realities of the new order. With governments accepting a limited and responsive role in business development, and with the business communities revealing (to this point) little enthusiasm for creative international marketing and a reliance on long-standing patterns of trade, it is unlikely that these national economies will react quickly and effectively to a dynamic, open, and highly competitive international marketplace. Advocates of neo-classical approaches to economic management assume that countries and economies will respond creatively to opportunities, and forget that some countries, regions, industries, and populations will inevitably experience severe dislocation due to shifts in largely unregulated international markets. More attention needs to be given to the "losers" in the race toward economic globalization, to the impact of international market pressures on localized markets and industries, and to the disruptions that can accompany major economic shifts.

Scholars have long been interested in national industrial policy and in the economic outcomes associated with government intervention in industrial development. Under the neo-classical model, the common economic strategy involves a reduction of government activism: the absence of policy or the imposition of severe limits on government involvement in economic affairs will increasingly become a field of inquiry. More research is required, on both domestic and international markets and on a variety of countries, to ascertain the effectiveness of the new approach, if it can be called such, to industrial planning. The vast majority of the existing analytical work on industrial policy is predicated on the idea of an activist state and the willingness of the government to take a lead role in managing the economy. These asumptions are no longer viable. Even if the analysts themselves favour a return to state leadership – and many of them do – it is important that they examine cases where governments have stepped out of the activist role and start to develop models and suggest approaches for economic guidance that work in such a non-interventionist environment. There are, as Australia, Canada, and New Zealand have demonstrated in relatively minor ways, tools, actions, and programs available for governments seeking to improve economic conditions, even in a neo-classical environment. There are also ways in which the business community or industry associations could take the lead in developing strategies for international business development. It is vital that theoretical and conceptual work keep up with changing political realities and provide analysis of the new political-economic milieu.

In the late 1980s, many western observers looked to Japan for an example of state management of economic development. The bursting of the bubble economy dampened enthusiasm for the Japanese model and resulted in widespread criticism of the Japanese approach to government-business relations. Much of the current political and journalistic commentary has assumed that Japan is in great difficulty, a misunderstanding of the country's current economic situation and future prospects. A close examination of the Japanese government's current activities, including its strong support for information technology and high technology manufacturing, makes it clear that the government has not abandoned its interventionist approach and continues its efforts to direct the development of the national economy. In the past, too much was made of Japan's economic and commercial success, and western observers often uncritically advocated adopting that model of government-business relations. At the end of the twentieth century, commentators moved too quickly to dismiss Japan's achievements and to assume that the country's pattern of state intervention did not work as effectively in the era of free markets and globalization.

Furthermore, as demonstrated with the three countries under investigation here, consideration must also be given to the economic opportunities missed by those countries, regions, and sectors that misread or ignore fundamental shifts in the international economy. The assumption seems to run through the literature – ignoring the earlier experience of countries like Argentina, Brazil, and Chile – that first world nations will retain their position throughout the process of globalization. This investigation questions whether Australia, Canada, and New Zealand will in fact be able to do so. The emergence of Japan, Singapore, and Taiwan as economic powers was hardly predicted thirty years ago, nor did forecasters recognize the potential decline in the economic importance of countries like the three under consideration here. But if their response to the Japanese market is an indication of economic prospects – and that is important and as yet unproven – then the economic future might not be very favourable. If these countries could not respond quickly, creatively, and effectively to the Japanese market, it is possible that they will not react appropriately to future shifts in global markets.

Trade liberalization and neo-classical economic management have dominated the western political scene for less than two decades. While enthusiasm for free markets remains widespread, problems are beginning to appear. The attempt to secure the Multilateral Agreement on Investment (MAI), which would have further liberalized international finance and investment, collapsed due to the protectionist sentiments and worries of a portion of the general public in many of the participating countries. Similarly, as the uneven development of the global economy under free trade conditions continues, concerns arise in countries that are not benefitting from market liberalization. Analysts who predicted the end of the nation-state and the continued rise of international organizations and multinational corporations might well have failed to account for the persistence of nationalist sentiment, the resilience of national governments, and the potential re-emergence of state intervention as government policy following a downturn in national or international markets. This is not to argue that the situation in western democracies will return to the level and nature of state intervention evident in the 1970s and early 1980s; it does suggest that governments will seek, and electorates will demand, measures to protect and improve national economies. The nation-state is not about to fade into political obscurity.

The relative failure of state-driven economic management to provide for the stability of national economies did much to lay the foundation for widespread acceptance of neo-classical policies. Political parties and leaders who continue to advocate a return to the interventionist strategies of the past have, in Australia, Canada, and New Zealand, experienced electoral difficulty and will likely continue to do so. At the same time, the relatively small adaptations of the national economies under the laissez-faire approach were insufficient. Governments have a significant role to play, as analysts from Adam Smith to Paul Omerod have argued, and will continue to be central players.

There are many policy options available to national governments other than state ownership and intense intervention. Industrial policies that emphasize signaling and the targeting of specialized markets, products, or technology can, as in Japan's case, prove to be highly effective means to stimulating national economic growth. Government involvement is clearly not inherently opposed to the functioning of the free market and should in fact be an important adjunct to private sector activity. If nothing else, governments have a responsibility to provide clear, nationally relevant intelligence and coordination designed to capitalize on the natural partnerships that should develop with the business community.

Creating an internationally competitive domestic economy is, for countries like Australia, Canada, and New Zealand, a formidable challenge. National electorates do not want to hear warnings about imminent dangers; they seek words of reassurance from their political leaders. But changing domestic and international realities will create a different future, one that may not fit well with the commercial structures and attitudes of the past. While there is little support for a return to high levels of state intervention, there is considerable evidence and strong intellectual support for the idea of a centrally coordinated national strategy, with an influential role for government, particularly in terms of signaling and establishing a firm foundation for international trade and investment. Governments *do* matter, but, as the experience of the last twenty years makes clear, they cannot act on their own. At the same time, business will not go out of its way to act on its own. Cooperative and creative involvement between the two is vital. In addition, the shift away from subsidies and protectionism and toward the identification of national strengths and international opportunities is crucial to national economic success. Shifting markets, dramatic alterations in financial markets, the fast pace of change in international economies, and the rapid emergence of new competitors makes it more important, not less so, that national governments accept a key role in the management of their country's economic future.

9 Japan's Dominions and International Trade at Century's End

The free market ethos of the 1990s was, by century's end, facing a considerable but not overly dramatic challenge from mildly left-wing governments and political parties. With the deficit woes of the 1980s and 1990s largely overcome, governments from New Zealand to the United Kingdom contemplated a return to a more activist state. At the same time, growing social movements promoting environmental responsibility and more accountability for the WTO and IMF, and targeting multinational corporations and laissez-faire ideologies, resulted in massive protests at WTO meetings and the growing confidence of nationalist and anti-free trade forces. The late 1990s saw Japan continue to struggle with a financial system in turmoil and a relatively stagnant economy. The technologies of globalization continued to expand apace, however, highlighted by rapid developments in telecommunications, international finance, and business-to-business electronic commerce that threatened to render national borders largely irrelevant. While the seemingly impenetrable consensus around the inevitability of free markets and globalized free trade had spawned its share of critics and counter-movements, most national governments operated on the assumption that the old order of state intervention would not soon return.

For Canada, Australia, and New Zealand, the realities of international markets served to limit flexibility. Each remained largely dependent on trade relations with one or two key partners, and continued to rely heavily on the dynamics of global resource markets. In New Zealand and Canada at least, a shift could be seen by the century's end back toward a more interventionist state, although such ideas and initiatives were, for good and for ill, a pale imitation of the proactive governments of the 1960s and 1970s. Although the debate between small government and an activist government played out differently in the three nations, the manner in which Australia, Canada, and New Zealand continued to struggle with the transition to a free market orientation made it clear that the future of the nation-state was far from over. New actions of government after 1997 concerning the management of international business opportunities, while hardly representing a dramatic challenge to the free market status quo, did indicate that careful consideration was being given to alternate models of national involvement in an interconnected and fast-changing international economy.

Japan's continued trials and evolution complicated efforts by Canadian, Australian, and New Zealand governments to respond to the opportunities its economy presented. Business headlines in all three countries trumpeted, and often exaggerated, difficulties in Japan. While there was substance to the issues – a financial system in difficulty, growing homelessness, comparatively high levels of unemployment, political turmoil and uncertainty, and the uneven effectiveness of massive government spending as an economic stimulus – the western press continued its pattern of highlighting economic grief and largely ignoring positive signs of adaptation and reorientation. Japan's quick move into information technology, overcoming a delayed reaction to the initial opportunities in this area, and massive investments in the technology of the digital revolution and telecommunications allowed the country to catch up with the "new economy" in other countries. The continued development of the domestic economy and the willingness of the Japanese government to open key sectors such as finance and insurance to international competition continued to change the nature of foreign opportunities in the country. Despite its economic difficulties, Japan remained a formidable international trading partner and retained its pivotal role in the economies of New Zealand, Australia, and Canada. In each country, however, the reports of Japan's economic difficulties diverted government attention and limited commercial interest in trade and investment opportunities involving Japan.

The years 1997 to 2000 saw Canadian and New Zealand attitudes shift in favour of government leadership in economic development but there is much less evidence that Japan was singled out for special attention. Despite the historic and contemporary significance of Japan to all three countries, not one of them made the cultivation and enhancement of this relationship a central priority. (The 1999 Team

Canada trade mission to Japan might appear to be an indication of a particular commitment to Japan on Canada's behalf, but in reality it was just one of a series of these large trade missions.) If anything, the imperatives and rhetoric of globalization, combined with misunderstandings about the difficulties of penetrating the Japanese marketplace, convinced these governments that the real opportunities lay elsewhere, with more readily accessible trading nations. This assumption perpetuated the current model of economic relations with Japan, which left this powerful, wealthy, innovative, and highly competitive trading nation in the driver's seat in terms of the development of national opportunities for trade and investment.

NEW ZEALAND

There is a prevailing sense in New Zealand that the controversial economic policies of the 1980s and 1990s have been paid for through national economic reorientation and a high level of societal dislocation. In the late 1990s, the National Party, long applauded for its willingness to adhere to a strict internationalist agenda, found itself facing renewed internal opposition as the New Zealand economy experienced a slowdown. The effect of the economic downturn in Asia, declining commodity prices, and a severe drought at the end of 1997 and into 1998, which had an impact on the country's export capacity in certain agricultural sectors, particularly meat, were only partially offset by a weakening New Zealand dollar. The national GDP growth rate fell to 0.2% in 1998 but surged forward to 3.5% in 1999. More generally, the length of National Party rule and the lingering effects of its unseemly alliance with New Zealand First in the aftermath of the 1996 election empowered its critics and sustained a growing criticism of national economic policies.

Opponents of the National Party, lead by Helen Clark and the Labour Party, offered an alternative vision of the economy. In the lead-up to the national election of November 1999, Labour made it clear that it believed that government has a major role to play in industrial development. In its April 1999 publication entitled *Industry Development*, Labour outlined its economic viewpoint:

Labour believes there is a role for the government in industry development. Indeed we assert not only that a role exists, but that government has an obligation to fill it... Labour believes that the role of modern government is: to offer leadership, strategic vision, active partnerships, brokerage, procurement, a supportive public sector apparatus and a series of programmes that collectively form industry policy.... Labour defines industry broadly, and industry development policy therefore embraces all sectors of the economy though with a focus on value-added exports and import substitutes. Our economy needs to move progressively towards elaborately transformed manufactures in niche markets.[1]

In public speeches, Helen Clark and Labour representatives hammered home the message that, if elected, the party would not follow National's policy of limited government involvement in New Zealand's economy. It envisioned the role of government as doing more than just offering price stability, fiscal constraint, and microeconomic reform. New Zealand's standard of living had dropped from the third highest in the world to twenty-fifth, Ms Clark stated. To change this trend, she asserted, conditions for the rapid growth of new industries had to be created. Pointing out that Ireland had been through "an economic and cultural renaissance by implementing policies which are in many ways the opposite of those trialled in New Zealand,"[2] Ms Clark said that, as Labour,

We are unashamedly for leading New Zealand away from the purity of hands off policies and towards smart and intelligent government action in partnership with business which will give this country a chance to reach its potential.... The government's role in driving the change which has to happen is crucial. Labour is prepared to accept that leadership role. We see the role of government in the economy as being that of a leader, a partner, a facilitator, a broker and occasionally a funder – working alongside the private sector, local and regional government, and our education and research institutes to improve the nation's prospects.[3]

Labour was quick to point that it was not advocating a return to the "Think Big" policies of earlier decades that had led the country into economic difficulty; this was "appallingly unsuccessful and intrusive state involvement in industry development"[4] and avoiding that approach was definitely justified. However, *Industry Development* argued "that reaction has now become an ideologically inspired over-reaction, as dysfunctional as the Think Big programme itself."[5]

Labour's viewpoint was not an isolated one. A shift in opinion had been occurring gradually since 1997 and could be seen in the media in the final years of the century. Numerous commentators pointed to the relative decline in New Zealand's living standards, often blaming this on the fact that "New Zealand slavishly adheres to the neoclassical model,"[6] or on the country's dependence on resource exports. Other observers pointed to the widening gap between rich and poor and asked whether this was the kind of country New Zealanders wanted. After the economic revolution of the mid-1980s, the top 10% of the most wealthy Kiwi households were better off, the next 20% just held their own, and the remaining 70% had been left relatively worse off. Those economically lower down the scale suffered while those up the ladder benefitted.[7] Middle income jobs declined and increasingly the work available was part-time and poorly paid. Related discussions on the level of research and development spending in New Zealand were also seen in the news. New Zealand spends less than 1% of its GDP on research while the average among the OECD countries is 2.2%. More tax breaks for research and development, encouraging research for its own sake, and more government funding for research were proposed as means of addressing the nation's shortcomings in this crucial area.[8]

In the mid-1990s the public and the government alike were certain of the agricultural sector's ability to deliver a prosperous future for New Zealanders. A couple of years later, cracks began to appear in that overweening confidence. The lead article in the 19 April 1999 issue of *Export News* described the conclusions of a recently published discussion paper, which stated that "New Zealand's relative standard of living will continue its 30-year decline if industry does not turn to advanced technology."[9] Another observer continued in this vein, stating that

New Zealand's traditional agricultural-based export commodities have been losing value for several decades. They have low growth potential and are essentially price takers on the world market, not price makers. New Zealand's economic future requires much greater value to be added to its exports in order to win improved returns and growth....The difference in performance between traditional commodity-based exports and added-value, higher technology exports over recent years has been striking. Electrical and engineered products doubled their value added to the economy between 1991 and 1997, while meat and dairy processing remained almost static.[10]

Opposition politicians tackled the issue. Prior to the election, Michael Cullen (as of 2000, the Labour finance minister) stated that New Zealand needed to focus on adding value, saying, "This requires a transformation of the economic base of New Zealand out of dependence upon commodity production and into the new knowledge-based industries."[11] Even the National Party now accepts that point, Cullen argued, although it is "unable to recognize the kind of policies that are implied by the need to engage in a knowledge economy project."[12]

Such mainstream debate on the costs of the government's neoclassical approach had not been seen in the mid-1990s. While many

New Zealanders, particularly older people and academics, had decried the economic revolution, the general feeling in the middle of the decade was that the changes implemented after 1984 had been necessary, even if that did not always justify the speed and manner in which they occurred. More striking was the almost evangelical way in which the majority of government bureaucrats, politicians, academics, and journalists embraced the neo-classical hands-off role of government. While it was difficult in the mid-1990s to find anyone willing to even discuss the concept of a significant role for government in managing the economy, only a couple of years later the newspapers and magazines carried numerous articles on the topic. In November 1999, the National Party government was defeated and Labour, the party that had campaigned on the premise that government has an obligation to play a role in the nation's industrial development, was elected, and to achieve a six-seat majority signed a coalition with the even more interventionist Alliance Party. The Labour Party's election meant that a substantial percentage of the general New Zealand population was, at the very least, not opposed to this approach. (Labour garnered 39% of the popular vote compared with 30.7% for the ousted National Party.)

In the first year following the inauguration of the Labour-Alliance coalition, the new government took several major steps to implement concrete policies to increase its involvement in the economy. The first was a decision to freeze unilateral tariff reductions for the next five years as of 1 July 2000. Although limited cuts might take place as part of a free trade agreement with other countries, the government ended the policy of unilateral tariff cutting that had characterized the last fifteen years. New Zealand was already one of the least protectionist countries in the world. The government's sense was that there was little left with which to bargain with trading partners for better access to their markets for New Zealand goods. "We will consider tariff changes where there are clear benefits to New Zealand," said acting Commerce Minister Trevor Mallard.[13] Less than 5% of all imports (by value) carried any duty at all.[14] The vast proportion of those tariffs that did exist were under 10%, and many were under 5%, with the exception of tariffs on clothing and footwear, which were scheduled to drop from 19 to 15%. Reductions of two percentage points were also planned for some household appliances, paper products, plastics, prepared foods, furniture, and carpets.[15] Reactions to the announced freeze were mixed. The Employers and Manufacturers Association was pleased but farmers were unhappy. The national Opposition spokesperson, Lockwood Smith, was very critical, saying that the tariff freeze was unnecessary for business and would only hurt exporters and consumers.[16]

The government's other substantial change was the establishment of a new Crown entity, Industry New Zealand. As of mid-2000, Industry New Zealand was still in the process of being established. The organizational plan called for a board of directors primarily drawn from the private sector and with funding of approximately $100 million by the end of 2002.[17] Industry New Zealand would focus on "implementing policies and delivering programmes in seven key areas: business development; enterprise financing; innovation; local economic development; workplace productivity; ecological sustainability; and procurement policy."[18] The programs include an emphasis on developing managerial and technical skills, business capacity audits, business mentorships, and a variety of financing options to help companies overcome serious impediments to growth. Local economic development strategies are also a key part of Industry New Zealand: Labour's policy paper on the economy said that such strategies "are powerful because they embrace and capture the empirical success of both Professor Michael Porter's approach to the competitive advantage of nations and the subsequent understanding of the importance of cluster identification and cluster development."[19]

Trade New Zealand, with its focus on facilitating export growth, remained in place. Labour's plans also called for the establishment and funding of a foreign direct investment division within Tradenz, to be responsible for identifying potential investors and investment opportunities and bringing the two together.[20] It is too soon to know how Industry New Zealand and Trade New Zealand will coordinate. The government also faces a formidable challenge in convincing a civil service well schooled in the doctrines of laissez-faire globalism to develop proactive and interventionist economic and business development policies.

As of 2000, then, the Labour government's moves to offer leadership and strategic vision on the international trade front were limited and cautious. Although their speeches and policy documents discussed the need to move toward value-added exports, clear directions for achieving this objective had not yet been converted into legislation or administrative action. Prime Minister Clark and her party knew that for dramatic change to occur, government needed to play an important leadership role. However, decisions on specifically what to do are difficult and will likely alienate at least some voters (for example, there would surely be considerable opposition in key constituencies to the idea of moving money away from agriculture and into technology programs, despite the logic of such investment). This makes it difficult to determine how much Labour will actually change New Zealand, either positively or negatively. Certainly, it is doubtful that such tentative steps will change New Zealand's export profile very radically.

Not everyone was happy with the changes the Labour Party had made, or with, more generally, the role it saw for government. Ralph Norris, chair of the New Zealand Business Roundtable, was nervous about an increased role for government: "We learned to our cost that interventions beget more interventions and micro-management, and that there needs to be a clear-eyed view about the proper limits of government and what governments can and cannot achieve."[21] Many New Zealanders seemed happy, however, to give Clark and her party the chance to prove that government could play a role somewhere between "Think Big" and "Hands Off." Even before the election and the new initiatives, the 1998 New Zealand Survey of Values found that 91% of those surveyed felt that government should provide industry with the help it needs to grow.[22]

Mixed in with this re-examination of the role of government was a national desire for a more decent and fair society. Pointing to a widening gap between rich and poor, declining living standards, and inequalities in health, housing, and education, Bruce Ansley of *Listener* magazine wrote that "Most people ... are simply desperate for decency. They want their heart back."[23] Ansley hoped that this was beginning to be recognized: "The new economic thinking, from the government to the Treasury and Reserve Bank, puts great emphasis on 'social cohesion' – the idea that only a secure society will produce a vibrant economy. This is the opposite of past policy, but is it genuine and can it work?" Clearly, the Labour government had inherited some high expectations and enjoyed considerable support for the idea of a more activist state. With one eye on the electorate and another on the volatile international marketplace, however, it is not exactly clear how much will or could be done to reorient the New Zealand economy.

There is, as yet, little indication that Japan figures prominently in New Zealand's plans for economic restructuring. In March 1998, then Prime Minister Jenny Shipley paid an official visit to Japan – the first by a New Zealand prime minister since the 1976 visit by Robert Muldoon.[24] Very little of a practical nature emerged from this visit, however. More generally, any economic enthusiasm for expanded trade with Japan was offset by New Zealanders' general concern about foreign direct investment and, in particularly, increasing economic dependence on Asian markets.

The New Zealand-Japan commercial relationship changed relatively little from 1997 to 2000, although the end of the century saw a significant decline in Japanese imports of New Zealand products. New Zealand's exports to Japan fell from slightly more than US$2 billion in

1997 to US$1.54 billion in 1999, a decline of almost 25%.[25] In fact, the United States surpassed Japan as New Zealand's second largest trading partner in 1999. The U.S. purchased 14% of New Zealand's total exports (NZ$3.2 billion) while Japanese imports dropped from the 15% – 17% that had been sustained for the rest of the 1990s to 13% (NZ$3 billion).[26] Various factors accounted for this change, including a robust U.S. economy and a strong U.S. dollar, which boosted American purchases, and the Japanese economic downturn, which saw a decline in Japan's overall imports. However, New Zealand's exports to Japan were down by an even larger degree – meat, wood, aluminum, dairy, and vegetables all fell by 15% or more.[27] Prices for wood and aluminum fell and Japanese food importers began searching for less expensive suppliers while Japanese consumers switched to less expensive cuts of meat or kinds of produce. These declines were seen throughout Asia, and as one analyst put it, "New Zealand, which posted a $1.3 billion trade deficit in the 12 months to April [1999] – the biggest since January 1985 – would have been in dire straits during the Asian crisis but for the booming American market."[28]

New Zealand seemed increasingly preoccupied with internal economic dynamics. Although both Prime Minister Clark and Finance Minister Cullen are known for their internationalist leanings, it appeared that the coalition's agenda would focus primarily on such issues as the distribution of wealth (one of the government's first actions was to announce a sizable increase in the tax rate for "wealthy" New Zealanders, defined as those earning more than NZ$60,000) and regional economic development, including a major initiative led by Alliance leader Jim Anderton. Whereas the National Party was preoccupied with preparing the nation for the realities of international competition, the Labour-Alliance government appeared to be more interested in smoothing off the lumps and addressing the inequities that had resulted from more than fifteen years of market liberalization. Wariness about international markets and the possible impact of dramatic government action on trade and investment had quieted the government's hand and ensured that rhetoric remained far more prominent than government action. In 2000, New Zealand represented the nervousness that many nations felt about the trajectory of internationalization and illustrated the constraints placed on national governments by the economic realities of global markets and international finance.

AUSTRALIA

If New Zealand appeared to be on the cusp of looking to the past for economic policies, Australia seemed to be determined to stay the

course, at least for the short term. October 1998 saw the re-election of
the John Howard Liberal-National government, but with a greatly
reduced majority. Labour remained the main Opposition party,
although much of the anti-government vote went to the extreme right-
wing, anti-foreigner One Nation Party, which received 8.4% of the
national vote (14% in Queensland, where it also did well in state elections and up to 25% in some rural electorates). However, this translated into only one Senate seat and no seats in the House of Representatives; the party's founder, Pauline Hanson, lost her seat. Although
One Nation gained a great deal of attention after the Queensland
election (it made headlines through Southeast Asia) and around the
federal election, by the end of the century little was being written
about the party. Nonetheless, Australia had work to do to overcome
the negative impression left by a high number of votes for a party that
many feel has a racist vision. According to one Australian source, after
the Queensland election, all of Japan's major daily newspapers "ran
stories on One Nation, with the Asahi Shimbun describing it as 'the
political party with a White Australia Policy.' It said the party promoted
racist policies and its poll success was a clear warning to the Federal
Government."[29]

Australia's economy performed very well throughout the 1990s,
including the final years of the century. Despite the economic downturn in its Asian trading partners, Australia's GDP grew by over 4% per
year from 1997 through 1999. Inflation remained low at under 2%,
unemployment at a moderate 7.5% and, according to one study, productivity performance was outstanding.[30] Many analysts attributed this
success to macroeconomic reforms including extensive privatization,
trade barrier removal, tougher competition policy, and labour market
changes.[31]

Others were less sure both about the extent of Australia's economic
success and about its origins. As travel writer Bill Bryson wrote about
Australians,

For four decades, they have watched in quiet dismay as one country after
another – Switzerland, Sweden, Japan, Kuwait, and many others – has climbed
over them in the per capita GDP table. When news came out in 1996 that Hong
Kong and Singapore had also squeezed ahead, you'd have thought from the
newspaper editorials and analyses that Asian armies had come ashore somewhere around Darwin and were fanning out across the country, appropriating
consumer durables as they went. Never mind that most of these countries were
only marginally ahead and that much of it was to do with relative exchange
rates. Never mind that when you take into account quality-of-life indicators
like cost of living, educational attainments, crime rates and so on, Australia

bounds back up near the top. ... At the time of my visit, Australia was booming as never before. It was enjoying one of the fastest rates of economic growth in the developed world, inflation was invisible, unemployment was at its lowest level in years. Yet according to a study by the Australian Institute, 36 percent of Australians felt life was getting worse and barely a fifth saw any hope of its getting better.[32]

Australian commentators agreed. Meg Lees, leader of the opposition Democratic Party, argued in an interview with *The Bulletin*, a leading Australian magazine, that "strong economic figures are hiding 'enormous pain' at the lower and middle end of Australian society."[33] An Australian National University professor in a 1999 editorial questioned whether GDP was really the best indicator of either the economy's productivity or the population's state of well-being. He wondered if Australians were actually better off than they were twenty years ago or if they were just working harder to stay in the same place.[34] In comparison to both New Zealand and Canadian commentary, however, the final years of the twentieth century in Australia saw less questioning of economic rationalization, globalization, and the unfettered marketplace. This can be most likely attributed to Australia's economic success in the 1990s.

The Howard government planned to continue its privatization of the public sector. In early 2000, the government announced its decision to expand outsourcing and contracting out of government services. The general government viewpoint appeared to be that clear evidence was needed to convince the government that the service should remain in-house.[35] In international trade, the government's focus remained on trade liberalization, particularly of the agriculture and services sectors. While still committed to the WTO and other multilateral forums, after APEC 1998's failure to deliver much progress on trade liberalization, and particular frustration with Japan's refusal to cut fishery and forestry tariffs, the Australian government began turning its attention to expanding bilateral trading relationships rather than focusing solely on multilateral forums.[36] The failed WTO talks in Seattle in 1999 reinforced this change in emphasis. Australia had had high hopes for the Seattle talks. Along with the rest of the Cairns Group of agricultural exporters, Australia was pushing to have trade in agriculture put on the same footing as trade in other products. As protectionism abounds in the agriculture sector – tariffs of over 300% are not unusual – this was an optimistic agenda.

Upon his return from Seattle, Australia's Trade Minister Mark Vaile appointed his predecessor Tim Fischer to begin negotiations to establish a free trade arrangement between the ASEAN countries and

Australia and New Zealand through their CER pact.[37] In its *2000 Trade Outcomes and Objectives Statement*, the government also stated its commitment to expanding bilateral trade efforts, particularly with a greater array of trading partners. The effort to look beyond traditional trading partners helped Australia weather the Asian crisis as well as it did, the report stated: "While we maintained our efforts in Asia, we put additional emphasis on developing new markets and reviving old ones. This has paid off handsomely since we came to office in 1996."

In this same vein, new Austrade offices were opened in Lima and Bucharest, Austrade offices in Egypt and the United Arab Emirates were expanded, and embassies were being opened in Copenhagen and Lisbon.[38] The Liberal-National coalition reiterated its desire to diversify its export markets in "Advancing Australia's Trade Interest," its trade policy document. While affirming that Australia is "committed to Asia for the long haul,"[39] the document stated that "the government will take direct action to diversify markets and increase opportunities for exporters beyond Asia."[40]

Different ways to improve trading conditions for Australia were also suggested by the private sector. The National Farmers' Federation tried to convince Australia's leading business groups to form a new free trade alliance, and a Canberra trade lawyer suggested that a trade rights office be established to identify and tackle trade access issues.[41] Negotiating some form of bilateral deal with the European Union was also proposed.[42] However, while the Australian government and much of the private sector may have been wholeheartedly behind freer trade, the general public was not necessarily so keen. A recent *Economist* poll "showed that protectionists outnumbered free traders almost two to one in Australia."[43] The Liberal-National coalition, desirous of being re-elected, was unlikely, therefore, to push the free trade envelope as far as it might have liked, especially if or when the Australian economy slowed down.

For this reason perhaps, in 1998 the Australian government imposed a five-year moratorium on tariffs that would see tariff levels held at 2000 levels until 2005. And in 1999, under its Strategic Investment Program, the government proffered $700 million to the textile, clothing, and footwear industries as a response to its public admission that without incentives to invest and innovate, these industries would have difficulty surviving. As part of the program, rebates were offered for capital investment, adding value, and research and development.[44] Surprisingly, even critics within the targeted industries themselves complained that this financial injection could be a waste of money. The guidelines were too broad, they said, so that companies with little hope of long-term viability would receive assistance. The larger manufacturers worried that nothing might come out of this fairly massive financial lifeline and that it could amount "to little more than a short-term subsidy for a diminishing industry."[45]

Commentators writing about the November 2001 Australian election, won by Howard's Liberal-National coalition, expected that the government would suffer electorally for promoting freer trade. Max Walsh wrote in *The Bulletin*, "The bush will decide the outcome of the next election, and the bush sees itself as a casualty of globalization."[46] Opinion polls suggested that Labour Party leader Kim Beazley was likely to become Australia's next prime minister. In a long interview published in an April 2000 issue of *The Bulletin*, Beazley was asked about his vision for Australia. He said that Australia has "to be a knowledge society for a knowledge economy. We need first class educational institutions, first-class research and development, private and public, first-class opportunities for education through life, first-class opportunities for training."[47] He went on to say that he worried that Australia was becoming a "comatose nation" and stated that "It is only intelligent nations which will survive and prosper this century. The unintelligent nations will gradually, quietly, go comatose and become vulnerable with unhappy, divided, non-achieving populations."[48] How exactly Beazley planned to make Australia one of the intelligent nations or a knowledge society for a knowledge economy will remain unknown, as the Howard government rode a tough stance on refugees and the "war" on terrorism to success at the polls. Beazley "argues the current government sees itself as having no role in nation-building or regional policy. 'Nothing happens naturally of that nature – you (governments) make decisions all the time ... Howard is taking minimal government to the nth degree.'"[49] That pattern is likely to continue.

Given the cautious politics of the Howard administration, it is hardly surprising to discover that the national government has shied away from major trade initiatives with Japan. The Australia-Japan relationship remained relatively stable to 2000. Japan continued to be Australia's largest single export market, purchasing 20% of total Australian-produced exports in 1998–99 (valued at A$16.6 billion). While this represented a decline of 6% over 1997–98, it was a substantial increase over the A$15.4 billion of 1996–97.[50] (Of the three countries under investigation, the decline in Australia's trade with Japan was the smallest.)[51] The composition of Australia's trade to Japan also remained relatively unchanged. Food exports increased slightly (primarily fish and meat) while sales of mineral fuels (coal, petroleum, and natural gas) and non-ferrous metals declined a little. The total value of fruit and vegetable exports to Japan increased. This may be at least partially due to a significant breakthrough on the horticultural side that occurred in early 1999: an export agreement permitting Tasmanian apples into Japan was signed, which the government estimates could be worth A$500,000 to Australian growers.[52] Sales of machinery and transport equipment were of approximately the same value in 1999 as in 1997, although road vehicle and office machine exports declined a little, and power generating machinery, electrical machinery, and general industrial machinery sales were up slightly.

The decline in the value of coal exports to Japan reflected plummeting coal prices. As a February 2000 article in *The Bulletin* stated, "Japan's steel and electricity producers have almost cut Australia's average export coal prices in half since the start of the '90s. And that is just in U.S. dollar terms. In yen terms, the cut has been much greater. Adjust for inflation and coal ranks among the worst investments of the late 20th century."[53] In 1999, Australian coal producers took an 18% (about US$9) cut in the contract price of coking coal sold to Japanese steel mills, and in February 2000 they were forced to accept another cut, this time of 5%, but secured agreement for acceptance of higher volumes.[54]

While the Australian government sees Japan as a vitally important market (the decision to expand the trade office in Fukuoka into a consulate general is one indication of this), according to a senior Austrade representative in Tokyo, many Australian exporters have been taking their eyes off Japan and looking at China and Vietnam instead. A 1996 survey of Australian exporters revealed that half were interested only in the ASEAN markets.

Japanese protectionism toward agricultural, fishery, and forestry products has been a touchy issue between the two countries. Although some progress has been made – lower sugar tariffs, more advantageous rice tender conditions, and access for four varieties of Australian citrus fruits were all recently negotiated – Australia still feels that much needs to be done to ensure fair access for Australian products.[55] Sectors that are seen to have potential for Australian sales to Japan include defense systems integration, organic food, custommade jewellery, top end gemstones, scientific equipment, building materials, high technology (multimedia, software, packaged software, telecommunications), services for the aged, health care, and financial services. Third country projects have also been proving to be successful, particularly in Asia. Residual bad feelings against Japan are tempered when the Japanese, Australians, and Asians work together in Asia.

Australia's ability to attract significant Japanese investment in the future is uncertain. Australia has neither a large domestic market nor secure, low-cost labour. Most Japanese industries locating abroad in the twenty-first century are electronics, heavy machinery, chemicals, and automotive and these do not match with Australia's strengths. New investments are likely to be in financial services and telecommunications; most likely, however, resource businesses will continue to attract the greatest Japanese interest as they continue their efforts to ensure the country a steady supply of essential raw materials.

CANADA

For much of the last two decades, Canada's approach to international trade was characterized by strong rhetoric and commercial preoccupation with the United States. Little changed by 2000. Canada's economy looked strong at the end of the 1990s: GDP grew by 3.1% in 1998 and 4.2% in 1999, inflation was at near historically low levels, unemployment was at its lowest point in years, and the government had made steps toward decreasing the national debt.[56] But these strong statistics hid more sobering realities. Many Canadian commentators noted that Canadian purchasing power had declined from 78% of that of the United States in 1978 to less than 66% in 2000; that real GDP per capita growth had been sluggish (only 5% between 1988 and 1998, placing Canada twenty-fourth out of twenty-five OECD countries); that the Canadian dollar had fallen from 87 cents against the U.S. dollar in 1991 to 65–69 cents in 2000 and that Canadian living standards fell from about 74% of U.S. levels in 1989 to 61% in 1999.[57]

The comparisons with the United States are important as it is to the United States that Canada worries it will lose its best and its brightest individuals and corporations. As John McCallum, chief economist for the Royal Bank of Canada wrote, "as the Canada-U.S. income gap and the cost of staying here get progressively higher, fewer will be willing to pay that price. In addition to the purely economic incentives, a continuing rise in the income gap would enhance the sentiment that only 'losers' stay in Canada, only those who can't make it south of the border."[58]

Concern already abounds about the loss of control of Canadian industries to American ownership. Pointing to numerous Canadian companies moving their head offices or their entire operations south of the border, former Supreme Court justice Willard Estey stated: "I supported free trade a decade ago. Now I am beginning to suspect that Canada may have contracted out our independence in those trade agreements. The problem is that we are letting corporations with no loyalty to this country strip it of its finite resources. We are witnessing the quiet hijacking of Canadian companies by foreign managers."[59] A 1999 Business Council on National Issues study showed that "40 per cent of chief executives (from Canadian and foreign-owned companies alike) would put the probability that their own jobs would leave Canada within 10 years at 50/50 or higher. The responses suggesting a high probability of CEO departures came from companies across all industries, from companies with more than half a trillion dollars in assets and $160-billion in annual revenue."[60]

The late 1990s were also difficult for the numerous Canadians who work in the natural resource and agricultural sectors. While the government liked to talk about the diversification of Canada's exports to include a high percentage of highly processed goods and services, the reality was that, outside of Ontario and about half of Quebec, "foreign trade is still all about fish, wheat, oil, logs, and livestock. Natural resources, including agricultural products, make up 79 per cent of Atlantic Canada's merchandise exports, 80 per cent of Alberta's, 74 per cent of Saskatchewan's, and 77 per cent of B.C.'s."[61] Falling commodity prices devastated farming on the prairies (Saskatchewan farm incomes fell by 72% in 1997–98 and the following year was worse) and coal and forestry in British Columbia.

Canada suffered more from the Asian economic downturn of 1997–99 than many other nations because of its dependence on resource exports and because it does not add value to the goods it exports. In its *1999 Asia Review*, the Asia Pacific Foundation called for the provincial and federal governments to encourage producers to determine ways to add value to their commodities before exporting them. "Shipping lightly processed commodities is equivalent to shipping jobs out of the country," noted the report. "As long as Canada fails to diversify its Asian exports into manufactured goods, especially branded products that are less vulnerable to economic fluctuations, our trade with Asia will remain hostage to sharp downturns."[62]

Concerns about the Canadian brain drain to the U.S., declining living standards, worries about the widening gap between rich and poor (a *Maclean's* magazine survey revealed that 46% of men and 55% of women think that the government should intervene to narrow this growing divide), along with, for many Canadians, the frightening realities of making a living in a precarious commodity market, have been escalating.[63] Canadians are searching for leadership and direction on many issues, particularly the economy. From whence that leadership should come is less clear. The neo-liberal Business Council on National Issues (BCNI), an organization composed of the chief executive officers of 150 Canadian companies, has begun to take a more

active role in encouraging discussion about Canada's future and suggesting ways to overcome some of the difficulties being faced. In April
2000, the council presented its plan for Canada, sections of which
were reprinted in one of the national newspapers. The BCNI report
outlined what it believed government must do – cut personal and corporate income taxes, "ensure that Canadian communities offer a high
quality of life and excellent public services and infrastructure,"
"encourage change not stagnation," "invest in people and encourage
initiative rather than subsidize jobs and reinforce dependence" – and
what the corporate sector should do – "become more aggressive in
seeking to be global leaders rather than regional followers."[64] BCNI
advocates less government, lower taxes, and fewer programs and services – and places little emphasis on national economic leadership.

Michael Porter, author of *The Competitive Advantage of Nations* and
Canada at the Crossroads, agrees that responsibility for improving
Canada's situation is shared between government and business. In
Canada at the Crossroads, a 1991 study of Canadian competitiveness, he
had outlined what he believed each needed to do but stated that "In
2000, the greatest challenges lies in Canadian firms themselves."[65] In
January 2000, he presented a paper, *Canadian Competitiveness: Nine
Years after the Crossroads*. Nine years later, he says, the recommendations
of his *Canada at the Crossroads* study have largely been ignored and as a
result Canada "will now be condemned to a declining standard of
living compared to other countries" if changes do not occur. Porter
was particularly critical of business, saying that "Canadian companies
have not effectively prepared for the kind of competition that will
produce strong industries" and that "Canadian firms must understand
that competing in Canada alone will eventually destroy them. They
must decide to compete globally and compete on the basis of unique
products and processes."[66]

Where Porter advocated dramatic steps and strong government
leadership, the federal government preferred to tinker with existing
policies and to shy away from bold initiatives. The federal government
has made some changes to its international business development initiatives that were outlined in chapter 4. The Canadian International
Business Strategy process was discontinued in 1998. There was a sense
that it had become a time consuming "academic" exercise with too
much emphasis on writing reports and not enough on actual outcomes. The National Sector Teams also changed. The teams were supposed to reflect national sectoral priorities, but by 1998, the desire not
to leave anyone out had resulted in too many teams (and many of
them were doing very little) to reflect priorities. "Political correctness
had got in the way of commercial realities," as one government official

commented. It would be better, it was argued, to have fewer teams that actually reflected the country's sectoral priorities. A two-stage competition (implemented by a private sector company) was initiated to select these teams and all the National Sector Teams were invited to apply. Sectors had to explain why they should be considered a trade priority for Canada and demonstrate what they had done to improve their performance. Their names were changed to Trade Team Canada Sectors, and as of 2000, eleven were established: aerospace and defense; agriculture, food, beverages; automotive; bio-industries; building products; electric power equipment and services; environmental industries; health industries; information and communications technologies; plastics; service industries and capital projects. Each sector indicates its priority geographic markets. The government sees these Trade Team Canada Sectors as their main export priorities and allocates 50% of its promotional budget on these eleven sectors.[67]

Government policies had little economic impact. Despite relatively high profile efforts to promote better commercial links with Japan, Canada's business community remained as focused as ever on the American market. Through the late 1990s, although Japan has remained Canada's second largest export market, Canada became increasingly dependent on the United States. While the value of Canadian exports to the United States were continuously increasing (to C$310 billion in 1999), those to Japan were steadily declining (to C$9.2 billion in 1999).[68] At the end of 1999, Canadian exports to Japan accounted for 2.6% of Canadian exports while exports to the U.S. were a staggering 86%.

Despite abundant evidence of the growing importance of the "new economy," specifically in Japan and globally, Canadian businesses remain wedded to traditional products. While foreign firms discovered a dramatic Japanese appetite for financial services, software, consulting, and numerous computer and information technology products, Canadian companies were not overly active in these critical and fast-growing areas in Japan. Canada's main exports to Japan continued to be forest products, coal, canola, wheat, fish, meat, and aluminum. This unchanged export profile in fact explains a great deal of the continuing decline in the value of Canadian exports to Japan. Commodity prices have been declining and new competitors are entering many of these markets.

The Canadian forest industry is a good example. Forest companies were sharply affected by Japan's economic downturn in 1998. The drop in timber sales was such that in British Columbia the industry convinced the provincial government to allow the export of surplus logs. Exporting logs, as opposed to milling them at home where they create jobs, flies in the face of both public opinion and government policy, but the province took this desperate measure to help keep the industry active.[69] While general commentary blamed the Japanese recession for the decline in sales, a closer look revealed that while Japanese purchases were down, purchases from Canada had declined disproportionately; Canada had begun to lose out to Scandinavian competition. A few years before, Scandinavians were not even in the lumber market; in 1996 they sold 1.3 million cubic feet and in 1997, 1.8 million cubic feet. Canada took a long time to achieve sales of 2 million cubic feet while the Scandinavians attained this level in only two years. According to some Canadian industry insiders, the Scandinavian companies are more flexible than those in Canada and are more willing to deliver small orders and to adjust products to fit the sizes the Japanese want.

Stricter Japanese building codes introduced in June 2000 also affected British Columbia's coastal forest industry. According to Brian Zak, the president of the Coast Forest and Lumber Association, "Lumber from green hemlock, one of the three main species on the coast, is going to be ranked lower than engineered lumber, a new product being made by foreign and domestic competitors."[70] The industry therefore had to embark on research into the drying of hemlock. At least one analyst, however, says that for years the Japanese had been asking the B.C. coastal producers to dry their green hemlock, citing Japanese preference for the appearance of the dried wood. Japanese building codes at that time called for a species of wood rather than certain performance standards. As there was no real competition for the hemlock, the B.C. industry stayed with the undried wood and is now paying the price.

Despite the demonstrable success of B.C.'s Canada Comfort Direct program, only a skeleton of it remains. Some of the funding has been redirected toward Forest Renewal B.C. initiatives,[71] and although these partially duplicate the work of Canada Comfort Direct, the structure of the program and the attendant demands on companies to demonstrate commitment to the Japanese market are no longer in place.

The coal industry also went through hard times. Quintette, one of British Columbia's major coal mines that sold exclusively to Japanese steelmakers, ceased operations on 31 August 2000, three years before the end of its scheduled twenty-year run. The Japanese had negotiated cuts in volume and in price numerous times and the mine management finally decided that Quintette was no longer a viable operation. Between 1998 and 2000, coal prices fell by almost 30% due to increased international competition and worldwide coal surpluses.[72]

Patterns established in the 1970s remained dominant in the Canada-Japan trading relationship in 2000. Japanese companies typically took the lead, and emphasized resource products. The federal government was, at least at a very general level, anxious to adapt trading activities to the realities of the early twenty-first century. Although movement was less than dramatic, a significant number of events occurred in the final years of the 1990s. In the fall of 1998, the Canadian embassy launched a concerted effort to update and enhance the image of Canada in Japan. The Canadian Brand Committee, the group entrusted with this task, began by commissioning a survey from the Japan Market Research Bureau in March 1999. The goal of the research was to find out how Canada is perceived in Japan by the Japanese and asked respondents to answer questions on their perceptions of five countries (Australia, France, Canada, Sweden, and the United States). The survey was broad-ranging and solicited opinions on issues ranging from the economy to culture to world affairs.

According to Donald Bobiash, chair of the committee and counsellor at the embassy, the results revealed that while the Japanese appear to generally "like" Canada, to recognize the country's natural beauty, and to value the role Canada has played in world and environmental affairs,[73] Canada did not score well in a number of areas (only 11% said Canada is an innovative country, for example) and few respondents associated Canada with any high technology industries (8% of respondents) or with research and development (10% of respondents).[74] Interestingly, the country's considerable and often successful efforts to market Canadian tourism opportunities – Banff, Jasper, and Anne of Green Gables – and agricultural products – which highlight clean air, fresh water, and wide open spaces – run counter to the nation's efforts to position itself as a high technology and manufacturing powerhouse.

With a clear sense of Japanese images of Canada, the embassy is now working to expand that picture, building on the positive but rather limited image that currently exists. To this end, the embassy actively promotes Canadian high technology goods and services and, in particular, "champion[s] areas where Canada has leading edge technology."[75] The embassy assists Canadian firms by co-hosting product presentations, software showcases, and press conferences. The embassy also regularly briefs the media on Canada's information technology sector, makes corporate calls on Japanese firms to brief them on Canada's information technology capabilities, assists with Canadian agencies, helps set up local meetings, and encourages Japanese companies, associations, and the media to visit Canada and learn about Canada's research and development and technological capabilities for themselves.

This desire to showcase Canada's high technology sector and demonstrate to the Japanese that Canada offers more than coal and timber was also evident in the Team Canada trade mission to Japan that took place in September 1999. This sixth Team Canada trade mission, the first to a G7 country, saw approximately 250 Canadian business people, the prime minister, eight provincial premiers, and three territorial leaders spend a week in Osaka and Tokyo. The mission focused on eight priority sectors: space, electric power and new energy, building technologies and materials, food biotechnology, information and communication technologies, environment, education, and health. The mission shone light on Canada's high technology industries and capabilities. Japanese business people were invited to a variety of seminars on successful Canadian companies and products in fields such as multimedia and biotechnology. Canadian astronaut Julie Payette accompanied the mission, speaking about her time in space and personifying Canada's high tech abilities. Representatives from about 4,000 companies met with Canadian business people during the week, and at the official luncheon in Tokyo, there were 1,200 guests, including members of the Japanese Diet and presidents of many of Japan's larger companies. All of these people heard the message about Canada's high technology abilities, and it was hoped that there would be far-reaching spin-off effects for Canadian companies.

Along with increasing Japanese understanding of Canadian capabilities, the focus of the Team Canada Japan trip was on building relationships between Canadian and Japanese business people and increasing Canadian awareness of the potential of the Japanese market. The government recognized going into the mission that doing business in Japan takes a great deal of time, so less importance was attached to the announcement of specific commercial contracts than on past missions. Nonetheless, Prime Minister Chrétien witnessed a signing ceremony for C$409-million worth of trade deals.[76] These deals covered a wide range of products and services, including kitchen cabinets, airplanes, software, housing, snack foods, and telecommunications. While the media pointed out that the $409-million total was much less than that achieved on previous Team Canada missions (the Team Canada mission to China in 1994 netted $8.6-billion worth of deals, including the sale of a Canadian nuclear reactor), the real worth of the mission should be judged by sales over the long term of products and services, especially those in the high tech sector. It will be crucial for the Canadian government and business community to follow up on the start that Team Canada made. From the government's side, sending the consistent repeated message that Canada is a high technology nation with leading edge products Japan needs will be very important. Unfortunately, the desire not to offend those in the traditional resource sectors that make up the bulk of current Canadian exports to Japan may soften Canada's message.

In the wake of the Team Canada Japan trip, the BCNI and the Japanese Keidanren (Federation of Economic Organizations) each agreed to commission studies on how to improve the Canada-Japan economic relationship. These reports were presented in May 2000 and the two business groups signed an agreement to explore the potential of a free trade agreement between Canada and Japan over the next five to seven years.[77] So far discussions are at a preliminary stage and the two governments are allowing business groups to examine the issue first. There are many challenges (debate over the inclusion of agriculture could be one area of difficulty) and no small amount of disinterest and/or potential opposition to overcome.

According to Canada's *National Post* newspaper, "Officials from both Canada and Japan said while a free trade deal is a possibility, there are other types of trade deals that could emerge, including deals limited to sectors such as technology."[78] Japan does not yet have many bilateral trade deals, although one has been signed with Singapore and another is under discussion with South Korea, so negotiations could take a long time. One Canadian newspaper columnist questioned the involvement of the BCNI in trade deal discussions and wondered whether Canadian companies are really in a position to take advantage of free trade with Japan. Noting that Canada trades more with many individual American states that with Japan, Rod McQueen pointed out that fully 45% of exports to the United States come from only fifty companies. "Let's face it," he wrote, "if most Canadian firms don't have enough gumption to ship next door to the U.S., how many of them are likely to focus on far-off Japan?"[79]

The Keidanren and the BCNI plan to table a detailed proposal to the two governments in May 2001. Whether or not a free trade deal is ultimately negotiated, the commencement of discussions with the government of Japan about a possible free trade agreement could be of great symbolic importance for Canada. It would signal to the Japanese government that Canada attaches a high level of importance to this bilateral trade relationship. Further, it would quickly raise the profile of Japan across Canada, and send a strong message to the Canadian population that Japan was deemed important to the country's economic future.[79]

Such initiatives are urgently needed if Canada is to reverse a steady decline in its Japanese trade. In 1997, the country exported US$7.3 billion worth of products to Japan. By 1999, that trade had fallen to only US$5.3 billion, a $2 billion decline in Canadian trade with its second largest partner.[80] Despite the high profile Team Canada expedition, and federal attempts at "re-branding" Canadian products, it remained clear that the national strategies for increasing trade with Japan had yet to bear fruit. More to the point, Canada's trade position in Japan continues to decline, with little apparent prospect for a quick reversal. If earlier Canadian practice provides a guide for future action, the country's political and business leaders will use evidence of declining trade as a reason to do less – not more – to promote trade activity with Japan.

Although a free trade deal is no great panacea and would not instantly solve all of the problems of the Canada-Japan trading relationship (tariffs, the usual focus of free trade negotiations, are not the major impediment to Canada-Japan trade), the potential deal has attractions for both sides. For the Japanese, Canada holds one major, impressive card: access to the American market through the North American Free Trade Agreement, and Japanese companies have, particularly in the automobile sector, been taking advantage of this opportunity for years. (For the same reason, of course, American officials might look askance at such a Canadian and Japanese move.) For Canada, Japan offers the potential to diversify beyond the United States and to expand Canadian sales of high technology products to an economy with the capital to purchase them. Canada is nowhere near as important to Japan as Japan is to Canada. The emergence of new resource-producing competitors has weakened Canada's claim on Japan's attentions and, as the Canadian Brand Committee survey indicated, the Japanese have yet to position Canada on their high technology radar screen. As the responsibility for rebuilding and expanding the trade relationship lies firmly in Canadian hands (Canada has been far too reliant on Japanese initiative in the past), the prospect of a free trade agreement, even if it does not lead quickly to an accord, could send a critical signal to Japan that Canada intends to become a major player on the international trading scene and that Canadians are, in particular, committed to capitalizing on the opportunities to be found in Japan.

Not one of the three countries, Australia, Canada, or New Zealand, made dramatic improvements in its trading relationship with Japan between 1997 and 2000. While the nations generally kept to a laissez-faire, free market approach to international market development, there were signs in Canada and New Zealand that government was prepared to consider other options. Both countries, however, appeared more enthusiastic about the policies and approaches of the 1970s –

subsidies, regional development initiatives, government-business con-
sultations – than with bold initiatives designed to alter historic patterns
of imports and exports. Like most democratic nations, the three countries continued to offer the rhetoric of international trade, but
remained committed to traditional products, traditional trading partners, and traditional approaches to business development. While the
glow appears to have come off the free market euphoria of the early
1990s, there is nothing approaching a coherent or widely shared alternate image of how governments might manage national economic
development. Moreover, the inherently short-term nature of political
life in all three countries (elections are generally held every three
years in Australia and New Zealand and every three to four years in
Canada; in New Zealand, the process of alliance-building and maintenance can easily cut several months out of an already short mandate)
mitigates against thoughtful and analytical political approaches to economic strategy.

The three countries face remarkably similar problems and concerns. They remain, despite years of seeking to diversify, largely dependent upon selling resources, despite volatile prices and increasing
international competition. Much is made of the need to promote
"value-added" production and to enhance the national commercial
return from resource exploitation, but relatively little has been done.
Australia, Canada, and New Zealand each have active high technology
sectors (the latter two are noted for the high percentage of wired
homes, business, and government offices), but their economic impact
has been relatively slight. There is disquiet in all three countries,
voiced as nagging doubt about economic direction and future
prospects. Observers in each nation – and others around the world –
are worried about the growing gap between rich and poor and
comment about the sense that average workers appear to be working
harder and longer to simply remain in one place economically. New
Zealanders and Australians have been looking to each other for economic lessons. As one Australian journalist noted, a bit harshly: "NZ
will be a similar disappointment to the free traders. The Kiwis have discovered that what they've enjoyed for the last decade is pretty much a
trickle-up effect. There are about six people in Auckland who are very
well off for beer and smokes while everyone else has got their noses
pressed to the window of the restaurant."[81]

Enhanced trade with Japan is no panacea for any country, let alone
Australia, Canada, or New Zealand, but the manner in which national
governments have – or have not – responded to changing opportunities and markets in the world's second largest economy shows how
government has responded to the changing realities of international

commerce. Shackled by a lack of national imagination and the pervasive ideology of the free market, hamstrung by historical dependency on natural resources, and possessed of little enthusiasm for dramatic economic action (New Zealand's passion for risk-taking having largely run its course), each of the countries has seen their relative international economic position decline. There have been bright spots – individual companies, entrepreneurs, or sectors – in each country, but neither Australia, Canada, nor New Zealand truly capitalized on the rapid globalization of an increasingly technology-dependent economy.

The main study explained the web of political, historical, cultural, commercial, and economic factors that limited national responsiveness and conditioned government responses to opportunities and challenges in Japan. By 2000, nothing substantial had changed; the cautious, resource-reliant policies of the past remained very much in place. Even as the lustre appeared to be wearing off the free market ethos that had dominated the 1990s, there was no substantial evidence from Australia, Canada, or New Zealand that the national government was about to make trade with Japan a national priority. If anything, the long-standing practice of disparaging Japan, over-emphasizing its economic trials and underestimating both its success and adaptive capacity, remained very much in effect in all three countries. Japan remains an illusive target, desired but not actively courted, appreciated more when trade declines than when opportunities emerge, and little understood either by national governments or business communities.

This investigation of trade relations between Japan and Australia, Canada, and New Zealand suggests that governments in free market countries are unlikely to take bold steps to re-enter the field of national business development. All three countries adopted and to varying degrees internalized the language and ideology of the free market, and appeared committed to paths of limited intervention. At the same time the national business communities did not respond creatively, aggressively, or innovatively to the changing dynamics of global trade and instead remained largely wedded to the old order. Relying on the market place entails risks, and the governments of the three countries seem to have accepted that the private sector, not government, will determine the direction of economic policy. If the manner in which Canada, Australia, and New Zealand responded to Japan's changing economy are any indication, there is little reason to believe that any of the three economies will do particularly well in the fast-paced, technology-driven, and increasingly open international economy of the twenty-first century.

Notes

INTRODUCTION

1 Francis Fukuyama, *The End of History and the Last Man*. Reprint Edition (New York: Avon, 1993).
2 "Rich" was defined in Labour Party election material as constituting those New Zealanders who earned more than NZ$60,000 per year.
3 On this topic, see Paul Hirst and Grahame Thompson's *Globalization in Question* (London: Polity Press, 1996).
4 See Martin Carnoy, Manuel Castells, Stephen S. Cohen, and Fernando Henrique Cardoso, *The New Global Economy in the Information Age: Reflections on Our Changing World* (Pennsylvania: Pennsylvania State University Press, 1993).
5 For various viewpoints, see Walter Wriston, *The Twilight of Sovereignty* (New York: Scribner, 1992); William Greider, *One World, Ready or Not: The Manic Logic of Global Capitalism* (New York: Simon & Schuster, 1997); Paul N. Doremus, William W. Keller, Louis W. Pauly, and Simon Reich, *The Myth of the Global Corporation* (Princeton: Princeton University Press, 1998); Hirst and Thompson, *Globalization in Question*.
6 See, on this topic, Eamonn Fingleton, *Blindside: Why Japan is on Track to Overtake the US by the Year 2000* (New York: Houghton Mifflin, 1993).
7 The case study, which is necessarily limited in scope, focuses only on the promotion of trade and investment relations. This means that the service and financial sectors will not be covered in detail.
8 For a very useful study that places Japan's recent developments in context, see Eamonn Fingleton, *In Praise of Hard Industries: Why Manufac-*

turing, Not the Information Economy, Is the Key to Future Prosperity (New York: Houghton Mifflin, 1999).

9 Clyde Prestowitz, *Trading Places: How We Are Giving Our Future to Japan and How to Reclaim It* (New York: Basic Books, 1989); William Holstein, *The Japanese Power Game: What It Means for America* (New York: Scribner, 1990).

10 Susan Strange, *States and Markets: An Introduction to International Political Economy* (London: Pinter, 1988).

CHAPTER ONE

1 See, for example, David Korten, *The Post-Corporate World: Life After Capitalism* (San Francisco: Berrett-Koehler Publishers, 1999).

2 Milton Friedman, *Capitalism and Freedom* (Chicago: The University of Chicago Press, 1962), 3.

3 Ibid, 2.

4 Robert Wade, *Governing the Market: Economic Theory and the Role of Government in East Asian Industrialization* (Princeton: Princeton University Press, 1990), 13.

5 Bela Ballasa, 'The Lessons of East Asian Development: An Overview,' *Economic Development and Cultural Change* 36 no. 3, 1988: s273–90, quoted in Linda Weiss and John Hobson, *States and Economic Development* (United Kingdom: Polity Press, 1995), 140.

6 Weiss and Hobson, *States and Economic Development*, 140. See also Michael Porter, Hirotaka Takeuchi, and Mariko Sakakibara, *Can Japan Compete?* (London: Macmillan, 2000).

7 David Crane, *The Canadian Dictionary of Business and Economics* (New York: Stoddart, 1993), 316.

8 Friedrich List, *The National System of Political Economy* (New York: Augustus M. Kelley, 1966), xxvi. Reprint of 1885 edition.

9 Chalmers Johnson, *MITI and the Japanese Miracle: The Growth of Industrial Policy, 1925–1975* (Stanford: Stanford University Press, 1982).

10 Chalmers Johnson, *Japan: Who Governs? The Rise of the Developmental State* (New York: W.W. Norton & Company Inc., 1995), 101.

11 Johnson, *MITI and the Japanese Miracle*, 20.

12 For a helpful review of Chalmers Johnson's work, see Meredith Woo-Cummings, "Introduction: Chalmers Johnson and the Politics of Nationalism and Development," and Chalmers Johnson, "The Developmental State: Odyssey of a Concept" in *The Developmental State* (Ithaca: Cornell University Press, 1999).

13 Chalmers Johnson, "Introduction: The Idea of Industrial Policy," in Chalmers Johnson, ed., *The Industrial Policy Debate* (Los Angeles: ICS Press 1984), 8.

14 Ibid., 10.

15 Wade, *Governing the Market*; Alice Amsden, *Asia's Next Giant: South Korea and Late Industrialization* (New York: Oxford University Press, 1989).

16 Other books on similar themes include Johnson, *The Industrial Policy Debate*; Marie Anchordoguy, *Computers Inc.: Japan's Challenge to IBM* (Boston: Harvard University Press, 1989); Stephen Cowen, *Cowboys and Samurai: Why the U.S. is Losing the Industrial Battle and Why it Matters* (New York: Harper Business, 1991); Pat Choates, *Agents of Influence* (New York: Alfred A. Knopf, 1990), which looks at the way the US has allowed Japanese business and government to influence American policy-making; James Fallows, *Looking at the Sun: The Rise of the East Asian Economic and Political System* (New York: Pantheon Books, 1994); William Holstein, *The Japanese Power Game: What It Means for America* (New York: Scribner, 1990).

17 Clyde Prestowitz, *Trading Places: How We Are Giving Our Future to Japan and How to Reclaim It* (New York: Basic Books, 1989), 315–16.

18 William Dietrich, *In the Shadow of the Rising Sun: The Political Roots of American Economic Decline* (Pittsburgh: Pennsylvania University Press, 1991), 249.

19 Ibid., 250.

20 Eamonn Fingleton, *Blindside: Why Japan is On Track to Overtake the US by the Year 2000* (New York: Houghton Mifflin, 1993), 328. This argument is continued in Eamonn Fingleton, *In Praise of Hard Industries: Why Manufacturing, Not the Information Economy, Is the Key to National Prosperity* (New York: Houghton Mifflin, 1999).

21 Anchordoguy, *Computers Inc.*, 135.

22 Daniel Drache, "From Keynes to K-Mart" in Robert Boyer and Daniel Drache, eds., *States Against Markets: The Limits of Globalization* (London: Routledge, 1996), 34–5. For a previous collection in the same vein see Daniel Drache and Meric S. Gertler, eds., *The New Era of Global Competition: State Policy and Market Power* (Montreal: McGill-Queen's University Press, 1991).

23 Drache, "From Keynes to K-Mart," 34–5.

24 Other books discussing the Asian approach to economic development are also relevant. Paul Hirst and Grahame Thompson argue in *Globalization in Question*, for example, that there are lessons to be learned about economic development beyond the laissez-faire model by observing the economic policy initiatives of various Asian nations. Hirst and Thompson, *Globalization in Question* (London: Polity Press, 1996), 114.

25 Weiss and Hobson, *States and Economic Development*, 1.

26 Ibid., 169–70.

27 Ibid., 154.

28 Robert Kuttner, *Everything for Sale: The Virtues and Limits of Markets* (New

York: Alfred A. Knopf, 1997), flyleaf.

29 Paul Omerod, *The Death of Economics* (London: Faber & Faber, 1994), 45–6.

30 Fallows, *Looking at the Sun*, 180.

31 The strongest statement in this regard is Porter et al., *Can Japan Compete?*

32 Kimon Valaskakis, *Canada in the Nineties: Meltdown or Renaissance?* (Ottawa: The Gamma Institute Press, 1980), 81.

33 Weiss and Hobson, *States and Economic Development*, 246.

34 Paul Krugman, 'Does Third World Growth Hurt First World Prosperity?' *Harvard Business Review*, July–August 1994, 113–21.

35 Friedman, *Capitalism and Freedom*, 200.

36 Pranab Bardham, 'Symposium on the State and Economic Development,' *Journal of Economic Perspectives* 4, no.3: 3–8, quoted in Weiss and Hobson, *States and Economic Development*, 252–3.

37 Valaskakis, *Canada in the Nineties*, 156, italics in original.

38 Wade, *Governing the Market*, 356.

39 Anchordoguy, *Computers Inc.*, 137–8.

40 Ibid., 185.

41 William Cline, *Reciprocity – A New Approach to World Trade Policy?* (Institute for International Economics, Washington, D.C. 1982), 39–40, quoted in Wade, *Governing the Market.*

42 Bela Gold in *Productivity, Technology and Capital* (Lexington: Lexington Books, 1979), 11–12, quoted in Wade, *Governing the Market* and Valaskakis, *Canada in the Nineties*, 70.

43 Michael E. Porter and the Monitor Company, *Canada at the Crossroads: The Reality of the New Competitive Environment* (Ottawa: BCNI, Government of Canada, 1991); Graham T. Crocombe, Michael J. Enwright, and Michael E. Porter, *Upgrading New Zealand's Competitive Advantage* (Oxford: Oxford University Press, 1991).

44 Michael E. Porter, *The Competitive Advantage of Nations* (New York: The Free Press, 1990), 621.

45 Ibid., 651.

46 Ibid., 636.

47 Ibid., 682.

48 See, for example, George Soros, *The Crisis of Global Capitalism* (New York: Public Affairs, 1998) and Bob Rae, *The Three Questions: Prosperity and the Public Good* (Toronto: Canbook, 1998). Bob Rae, formerly premier of Ontario, is now a political analyst.

49 Richard Rosencrance, 'The Rise of the Virtual State,' *Foreign Affairs*, 75, no. 4 (July/August 1996): 55.

50 Michael Parkin and Robin Bade, *Economics: Canada in the Global Environment*, third ed. (Don Mills, Ontario: Addison-Wesley, 1997), 807.

51 Valaskakis, *Canada in the Nineties*, 164.

52 Ibid.
53 For an excellent theoretical and conceptual analysis of globalization, see David Held, Anthony McGrew, David Goldblatt, and Jonathan Perraton, *Global Transformations* (Stanford: Stanford University Press, 1999).
54 Edward J. Graham, *Global Corporations and National Governments* (Washington: Institute for International Economics, 1996), 4, 13.
55 Drache, 'From Keynes to K-Mart,' 49.
56 Anthony G. McGrew, 'Global Politics in a Transitional Era' in Anthony G. McGrew et al., eds., *Global Politics: Globalization and the Nation State* (London: Polity Press, 1992), 313.
57 Ibid., 321.
58 Other books that argue, from varying starting positions, that globalization is taking place include Christopher Chase-Dunn, *Global Formation: Structures of the World Economy* (Cambridge, Mass.: B. Blackwell, 1989); Paul Kennedy, *Preparing for the Twenty-First Century* (New York: Vintage Books, 1993); and P. Dicken, *Global Shift: The Internationalisation of Economic Activity* (New York: The Guildford Press, 1992).
59 Susan Strange, *The Retreat of the State: The Diffusion of Power in the World Economy* (Cambridge: Cambridge University Press, 1996), 4.
60 Robert Boyer, "State and Market: A new engagement for the twenty-first century?" in *States Against Markets*, 86.
61 Kenichi Ohmae, *The Borderless World* (New York: McKinsey & Company, 1990), 12.
62 Ibid., 194.
63 Robert Reich, *The Work of Nations: Preparing Ourselves for 21st Century Capitalism* (New York: Alfred A. Knopf Inc., 1991), 138, 168.
64 Reich, *The Work of Nations*, 311–12.
65 Linda McQuaig, *The Cult of Impotence: Selling the Myth of Powerlessness in the Global Economy* (Toronto: Penguin Books, 1998), 26.
66 Drache, "From Keynes to K-Mart," 38.
67 Manfred Bienefeld, 'Strong National Economy: A Utopian Goal' in *States Against Markets*, 428.
68 Hirst and Thompson, *Globalization in Question*, 4.
69 Paul N. Doremus, William W. Keller, Louis W. Pauly, and Simon Reich, *The Myth of the Global Corporation* (Princeton: Princeton University Press, 1998), 4.
70 Martin Carnoy, "Multinationals in a Changing World Economy: Whither the Nation-State?" in Martin Carnoy, Manuel Castells, Stephen S. Cohen, and Fernando Henrique Cardoso, *The New Global Economy in the Information Age: Reflections on Our Changing World* (Pennsylvania: Pennsylvania State University Press, 1993), 53.
71 Carnoy et al., *The New Global Economy*, 9.
72 Richard Falk, "State of Seige: Will Globalization Win Out?" *International*

Affairs 73, no. 1 (1997): 123–36.

73 Vivean Schmidt, "The New World Order, Incorporated: The Rise of Business and the Decline of the Nation State," *Daedalus*, 124, no. 2 (Spring 1995): 75–106.

74 Susan Strange, *The Retreat of the State*; on the reality that the state is a social construction, and therefore logically subject to de-construction if circumstances are right, see Thomas Biersteker and Cynthia Weber, eds., *State Sovereignty as Social Construct* (Cambridge: Cambridge University Press, 1996). See also Vincent Cable, 'The Diminished Nation-State: A Study in the Loss of Economic Power,' *Daedalus* 124, no. 2 (Spring 1995): 23–54.

75 One of the best and most thoughtful reviews of this subject is David Elkins, *Beyond Sovereignty: Territory and Political Economy in the Twenty First Century* (Toronto: University of Toronto Press, 1995).

76 Peter Drucker, 'The Global Economy and the Nation-State,' *Foreign Affairs* (September/October 1997): 159.

77 Cable, 'The Diminished Nation-State,' 38.

78 Francis Fukuyama, *The End of History and the Last Man* (New York: Free Press, 1992).

79 Lisa Hoecklin, *Managing Cultural Differences: Strategies for Competitive Advantage* (London: Economist Intelligence Unit/Addison Wesley, 1995), 21.

80 Geert Hofstede, *Culture's Consequences: International Differences in Work-Related Values* (London: Sage Publications, 1980).

81 Geert Hofstede, *Cultures and Organizations: Software of the Mind* (London: McGraw Hill, 1991).

82 Michael Bond's questionnaire was designed by Chinese social scientists (Hofstede's survey had been designed by westerners). The Chinese Value Survey was administered to 100 students in 22 countries. The results correlated quite closely to Hofstede's findings, even though Bond did not include uncertainty avoidance, and added Confucian dynamism, which Hofstede referred to as long-term vs. short-term orientation. The article discussing the survey's findings can be found under this reference: The Chinese Culture Connection (a team of 24 researchers) (1987), 'Chinese values and the search for culture-free dimensions of culture,' *Journal of Cross-Cultural Psychology* 18, no. 2: 143–64.

83 In this study, the IRIC conducted interviews and issued questionnaires to staff in twenty units (entire organizations or parts of organizations assumed to be culturally homogeneous) from five organizations in Denmark and five in the Netherlands. The number of people in each unit varied from 60 to 2,500. The study revealed that while the twenty units showed only slight cultural differences among their members, there were considerable variations in the practices of members.

84 Charles Hampden-Turner and Alfons Trompenaars, *The Seven Cultures of Capitalism* (New York: Doubleday, 1993), 16.
85 Hampden-Turner and Trompenaars also published *Riding the Waves of Culture. Understanding Cultural Diversity in Global Business* (New York: McGraw Hill, 1993, 1998), which looks at managing in the global multi-cultural business community of the 1990s.
86 A few examples include Allan Goldman, *Doing Business with the Japanese* (New York: State University of New York Press, 1994); Mark Zimmerman, *How to Do Business with the Japanese* (Tokyo: Tuttle, 1985); Jared Tayor, *Shadows of the Rising Sun: A Critical View of the Japanese Miracle* (Tokyo: Tuttle, 1993); Robert Christopher, *The Japanese Mind* (New York: Fawcett Columbine, 1984); Robert Dore, *Taking Japan Seriously: A Confucian Perspective on Leading Economic Issues* (London: Athlone Press, 1987).
87 Canadian examples include Allan Smith, *Canadian Culture, the Canadian State and the New Continentalism* (Orono: University of Maine, 1990); Andrew Fenton Cooper, ed., *Canadian Culture: International Dimensions* (Toronto: Centre on Foreign Policy and Federation, 1985), which examines Canadian efforts at cultural diplomacy; Duncan Cornell Card, *Canada-U.S. Free Trade and Canadian Cultural Sovereignty* (Victoria: Institute for Research on Public Policy, 1987); W.L. Morton, *The Canadian Identity* (Toronto: University of Toronto Press, 1972), which attempts to state "the character of Canadian nationhood in its peculiarly intimate association with the Commonwealth of Nations and the United States of America"; and the amusing Mervyn J. Huston, *Canada Eh to Zed: A Further Contribution to the Continuing Quest for the Elusive Canadian Identity* (Edmonton: Hurtig Publishers, 1973). New Zealand examples include David Novitz and Bill Willmott, *Culture and Identity in New Zealand* (Wellington: GP Books, 1989); Keith Sinclair, *A Destiny Apart: New Zealand's Search for National Identity* (Wellington: Allen and Unwin, 1986); Gordon McLauchlan, *The Passionless People* (Auckland: Cassell New Zealand, 1976). Australian examples include Charles Price, ed., *Australian National Identity* (Canberra: Academy of the Social Sciences in Australia, 1991); Donald Horne, *The Lucky Country* (Sydney: Penguin Books, 1964); Vance Palmer, *The Legend of the Nineties* (Melbourne: Melbourne University Press, 1954); John McLaren, ed., *A Nation Apart: Personal Views of Australia in the Eighties* (Sydney: Longman Cheshire Publishers, 1983); Robin Boyd, *The Australian Ugliness* (Victoria: Penguin Books, 1963); Ian Craven, ed., *Australian Popular Culture* (Cambridge: Press Syndicate of the University of Cambridge, 1994), which includes a chapter called "A brief cultural history of vegemite"!
88 Porter and the Monitor Company, *Canada at the Crossroads*, 283.
89 Jenny Stewart, *The Lie of the Level Playing Field: Industrial Policy and Australia's Future* (Melbourne: The Text Publishing Company, 1994), 217.

90 Ian Marsh, *Beyond the Two Party System: Political Representation, Economic Competitiveness and Australian Politics* (Cambridge: Cambridge University Press, 1995), 185.
91 Ibid., 183.
92 Rosabeth Moss Kanter, *World Class – Thriving Locally in the Global Economy* (New York: Simon & Schuster, 1995), 23.
93 Ibid., 127.
94 The American expansion was not without its difficulties, including a steady escalation in the U.S. trade deficit and an increase in the value of the U.S. dollar relative to almost all of the world's major currencies, a development that hindered American exporters.

CHAPTER TWO

1 Tom Larkin, 'Japan: Changing Problems' in John Henderson, Keith Jackson, and Richard Kennaway, eds., *Beyond New Zealand: The Foreign Policy of a Small State* (Auckland: Methuen, 1980).
2 Gavan McCormack, 'The Australia-Japan Relationship – The First Hundred Years' in G. McCormack, ed., *Bonsai Australia Banzai: Multifunctionpolis and the Making of a Special Relationship with Japan* (Leichhardt, NSW: Pluto Press, 1991), 15.
3 This section on Canada-Japan relations is drawn from Carin Holroyd and Ken Coates, *Pacific Partners: The Japanese Presence in Canadian Business, Society, and Culture* (Toronto: James Lorimer and Company, 1996). Also useful in providing an overview to Canada-Japan relations before 1985 are Klaus Pringsheim, *Neighbours Across the Pacific: The Development of Economic and Political Relations Between Canada and Japan* (Westport: Greenwood Press, 1983) and Frank Langdon, *The Politics of Canadian-Japanese Economic Relations, 1952–1983* (Vancouver: UBC Press, 1983).
4 Canada sent 36.7% of its exports to the U.S. and 31.5% to the United Kingdom in the same year. The figures for its third- and fourth-ranked export partners, Germany and the Netherlands, were only slightly higher than Japan.
5 David Edgington, *Japanese Direct Investment in Canada: Recent Trends and Prospects* (Vancouver: University of British Columbia, Department of Geography, 1992).
6 Canada maintained a trade surplus with Japan through this period, except for 1920 and 1921, when a short term rise in the silk trade temporarily boosted Japan's trade figures.
7 Pringsheim, *Neighbours Across the Pacific*, 195–6.
8 Maarten Wevers, *Japan, Its Future, and New Zealand* (Wellington: Institute of Policy Studies, University of Victoria), 1988.
9 Information supplied by Dr Ken McNeil, 4 September 1997.

10 Wevers, *Japan, Its Future, and New Zealand*, 113.
11 Dr Ken McNeil, 4 September 1997.
12 Larkin, 'Japan: Changing Problems.'
13 Wevers, *Japan, Its Future, and New Zealand.*
14 M.P. Lissington, *New Zealand and Japan 1900–1941* (Wellington: New Zealand Government Printer, 1972), 126
15 Ibid.
16 Ibid., 125–6.
17 Ibid.
18 Wevers, *Japan, Its Future, and New Zealand.*
19 Lissington, *New Zealand and Japan*, 125–35.
20 Ibid.
21 Ann Trotter, *New Zealand and Japan 1945-52: The Occupation and the Peace Treaty* (London: Athlone Press, 1990), 117, 175.
22 Ibid., 175; MFAT, *Report on and Analysis of External Trade Statistics of New Zealand 1949–52.*
23 Trotter, *New Zealand and Japan 1945–52.*
24 MFAT, *Report on and Analysis of External Trade Statistics of New Zealand 1949–52.*
25 Trotter, *New Zealand and Japan 1945–52.*
26 MFAT, *Report on and Analysis of External Trade Statistics of New Zealand 1962–63* and *1963-64.*
27 New Zealand Centre for Japanese Studies, *Japan and New Zealand Historical Connections*, Proceedings of a Colloquium held in Wellington, 20 February 1997, 13.
28 MFAT, *Report on and Analysis of External Trade Statistics for the Year 1961.*
29 Larkin, 'Japan: Changing Problems,' 190.
30 Ibid., 191.
31 BIE, *Australia and New Zealand in Asia – an analysis of changes in the relative importance of Australia and New Zealand as suppliers of goods to East Asia, 1970–1980* (Canberra: Australian Government Publishing Service, 1984), 58–9.
32 Larkin, 'Japan: Changing Problems,' 191.
33 Wevers, *Japan, Its Future, and New Zealand*, 183.
34 Ibid.
35 Ibid., 186.
36 For an overview of Australia's political approaches to Japan, see Alan Rix, ed., *The Australia-Japan Political Alignment, 1952 to the Present* (Canberra: AJRC, 1978) and Alan Rix, *Coming to Terms: The Politics of Australia's Trade with Japan, 1945 to 1957* (Canberra: AJRC, 1986).
37 D.C.S. Sissons, 'Immigration in Australian-Japanese Relations, 1871–1971' in J.A.A. Stockwin, ed., *Japan and Australia in the Seventies* (Sydney: Angus and Robertson, 1972), 193.

38 Ibid., 193.

39 Five nuns from Sydney's Society of the Sacred Heart are some of the most well-known missionaries and are particularly noted for the schools they built. *Episodes: A Glimpse of Australia-Japan Relations 1859–1979*, produced by Eric White Associates under the auspices of the Embassy of Japan in Australia, 4.

40 Sissons, 'Immigration in Australian-Japanese Relations,' 194.

41 *Episodes: A Glimpse of Australia-Japan Relations 1859–1979*, 5.

42 Ibid., 7.

43 Ibid.

44 David Abe and Ted Wheelwright, 'Japanese Global Economic Strategies and Australia' in *Bonsai Australia Banzai*, 76.

45 T.B. Millar, *Australia's Foreign Policy* (Sydney: Angus and Robertson Ltd., 1968), 325–31.

46 'Natural Partners – Australia and Japan: Past, Present and Future,' Address by the Hon. Alexander Downer, MP, Minister for Foreign Affairs, to the 20th Australia Japan Relations Symposium, Canberra, 26 May 1997 (www.dfat.gov.au/media/speeches/foreign/1997/downer_ajrs.html).

47 Shinobu Ohe, 'Future City Planning: The Japanese Experience and the MFP' in *Bonsai Australia Banzai*, 88.

48 Abe and Wheelwright, 'Japanese Global Economic Strategies,' 77.

49 'Natural Partners – Australia and Japan'; and the Australia-Japan Partnership Agenda, 1 August 1997, 1.

50 David Edgington, *Japanese Business Down Under – Patterns of Japanese Investment In Australia* (London: Routledge, 1990), 50.

51 Ibid., 81.

52 Ibid., 82.

53 Ibid., 82.

54 McCormack, 'The Australia-Japan Relationship.'

55 Abe and Wheelwright, 'Japanese Global Economic Strategies,' 76.

56 Edgington, *Japanese Business Down Under*, 82 and *Episodes: A Glimpse of Australia-Japan Relations*, 11.

57 Edgington, *Japanese Business Down Under*, 82.

58 Abe and Wheelwright, 'Japanese Global Economic Strategies,' 76.

59 Ibid., 77.

60 Ibid., 77.

61 Ibid., 51.

62 Australian Bureau of Statistics, *Overseas Trade Australia Part 2: Comparative and Summary Tables 1981–82*.

63 Sir Robert Norman, 'A Growing Complementarity' in *Japanese Investment in Australia* (Canberra: The Australia-Japan Economic Institute, 1971), 13.

64 BIE, *Australia and New Zealand in Asia – an analysis of changes in the relative*

importance of Australia and New Zealand as supplier of goods to East Asia, 1970–1980, 17.

65 The following analysis draws on Edgington, *Japanese Business Down Under*, 54–5. This detailed study of Japanese involvement in the Australian economy provides an informative and reliable overview of economic relations involving the two countries.

66 Ibid., 60–1.

67 Ibid., 55.

68 Ibid., 123–4.

69 Ibid., 141–3.

70 Ibid., 147.

71 Ibid., 128.

72 The politics underlying these economic relations are discussed in Rix, *The Australian-Japan Political Alignment*.

CHAPTER THREE

1   For a study of Japan's economic transformation from Meiji through to World War 11, see E. Herbert Norman, *Japan's Emergence as a Modern State*, edited by Lawrence T. Woods (Vancouver: UBC Press, 2000). For an explanation of how Westerners have traditionally misunderstood Japan's economic transformation, see Patrick Smith, *Japan: A Reinterpretation* (Toronto: Harper Collins, 1997).

2   Takatoshi Ito, *The Japanese Economy* (Massachusettts: The MIT Press, 1994), 65–7.

3   Ibid., 65–7.

4   Edwin Reischauer, *The Japanese Today* (Cambridge, MA: Belknap Press, 1988), 114.

5   Ibid., 115. For an excellent study of Japan's post-war economic resurgence, see John Dower, *Embracing Defeat: Japan in the Wake of World War II* (New York: W.W. Norton, 1999).

6   Reischauer, *The Japanese Today*, 118.

7   For an overview of Japan's economic changes from a Canadian viewpoint, see Richard Wright, 'Japan's Post-Bubble Economic Changes: Implications for the United States and Canada' in Michael Fry et al., eds., *The North Pacific Triangle: The United States, Japan and Canada at Century's End* (Toronto: University of Toronto Press, 1998).

8   Economic Trends, *Japan Economic Almanac 1996*.

9   Taggart Murphy, *The Weight of the Yen: How Denial Imperils America's Future and Ruins an Alliance* (New York: W.W. Norton & Company, 1996), 195.

10 Ibid., 196.

11 Eamonn Fingleton, *Blindside: Why Japan is On Track to Overtake the US by the Year 2000* (New York: Houghton Mifflin, 1993), 288.

12 Ibid., 289.
13 Murphy, *The Weight of the Yen*, 199.
14 Fingleton, *Blindside*, 290. Eamonn Fingleton, Tokyo, Japan, conversation with author, 19 November 1997.
15 Murphy, *The Weight of the Yen*, 199–200.
16 Paul Bowles and Brian MacLean, 'Regional Blocs: Can Japan be the Leader?' in Robert Boyer and Daniel Routledge, eds., *States and Markets: The Limits to Globalization* (The Nikkei Weekly, Tokyo 1990), 159.
17 Isaya Shimizu, 'Overseas Investment,' *Japan Economic Almanac 1990*, 42–3.
18 Hideshi Shirae, 'Production Flees Abroad as dollar crashes through ¥100 floor,' *Japan Economic Almanac 1995*, 16–17.
19 Hidenaka Kato, "Strong yen weakens manufacturers, may hollow industrial base," *Japan Economic Almanac 1994*, 22.
20 Kiyohiko Fukushima and C.H. Kwan, 'Foreign Direct Investment and Regional Industrial Restructuring in Asia' in *The New Wave of Foreign Direct Investment in Asia* (Singapore: Nomura Research Institute and Institute of Southeast Asian Studies, 1995), 3.
21 Hideaki Ohta, Akihiro Tokuno, and Ritsuko Takeuchi, 'Evolving Foreign Investment Strategies of Japanese Firms in Asia' in *The New Wave of Foreign Direct Investment in Asia*, 44.
22 Fukushima and Kwan, 'Foreign Direct Investment,' 8.
23 This theory is referred to as the "flying geese pattern of development" and was first put forward by Japanese economist Akamatsu Kaname.
24 Ohta, Tokuno, and Takeuchi, 'Evolving Foreign Investment,' 46.
25 Shirae, "Production Flees Abroad," 16–17.
26 Ohta, Tokuno, and Takeuchi, 'Evolving Foreign Investment,' 56.
27 *Japan Economic Almanac 1995*, 103.
28 Compiled from Nikkei Publications. 'Makers seek to add machine value as market shrinks for 2nd Year,' *Japan Economic Almanac 1995*, 102.
29 Fingleton, *Blindside*, 297–8. Fingleton, conversation, 19 November 1997.
30 Ibid., 299.
31 Toru Hirose, 'Growth seen in industrial items, but consumer goods still failing,' *Japan Economic Almanac 1995*, 78; Fingleton, *Blindside*, 299.
32 *Nippon: a charted survey of Japan 1994/95*, edited by the Tsuneta Yano Memorial Society, 73.
33 James Lambert, 'Japan's Changing Marketplace: Japan's Major Trading Partners' in *Doing Business in Japan*, The Canadian Chamber of Commerce in Japan (Toronto: Key Porter Books Ltd., 1994), 28.
34 Ron Wickes and Aldith Graves, *The Japanese Market for Manufactures Imports: The Door Opens Wider*, East Asia Analytical Unit Working Paper No. 1, Department of Foreign Affairs and Trade, Australia 1993, 7–8.

35 Ibid., 2.

36 Conversations with embassy staff, Canadian embassy, Tokyo, Japan, 23 September 1997.

37 Lambert, 'Japan's Changing Marketplace,' 31

38 Toshinori Dozen, 'Economic Outlook – Healthy once more – Japan's Economy swings back into gear,' *Japan Economic Almanac 1988*, 5.

39 Kenneth S. Courtis, 'Japan in the 1990s: To Still Higher Levels of Performance' in *Doing Business in Japan: An Insider's Guide*, 8.

40 Ichiro Sasaki, 'High-performance, status products find buyers; other markets still slow,' *Japan Economic Almanac 1996*, 146 and 'Digital TV makes debut; wider use expected in 2000s,' *Japan Economic Almanac 1999*, 86.

41 Ibid.

42 This section describing Japanese products and services follows Carin Holroyd and Ken Coates, *Pacific Partners: The Japanese Presence in Canadian Business, Society, and Culture* (Toronto: James Lorimer and Company, 1996), ch. 9.

43 Leonard Koren, *283 Useful Ideas from Japan* (San Francisco: Chronicle Books, 1988).

44 Ibid.

45 Ibid.

46 Douglas Bingeman, speech in the 'Atlantic Canada Products for Japan' edited conference proceedings, New Brunswick, 9 October 1996.

47 Glen S. Fukushima, 'Economic Trends, Internationalisation and Deregulation' in Gerald Paul McAlinn, ed., *The Business Guide to Japan* (Singapore: Reed Academic Publishing Asia, 1996), 22–3.

48 Marie Anchordoguy, *Computers Inc: Japan's Challenge to IBM* (Cambridge: Harvard University Press, 1989), 5.

49 Fukushima, 'Economic Trends,' 20.

50 Richard Wright, 'New Hope But Modest Progress on Japanese Deregulation,' *Canada-Japan Trade Council Newsletter*, March–April 1995, 1.

51 *Canada-Japan Trade Council Newsletter*, January–February 1997, 1.

52 Ibid.

53 'Making Deregulation Happen,' Keidanren website: http://keidanren.or.jp./english/journal/jou005.html.

54 Book titles have run the gamut from Ezra Vogel's *Japan as Number One*, Clyde Prestowitz's *Trading Places: How We Are Giving Our Future to Japan and How to Reclaim it*, Eamonn Fingleton's *Blindside: How Japan is On Track to Overtake the US by the Year 2000* to Jon Wornoff's *Japan as – anything but – Number One*, Brian Reading's *Japan: the Coming Collapse*, and Bill Emott's *The Sun Also Sets*.

55 Asahi Shinbun, *Japan Almanac 2001*, 272.

56 *Japan 2000: An International Comparison*, Keizai Koho Center, 30.

57 *Nippon 2000 Business Facts and Figures,* Japan External Trade Organization, 2000, 152.

58 Fingleton, *Blindside,* 68–75.

59 JETRO website:
    http://www.jetro.go.jp/it/e/pub/whitepaper/trade2000/tra1-6.html

60 JETRO website:
    http://www.jetro.go.jp/it/e/pub/whitepaper/trade1997/tra1-6.html

61 Leon Hollerman, *Japan's Economic Strategy in Brazil: Challenge for the United States* (Lexington: Lexington Books, 1988), 11.

62 Roger Boisvert, 'Doing High Technology Business in Japan.' Presentation sponsored by Ladner Downs and Deloitte Touche, Vancouver, 1998.

CHAPTER FOUR

1 Minister of Supply and Services Canada, *Canada's International Business Strategy 1996–97 Overview,* 3.

2 Michael E. Porter and the Monitor Company, *Canada at the Crossroads: The Reality of the New Competitive Environment* (Ottawa: BCNI), 5–6.

3 Porter and the Monitor Company, *Canada at the Crossroads,* 5–6.

4 Kimon Valaskakis, *Canada in the Nineties: Meltdown or Renaissance?* (Ottawa: The Gamma Institute Press, 1980), 61.

5 Ibid., 63.

6 DFAIT, *Canada's Action Plan for Japan 1996,* 1.

7 Ibid., 1.

8 The provinces are British Columbia, Alberta, Saskatchewan, Manitoba, Ontario, Quebec, New Brunswick, Nova Scotia, Prince Edward Island, and Newfoundland. The territories are the Yukon, the Northwest Territories, and Nunavut. The territories have less autonomy than do the provinces.

9 The Department of External Affairs became the Department of Foreign Affairs and International Trade on 12 November 1993.

10 http://www.dfait-maeci.gc.ca/english/infoweb/mandate.htm

11 http://www.ic.gc.ca/ic-data/ic-eng.html

12 Memo from Robert Collette, DFAIT, 12 November 1996.

13 Ibid.

14 Tony Clarke and Maude Barlow, *MAI: The Multilateral Agreement on Investment and the Threat to Canadian Sovereignty* (Toronto: Stoddart Books, 1997), 22, 36, 57.

15 Minister of Supply and Services Canada, *Canada's International Business Strategy 1996–97 Overview.*

16 Robert W. Eberschlag, Trade Policy Planning Division, DFAIT, letter to author, 18 March 1996.

17 Ibid.

18 Jennifer Rosebrugh, deputy director, Trade Planning and Coordination Division, DFAIT, e-mail to author, December 1996.

28 Minister of Supply and Services Canada, *Canada's International Business Strategy 1996–97 Overview*, 3.

19 'Team Canada: Working Toward Canadian Success in International Markets,' Address by the Honourable Roy MacLaren, Minister for International Trade, to the 52nd Annual meeting of the Canadian Exporters' Association. 2 October 1995, 2.

20 *International Business Development Review Report*, submitted to the Honourable Roy MacLaren, Minister for International Trade, 30 September 1994, 1.

21 Alan Virtue, DFAIT, letter to author, 16 January 1997.

22 *International Business Development Review Report*, 3.

23 Ibid., 5.

24 Virtue, letter to author, 29 January 1997.

25 Ibid.

26 Ibid.

27 The IBDR report was submitted on 30 September 1994 and the Team Canada initiatives were announced on 2 October 1995.

28 Minister of Supply and Services Canada, *Canada's International Business Strategy 1996–97 Overview*, 3.

29 John Skeggs, DFAIT, letter to author, 13 December 1996.

30 'Team Canada: Working Toward Canadian Success in International Markets,' 1.

31 Rosebrugh, interview with author, 11 October 1996.

32 Maurice J. Hladik, director of Trade Coordination and Advisory Committees Secretariat, DFAIT, telephone conversation with author, 14 April 1997.

33 Rosebrugh, interview.

34 Skeggs, letter to author.

35 Government of Canada Memorandum of Understanding, Canada-Northwest Territories Cooperation, March 1996.

36 Skeggs, letter to author.

37 Government of Canada, 'International Business Development – Team Canada,' n.d.

38 Skeggs, letter to author.

39 Rosebrugh, interview.

40 Ibid.

41 Canada, DFAIT, *Canada's International Business Plan*, 1996 Overview, 22,24, 37. ("Italy offers tremendous potential for Canadian commercial interests ... A small and prosperous country, Austria offers good potential for Canadian business interests ... While South Asia has not been a traditional market for Canadian goods, services and investment, this situation

is rapidly changing.")

42 'Team Canada: Working Toward Canadian Success in International Markets.'

43 Patricia Cronin, Japan Division, DFAIT, interview with author, 10 October 1996.

44 'Team Canada, Working Toward Canadian Success in International Markets,' 4.

45 *International Business Development Review Report*, 8.

46 Bruce Christie, Japan Division, DFAIT, interview with author, 10 October 1996.

47 'Canada's Regional Program in Japan,' Ni-Ka Online. http://www.dfait-maeci.gc.ca/ni-ka/offices/regnprg-e.as

48 Minister of Supply and Services Canada, *Investing and Doing Business with Canada* (Ottawa: Prospectus Inc., 1996), 60.

49 Ibid., 61.

50 Statistics Canada, *Canada's International Investment Position 1994 Catalogue 67–202*.

51 For a very good overview of changes to Japan's pattern of investment in Canada, see David Edgington, "Japanese Direct Investment in Canada: Patterns and Prospects" in Michael Fry et al., eds., *The North Pacific Triangle: The United States, Japan and Canada at Century's End* (Toronto: University of Toronto Press, 1998), 18–105.

52 Carin Holroyd and Ken Coates, *Pacific Partners* (Toronto: James Lorimer and Company, 1996), 134.

53 Although table 4.1 and 4.2 were both drawn from Statistics Canada material, the statistics reported by Statistics Canada were not consistent.

54 Japan Automobile Manufacturers Association, *JAMA Canada Annual Report 1996*, 5.

55 Ibid., 4.

56 *Canada-Japan Trade Council Newsletter*, January–February 1997, 6.

57 *The Globe and Mail*, 24 December 1997, B1.

58 Larry Pratt and Ian Urquhart, *The Last Great Forest: Japanese Multinationals and Alberta's Northern Forests* (Edmonton: NewWest Publishers Ltd, 1994), 86.

59 Pratt and Urquhart, *The Last Great Forest*, 151.

60 *Canada-Japan Trade Council Newsletter*, January–February 1997, 6.

61 Stephanie LeBlond, 'Trends in Japanese Foreign Direct Investment to the year 2000,' Canadian embassy, Japan, 1994, 14.

62 Ibid., executive summary.

63 Ibid., 14.

64 Koichiro Ejiri, Speech to the Canadian Chamber of Commerce in Japan in *Canadian* (The Canadian Chamber of Commerce in Japan Journal) 10, Issue 1 (winter 1997): 30.

65 Ibid., 32.
66 *Canada-Japan Trade Council Newsletter*, November–December 1996, 10.
67 Ibid., 11.
68 The best evidence of this is Shintaro Ishihara, *The Japan That Can Say No: Why Japan will be First Among Equals* (New York: Simon and Schuster, 1991).
69 Ministry of Supply and Services Canada, *A Review of Canadian Trade Policy* (Ottawa: Ministry of Supply and Services, 1983), 218.
70 Statistics Canada, *International Trade Division, Exports by User Defined Groupings to Japan 1995.*
71 Klaus Pringsheim, 'Canada's Processed Food Trade with Japan (1995–96),' in *Canada-Japan Trade Council Newsletter*, May–June 1997, 2.
72 Statistics Canada, *International Trade Division, Exports by User Defined Groupings to Japan 1995.*
73 DFAIT, *Canada Export* 14, no. 4 (March 4, 1996): 1.
74 John Tak, B.C. Trade and Investment Office, interview with author, Tokyo, June 1996.
75 Jim Anholt, Japan representative, Government of B.C., interview with author, Tokyo, 6 October 1997.
76 Ibid.
77 David Beardsall, director of the Economic Section, Délégation Générale du Québec, interview with author, Tokyo, 23 October 1997.
78 Asia Pacific Foundation of Canada, *Canada Asia Review 1997*, 9.
79 Peter Campbell, consul general, Osaka, Japan, interview with author, November 1997.
80 Cronin, interview.
81 Holroyd and Coates, *Pacific Partners*, ch. 7.
82 J.M. Lambert and M. Taylor, *Penetrating the Japanese Value-Added Marketplace: Strategies and National Approaches of Canada's Competitors*, Canadian Embassy Report, September 1992, executive summary. The embassy and DFAIT's Japan Division initiated *Canada's Action Plan for Japan.*
83 James M. Lambert,'Japan's Changing Marketplace: A Survey of Japan's Major Trading Partners' in *Doing Business in Japan – An Insider's Guide*, Canadian Chamber of Commerce in Japan, 1994, 26.
84 Lambert and Taylor, *Penetrating the Japanese Value-Added Marketplace*, executive summary.
85 Ibid.
86 Peter Campbell, consul general, Osaka, Japan, letter to author, 28 February 1997.
87 DFAIT, *Canada's Action Plan for Japan*, November 1995, introduction.
88 Campbell, letter.
89 DFAIT, *Canada's Action Plan for Japan*, January 1994, introduction.
90 Campbell, letter.

91 DFAIT, *Canada's Action Plan for Japan*, November 1995, introduction.
92 Pringsheim, 'Canada's Processed Food Trade with Japan,' 4.
93 Ibid.
94 Asia Pacific Foundation of Canada, *Canada Asia Review 1997*, 32.
95 For a follow-up report on Canada-Japan Forum 2000, see
    http://www.dfait-maeci.gc.ca/geo/html_documents/cajp2000-e.htm

CHAPTER FIVE

1 "Forex" is an abbreviation of foreign exchange.
2 New Zealand Trade Development Board, *Ten by 2010: A Goal for New Zealand*, May 1990, 10–11.
3 The manner and impact of the shift from a government-directed to private sector-directed economy has been widely debated in New Zealand. For a review of this debate, see Andrew Sharp, ed., *Leap Into the Dark: The Changing Role of the States in New Zealand Since 1984* (Auckland: Auckland University Press, 1994).
4 Peter McKinlay, *Redistribution of Power? Devolution in New Zealand* (Wellington: Institute of Policy Studies, 1990).
3 Graham T. Crocombe, Michael J. Enright, and Michael E. Porter, *Upgrading New Zealand's Competitive Advantage* (Oxford: Oxford University Press, 1991), 143.
6 Roger Kerr, "The Business Experience of Economic Reform in New Zealand," Speech to the Japan/New Zealand Business Council 23rd Joint Meeting, 17 October 1996.
7 The New Zealand Treasury Department's analysis and comments on the economic issues that faced New Zealand in 1984 are contained in a document entitled *Economic Management*, published by the Treasury in July 1984.
8 McKinlay, *Redistribution of Power?* 12.
9 Brian Easton, *The Commercialisation of New Zealand* (Auckland: Auckland University Press, 1997), 26.
10 Rick Christie, quoted in the New Zealand Trade Development Board's *New Zealand in the Global Marketplace*, August 1992, 2.
11 McKinlay, *Redistribution of Power?* 9.
12 This perspective was confirmed through interviews with over ten Wellington-based senior civil servants and five Japan-based consular officials between 1995 and 1997.
13 From 1943 to 1970, this department was called the Department of External Affairs. In 1970, it became the Ministry of Foreign Affairs, which it remained until 1988 when it was amalgamated with the International Trade Relations Division of the Department of Trade and Industry and renamed the Ministry of External Relations and Trade. The department

assumed its current name in 1993. Ministry of Foreign Affairs and Trade, *A Guide to the Ministry*, 4.

14 Richard Nottage, secretary of Foreign Affairs and Trade, interview with author, 5 September 1997.

15 New Zealand Trade Development Board, *Ten by 2010: A Goal for New Zealand*, May 1990, 1.

16 New Zealand Trade Development Board, *The Strategy for the New Zealand Trade Development Board*, May 1990, 2.

17 Nottage, interview.

18 The comment comes from a New Zealand civil servant who asked not to be identified.

19 Sandra Williams, To'aiga Su'a-Huira, and Colin Campbell-Hunt, TRADENZ: *Building a state agency for export development*, Case Research Publication CRP1/95 (Wellington: The Victoria University of Wellington Printers, 1995), 22.

20 John Arathimos, executive officer, Foreign Direct Investment Advisory Group, Tradenz, letter to author, 18 March 1997.

21 http://www.mft.govt.nz/Guide/function.htm

22 MFAT, *Corporate Plan 1995–96* (Wellington: MFAT, 1995), 12.

23 MFAT, *New Zealand Trade Policy: Implementation and Directions: A Multi-Track Approach* (Wellington: MFAT, 1993), vi.

24 Ibid., viii.

25 Ibid., iii.

26 Ibid., iv.

27 The Cairns group refers to the agricultural policy section of the Uruguay Round talks aimed at updating the GATT.

28 Williams, Su'a-Huira, and Campbell-Hunt, TRADENZ, 1–3.

29 New Zealand Trade Development Board, *Ten by 2010: A Goal for New Zealand*, May 1990, 3.

30 Ibid., 1.

31 Tradenz, *Report of the Review Committee on Tradenz* (Wellington, Tradenz, 1994), 5.

32 New Zealand Trade Development Board, *Growth Through Forex – Brief to the Incoming Government*, November 1990, 34.

33 Ifor Ffowcs Williams, 'Hard and Soft Networks: Helping Firms Co-operate for Future Growth,' *New Zealand Strategic Management* Summer 1996, 32.

34 Williams, Su'a-Huira, and Campbell-Hunt, TRADENZ, 7–9.

35 7–9

36 Eugene Bowen, senior trade commissioner (Japan) and regional manager, Tradenz, interview with author, 27 October 1997.

37 New Zealand Trade Development Board, *New Zealand in the Global Marketplace* (Wellington: New Zealand Trade Development Board, 1992), 6.

38 Tradenz, *Report of the Review Committee on Tradenz*, 26.

39 *New Zealand in the Global Marketplace* (1992), *Stretching for Growth* (1993), and *Stretching for Growth – Two Years into an Eight Year Journey* (1995).

40 Bowen, interview.

41 Rick Christie, quoted in the New Zealand Trade Development Board's *New Zealand in the Global Marketplace*, August 1992, 2.

42 Ifor Ffowcs Williams, general manager, Strategic Development Unit, Tradenz, interview with author, 12 March 1997.

43 Tradenz, *Competing in the New Millenium* (Wellington: Tradenz, 1997), 1.

44 Michael E. Porter, *The Competitive Advantage of Nations* (New York: The Free Press, 1990).

45 Ibid., 620. Italics in original.

46 Crocombe, Enwright, and Porter, *Upgrading New Zealand's Competitive Advantage*.

47 New Zealand Trade Development Board, *New Zealand in the Global Marketplace*, 13

48 Crocombe, Enwright, and Porter, *Upgrading New Zealand's Competitive Advantage*, 177.

49 Asia 2000 focuses on increasing awareness of Asia in New Zealand. Among other activities, Asia 2000 assists New Zealand journalists to visit countries in the Asian region, offers trade and investment seminars to help New Zealand business people establish contacts in Asia, organizes Asia 2000 week for the community at large, and works to increase the study of Asia (including Asian languages) in New Zealand schools and universities.

50 Nottage, interview.

51 Douglas Myers, Chairman of the New Zealand Business Roundtable, "The Role of Government in the Business Sector," MBA Programme 1992 Contemporary Issues Lecture, University of Canterbury, 30 October 1992.

52 Ibid.

53 This was the definition offered by Douglas Graham, minister of justice and long-time National Party cabinet minister, in a November 1998 discussion.

54 Ministry of Foreign Affairs and Trade, *Corporate Plan 1995-96*, 6.

55 Pat Colgate and Kathryn Featherstone, 'Changing Patterns of Foreign Direct Investment in the Pacific Region: New Zealand Country Paper,' *Report to PECC* (Wellington: New Zealand Institute of Economic Research, May 1992), 3.

56 Ibid., 3.

57 'Japanese investment likely to halve as boom-year growth subsides,' *The National Business Review*, 24 July 1992, 2.

58 Roger Peren in the introduction to Ian Duncan, "Foreign Direct Invest-

ment Benefits and Costs," New Zealand Centre for Japanese Studies, Working Paper No. 5, November 1992.

59 R.D. Cremer and B. Ramasamy, *Tigers in New Zealand? The Role of Asian Investment in the Economy* (Wellington: The Institute of Policy Studies, 1996), 1.

60 Published data on direct foreign investment in New Zealand is difficult to find and often requires the use of data supplied by the investor countries.

61 Brian Easton, *The Commercialisation of New Zealand*, 120.

62 Daniel Riordan, "Who is Left to Lead Corporate New Zealand?" *Sunday Star Times*, 3 May 1998, D1–2.

63 "Foreigners own more than many realise," *Sunday Star Times*, 3 May 1998, D5.

64 Ian Kennedy, *Japan and New Zealand: Adding Value* (Wellington: Institute of Policy Studies, 1992), 186.

65 Cremer and Ramasamy, *Tigers in New Zealand?* 64.

66 Nottage, interview.

67 Japan/New Zealand Business Council, *Japanese Direct Investment in New Zealand* (Wellington: Japan New Zealand Business Council, 1990), 3.

68 "Japanese investment likely to halve," 2.

69 Ibid.

70 Jim McCrea, managing director of Air New Zealand, in a speech entitled "The Direction of Expanding Trade and Investment between Japan and New Zealand, and Cooperation in Third Markets," given to the 22nd Meeting of the Japan/New Zealand Business Council, October 1995.

71 Richard Le Heron and Eric Pawson, eds., *Changing Places – New Zealand in the Nineties* (Auckland: Longman Paul Ltd., 1996), 37.

72 Masahiko Ebashi, *Japanese Direct Investment in New Zealand* (New Zealand Institute of Economic Research, 1993), 9.

73 Comments received from Roger Peren, New Zealand Centre for Japanese Studies, Massey University, 24 June 1997.

74 Japan/New Zealand Business Council, *Japanese Direct Investment in New Zealand* (Wellington: Japan/New Zealand Business Council, 1990), 32.

75 Ibid., 34

76 Cremer and Ramasamy, *Tigers in New Zealand?* 91.

77 Tradenz, *New Zealand – A Wealth of Opportunities*, March 1997.

78 Tradenz, *New Zealand – Regions of Opportunities*, July 1997.

79 Information provided by Tradenz.

80 Nils Holm, New Zealand embassy, Tokyo, interview with author, June 1996.

81 J.M. Lambert and M. Taylor, *Penetrating the Japanese Value-Added Marketplace: Strategies and National Approaches of Canada's Competitors*, Canadian embassy report, September 1992.

82　Ifor Ffowcs Williams, general manager, Tradenz, interview with author, 12 March 1997.

83　Jeremy Rifkin, *The End of Work* (New York: Putnam Publishing Group, 1995), 109.

84　William Knoke, *Bold New World: The Essential Road Map to the Twenty-First Century* (New York: Kodansha International, 1996), 66–7.

85　Eugene Bowen, 'The Japanese Imported Fruit and Vegetable Market, 1997,' Tradenz Tokyo Market Research, unpublished paper, 1.

86　Ibid., 2.

87　Klaus Pringsheim, 'Canada's Processed Food Trade with Japan (1995–96),' *Canada-Japan Trade Council Newsletter*, May–June 1997, 2.

88　Colin James, *New Territory: The Transformation of New Zealand 1984–92* (Wellington: Bridget Williams Books Limited, 1992), 297–8.

89　Bowen, 'The Japanese Imported Fruit and Vegetable Market,' 2.

90　Ibid., 6.

91　Bowen, interview.

92　Ibid.

93　John Jenner, deputy chief executive officer, Tradenz, interview with author, 5 September 1997.

94　Roger Peren, director, New Zealand Centre for Japanese Studies, Massey University, e-mail to author, 24 June 1997.

95　Michael Porter speaking at a Trade Development Board function, as quoted in the *New Zealand Education Review*, 16 April 1997.

96　Ibid.

CHAPTER SIX

1　Ian Marsh, *Beyond the Two Party System: Political Representation, Economic Competitiveness and Australian Politics* (Cambridge: Cambridge University Press, 1995), 135.

2　John Keniry, 'An Exportable Feast: Towards a Sectoral Policy for an Export Oriented Food Processing Industry' in Ian Marsh, ed., *Australian Business in the Asia Pacific Region: The Case for Strategic Industry Policy* (Sydney: Longman Professional Publishing, 1994), 237.

3　Michael Pusey, *Economic Rationalism in Canberra: A Nation-Building State Changes its Mind* (Cambridge: Cambridge University Press, 1991), 7.

4　Foreign Investment Review Board website: http://www.treasury.gov.au/organizations/fibr/PolicyAll.html#general.

5　Ibid. In 1997–98 Australia's foreign investment policy was under review.

6　Australian Department of Foreign Affairs and Trade website: http://www.dfat.gov.au.

7　BIE, *Evaluation of the Investment Promotion and Facilitation Program* (Canberra: Australia Government Publishing Service, 1996), xiii.

8 Australian Department of Foreign Affairs and Trade website:
   http://www.dfat.gov.au.
9 Austrade website: http://www.austrade.gov.au.
10 *Australian Trade Commission Annual Report 1994–95*, 12–13.
11 Ibid., 34.
12 Peter Harrison, manager of the Austrade Export Network Centre in Melbourne, letter to author, 7 July 1998.
13 Commonwealth of Australia, *Trade Outcomes and Objectives Statement* (Canberra: Commonwealth of Australia, 1997), 17.
14 Ibid., 17–18.
15 Speech by the minister for foreign affairs, Bill Hayden, at the ninth Australia-Japan ministerial committee in Canberra on 8 January 1987, in
   AFAR, January 1987, 3.
16 Australian Manufacturing Council, *The Global Challenge: Australian Manufacturing in the 1990s,* Final Report of the Pappas Carter Evans and
   Koop/Telesis Study, July 1990, preface.
17 Ibid.
18 Philip Yetton, Jeremy Davis, and Peter Swan, *Going International: Export
   Myths and Strategic Realities,* Report to the Australian Manufacturing
   Council (Australia: AGSM Limited, 1992), preface.
19 Ibid.
20 David W. Edgington, *Japanese Business Down Under: Patterns of Japanese
   Investment in Australia* (London: Routledge, 1990), 2.
21 East Asia Analytical Unit, Australian Department of Foreign Affairs and
   Trade, *A New Japan? Changes in Asia's Mega Market?* (Canberra: Commonwealth of Australia, 1997), 151.
22 Statement by the minister for industry, technology and commerce,
   Senator John Button, in Hansard, 13 November 1986.
23 Australia-Japan Business Forum, *Report of the AJBF Economic Survey Mission
   to Japan, June 1987: Endaka, A difficult question for Japan and for Australia,*
   28.
24 Jamie Anderson, 'From Sensitivity to Vulnerability: The Emergence of
   Asymmetrical Interdependence in the Australia-Japan Trading Relationship 1983-1996,' MA thesis, University of Melbourne, n.d., ch. 3, 19.
25 Ibid. ch. 3, 7.
26 Leonie Muldoon, minister-counsellor, Austrade, interview with author, 21
   November 1997.
27 Ibid.
28 Ibid.
29 BIE, *Evaluation of the Investment Promotion and Facilitation Program* (Canberra: Australian Government Publishing Service, 1996), xv.
30 Ibid., xiii.
31 Ibid., xiv.

32　Ibid., 57; Anderson, 'From Sensitivity to Vulnerability,' ch. 5, 3.

33　Anderson, 'From Sensitivity to Vulnerability,' ch. 3, 6.

34　Commonwealth Department of Industry, Technology and Regional Development, *Partnership for Development Program*, n.d., 3.

35　Ibid., 42.

36　Australia-Japan Economic Institute, *Economic Bulletin* 4, no. 6 (June 1996), 2.

37　Australia-Japan Economic Institute, *Economic Bulletin* 5, no. 6 (June 1997), 3.

38　Ibid., 3.

39　Peter Drysdale, *Japanese Direct Foreign Investment in Australia in Comparative Perspective*, Pacific Economic Papers, No. 223 (Canberra: Australia-Japan Research Centre, 1993), 22.

40　Australia-Japan Economic Institute, *Economic Bulletin* 4, no. 6 (June 1996), 6.

41　Ibid., 4.

42　Ibid.

43　MFAT, *Country Economic Brief – Japan* (Wellington: MFAT, 1997), 36.

44　Gavan McCormack, 'Coping with Japan: The MFP Proposal and the Australian Response' in G. McCormack, ed., *Bonsai Australia Banzai: Multifunctionpolis and the Making of a Special Relationship with Japan* (Leichhardt, NSW: Pluto Press, 1991), 38.

45　Shinobu Ohe, 'Future City Planning: The Japanese Experience and the MFP' in *Bonsai Australia Banzai*, 85.

46　McCormack, 'Coping with Japan,' 39.

47　Ibid., 44.

48　Ibid., 46.

49　Ibid., 46.

50　Australia Bureau of Statistics, *International Merchandise Trade*, December Quarter 1996, 10–11. (See table 6.7, which, to provide for greater comparability with Canadian and New Zealand tables, reports the trade data in American dollars.)

51　Australian embassy, Tokyo, *Australia-Japan Priority Market Access Issues* (Tokyo: Australian Embassy, 1997), 1.

52　Australia-Japan Economic Institute, *Economic Bulletin* 4, no. 8 (August 1996): 1–3.

54　Ibid., 4.

55　Anderson, 'From Sensitivity to Vulnerability,' ch. 3, 19.

56　Bob Hawke, Speech to the Australian-Japan Cooperation Committee, Canberra, 25 August 1983, in *AFAR*, August 1983, 465.

57　Prime Minister Bob Hawke, Speech to the 12th Australian-Japan Relations Symposium, 23 March 1984.

58　*AFAR*, January 1985, 4.

59 Australian Government Publishing Service, *Persistence, Performance and Price -Report of the Japanese Market Access Promotion Mission to Australia* (Canberra: Australian Government Publishing Service, 1984), 5.

60 Ibid., 7.

61 Report of the Japanese market access promotion mission, *AFAR,* February 1985.

62 Anderson, 'From Sensitivity to Vulnerability,' ch. 2, 5.

63 Australia Japan Business Forum, *Report of the AJBF Economic Survey Mission to Japan,* June 1987, 1.

64 Ibid., vii.

65 Ibid., 21.

66 Ibid., viii.

67 Rawdon Dalrymple, Australian ambassador to Japan, 'The Australian Government's Role in the Relationship with Japan,' Speech to the Australian Chamber of Commerce, Tokyo, 31 January 1991, 8–9.

68 Rawdon Dalrymple, Australian ambassador to Japan, 'Celebrate Australia: Taking a Different Approach,' Speech to the 31st joint meeting of the Japan-Australia and Australia-Japan Business Cooperation Committees, Tokyo, 19 October 1993.

69 Senator Gareth Evans and Senator Peter Cook, Joint Statement, 'Celebrate Australia Campaign Opens in Japan,' News Release, 31 October 1993.

70 Ibid.

71 Ibid.

72 Anderson, 'From Sensitivity to Vulnerability,' ch. 1, 12.

73 Minister for Small Business, Construction and Customs, 'Australian Business Office Set to Take on Japan,' News Release, 8 December 1992.

74 Minister for Trade, 'Australian Business Centre in Tokyo,' Media Release, 14 July 1994.

CHAPTER SEVEN

1 Michael E. Porter and the Monitor Company, *Canada at the Crossroads: The Reality of the New Competitive Environment* (Ottawa: BCNI, Government of Canada, 1991), 317.

2 Jenny Stewart, *The Lie of the Level Playing Field: Industrial Policy and Australia's Future* (Melbourne: The Text Publishing Company, 1994), xv. Leonie Muldoon, minister-counsellor, Austrade, interview with author, 21 November 1997.

3 Michael Pusey, *Economic Rationalism in Canberra: A Nation-Building State Changes its Mind* (Massachusetts: Cambridge University Press, 1991), 30.

4 The New Zealand Treasury Department's analysis and comments on the economic issues facing New Zealand in 1984 are contained in a docu-

ment entitled *Economic Management*, published by the Treasury in July 1984.

5 'Canada's International Trade and Investment: A Summary,' Canadian Department of Foreign Affairs and International Trade website: http://www.dfait-maeci.gc.ca

6 Ibid.

7 Ibid.

8 Asia Pacific Foundation of Canada, *Canada Asia Review 1997* (Vancouver: Asia Pacific Foundation, 1997), 8.

9 Ibid., 30.

10 Ibid., 31.

11 Michael Martin, Canadian embassy, Tokyo, interview with author, 24 June 1996.

12 MFAT, *New Zealand Trade Policy. Implementation and Directions: A Multi-Track Approach* (Wellington: MFAT, 1993), iv, 85.

13 Ibid., 86.

14 MFAT, *New Zealand Trade Policy: Implementation and Directions: A Multi-Track Approach*, 85–6.

15 See ch. 7, 149–50.

16 Takatoshi Ito, *The Japanese Economy* (Massachusetts: The MIT Press, 1992), 196–201.

17 Government funds as a percentage of total research and development are only about 20%. (Victor Argy and Leslie Stein, *The Japanese Economy* [New York: New York University Press, 1997], 95.)

18 Charles Hampden-Turner and Alfons Trompenaars, *The Seven Cultures of Capitalism: Value Systems for Creating Wealth in the United States, Japan, Germany, France, Britain, Sweden, and the Netherlands* (New York, Doubleday, 1993), 193.

19 Thomas M. Huber, *Strategic Economy in Japan* (Boulder: Westview Press, 1994), 115.

20 Leon Hollerman, *Japan Disincorporated: The Economic Liberalization Process* (Stanford: Stanford University Press, 1999), 243–70.

21 Muldoon, interview.

22 Michael E. Porter, *The Competitive Advantage of Nations* (New York: The Free Press, 1990), 677.

23 Kenichi Ohmae, *The Borderless World* (New York: McKinsey & Company, 1990), 193.

24 Stewart, *The Lie of the Level Playing Field*, 48, 56.

25 Australian Bureau of Statistics, *International Merchandise Trade Catalogue 5422*, March, June, September, and December 1985 quarterly reports and December 1997 report.

26 Ibid.

27 Australian Department of Foreign Affairs and Trade website: http://www.dfat.gov.au/geo/na/japan_brief.htm#2, page 2.

CHAPTER EIGHT

1 Linda Weiss, *The Myth of the Powerless State* (Ithaca: Cornell University Press, 1998), 20.
2 Eamonn Fingleton, *Blindside: Why Japan is On Track to Overtake the US by the Year 2000* (New York: Houghton Mifflin, 1993); Taggart Murphy, *The Weight of the Yen: How Denial Imperils America's Future and Ruins an Alliance* (New York: W.W. Norton & Company, 1996).
3 Murphy, *The Weight of the Yen*, 199–200.
4 It is interesting to note that while newspaper articles blame much of B.C.'s forestry woes on declining demand in Japan, this is not wholly accurate. Japanese housing starts rose dramatically in 1995 as consumers tried to beat an increase in the consumption tax. Housing starts now are simply back to levels prior to this blip. At least part of B.C.'s troubles with regard to Japan are due to increased competition from Scandinavia.
5 Jenny Stewart, *The Lie of the Level Playing Field: Industrial policy and Australia's Future* (Melbourne: The Text Publishing Company, 1994), 2.

CHAPTER NINE

1 Labour New Zealand 2000, *Industry Development*, 4–5.
2 Helen Clark, Auckland Trade Centre Address, 26 July 1999.
3 Ibid.
4 Labour New Zealand 2000, *Industry Development*, 6.
5 Ibid.
6 John Gascoigne, "Pocket Nation fights way to top of living standards," *National Business Review*, 22 October 1999, 64.
7 Gordon Campbell, "For Richer or Poorer," *The Listener*, 8 August 1998, 18–21; Bruce Ansley, "Human Values," *The Listener*, 25 March 2000, 16–19.
8 "Route 10 – Following the signposts to a healthy, wealthy and wise New Zealand economy," *The Listener*, 16 October 1999, 17.
9 "Technology key to arresting decline in standards of living," *Export News*, 19 April 1999, 1.
10 Ibid., 3.
11 Michael Cullen, "The State of the New Zealand Economy," speech on 21 July 1999: www.labour.org.nz/Media1/Speeches/99072.htm
12 Ibid.
13 "Joy and Anger Greet Tariff Freeze," *The New Zealand Herald*, 12 April 2000.
14 Colin James, "A Tectonic shift in the political faultline," *The New Zealand Herald*, 29 March 2000.

15 "Joy and Anger Greet Tariff Freeze," *The New Zealand Herald*, 10 May 2000.

16 "Lower exchange rate makes tariff freeze unnecessary," New Zealand National Party Media Release, 14 April 2000.

17 Brian Fallow, "Business wary of Anderton's plans," *New Zealand Herald*, 1 March 2000.

18 Labour New Zealand 2000, *Labour on the Economy*, 5.

19 Ibid., 9.

20 Ibid., 8.

21 Ralph Norris, Chairman, New Zealand Business Roundtable, "Can We Afford to Replay the Economic Past?" Speech to the New Zealand Society of Corporate Treasurers, Auckland, 3 February 2000.

22 Brian Easton, "Value Added," *The Listener*, 25 March 2000, 20–21.

23 Bruce Ansley, "Human Values," *The Listener*, 25 March 2000 16–19.

24 James Weir, "Japan's tough times offer benefits and risks for NZ," *The Dominion*, 11 March 1998, 25.

25 International Monetary Fund, Direction of Trade Statistics (Washington: IMF, 2000).

26 "Top 20 Export Markets," *Export News*, 20 March 2000, 11.

27 "USA now our second largest export market," *Export News*, 31 May 1999, 1.

28 David Barber, "Pickup in Japan Offers Exporters a Lifeline," *National Business Review*, 18 June 1999.

29 David Luff, "The Hanson juggernaut; Poll sends shockwaves around the world," Adelaide *Advertiser*, 15 June 1998.

30 "Surplus removes dead weight to lift economy," *The Canberra Times*, 15 June 1999.
(www.canberratimes.com.au/archives/news/1999/06/15/bus1.shtr)

31 Katharyn Heagney, "Government policy reforms behind Australia's 'miracle economy,'" *The Canberra Times*, 8 October 1999
(www.canberratimes.com.au/archives/news/1999/10/08/bus4.shtr).
Norris, "Can We Afford to Replay the Economic Past?"

32 Bill Bryson, *In a Sunburned Country* (Toronto: Doubleday Canada, 2000), 128.

33 John Lyons, "The World According to Meg Lees," *The Bulletin*, 1 June 1999, 25.

34 Geoff Davies, "It really is the economy, stupid," *The Canberra Times*, 16 June 1999.
(www.canberratimes.com.au/archives/news/1999/06/16/opinion1.shtr).

35 Fred Benchley, "Private Service," *The Bulletin*, 18 April 2000, 42.

36 Meenakshi Ganjoo, "Australia orders expansion of bilateral trade network," *Asia Pulse*, 19 November 1998.

37 Fred Benchley, "Think global, act regional," *The Bulletin*, December 14, 1999, 32.

38. Honourable Mark Vaile, Trade Minister, "Turning the Corner on Trade - the 2000 Trade Outcomes and Objectives Statement," Speech at the National Press Club, April 5, 2000. www.dfat.gov.au/media/speeches/trade/000405_toos_pressclub.htr

39 "Advancing Australia's Trade Interests," National Party website: http://www.ozmail.com.au/~npafed/Policy/trade2.htr

40 Ibid.

41 "Lawyer in for the chop," *The Bulletin*, 27 July 1999, 39.

42 Benchley, "Think global, act regional," *The Bulletin*, 14 December 1999, 32.

43 Fred Benchley, "Protection Racket," *The Bulletin*, 26 January 1999, 16.

44 Virginia Trioli, "Too much, too late," *The Bulletin*, 9 March 1999, 34–35.

45 Ibid., 35.

46 Max Walsh, "We've blown it before," *The Bulletin*, 15 February 2000, 33.

47 John Lyons, "The Accidental Leader," *The Bulletin*, 18 April 2000, 35.

48 Ibid.

49 Ibid., 38.

50 Australia Bureau of Statistics, *International Merchandise Trade*, September Quarter 1999, 27.

51 Australian exports to Japan fell from US$12.4 billion in 1997 to US$10.8 billion in 1999. International Monetary Fund, Direction of Trade Statistics (Washington: IMF, 2000).

52 "Australian Growers to Ship First Apples," *Asia Pulse*, 6 January 1999.

53 Bruce Jacques, "Coal at the Crossroads," *The Bulletin*, 1 February 2000, 48.

54 Ben Ready, "Coal prices forced down 5 pc" *The Canberra Times*, 8 February 2000. (www.canberratimes.com.au/archives/news/2000/02/08/bus1.shtr).

55 "Advancing Australia's Trade Interest."

56 Statistics Canada, "Canadian Economic Observer," Catalogue no.11-010-XPB, April 2000, 3.1

57 Michael Adams, "If times are so good, why do we feel so bad?" *The Globe and Mail*, 27 December 1999, A15. Business Council on National Issues, "This is your captains speaking," *The Globe and Mail*, 4 April 2000, A13; Alan Toulin, "Ottawa Ignored Productivity warning, leading economist says," *National Post*, 22 January 2000, A7; John McCallum, "Will Canada Matter in 2020," *National Post*, 19 February 2000, B7

58 McCallum, "Will Canada Matter in 2020."

59 Willard Z. Estey, "The quiet hijacking of corporate Canada," *The Globe and Mail*, 16 December 1999, A15.

60 BCNI, "This is your captains speaking."

61 Naomi Klein, "The Real APEC scandal," *Saturday Night*, February 1999, 48.

62 Wyng Chow, "Lack of value-added exports costs jobs, think-tank reports," *The Vancouver Sun*, 25 February 1999, D3.

63 "With an eye on the wallet," *Maclean's Magazine* 111, issue 52, 36.

64 BCNI, "This is your captains speaking."

65 McCallum, "Will Canada matter in 2020."

66 Alan Toulin, "Ottawa ignored productivity warning, economist says," *The National Post*, 22 January 2000, A7.

67 Peter McLachlan, DFAIT, and John Skeggs, Industry Canada, interview with author, 6 July 2000.

68 "Imports and exports of goods on a balance-of-payments basis," Statistics Canada:
http://www.statcan.ca/english/Pgb/Economy/International/gbleco2a.htm

69 Gordon Hamilton, "Desperate B.C. boosts overseas log shipments," *The Vancouver Sun*, 5 February 1998, D1.

70 Gordon Hamilton, "Stricter Japanese building codes forcing some mills to close," *The Vancouver Sun*, 10 May 2000, D1–2.

71 Forest Renewal B.C. funds four marketing programs in Japan. The first, the B.C. Wood Specialties Group, grew out of a desire by the B.C. government in the mid-1990s to push the forestry industry toward more value-added products. The organization is made up of over one hundred value-added wood manufacturers in sectors ranging from furniture to structural components and housing components. Funding comes from the Association's members and from the provincial and federal governments. The B.C. Wood Specialties Group has two small offices, one in Tokyo and one in Osaka, and it provides a referral service for companies looking for value-added wood products. It also arranges overseas trade missions and incoming visits and plant tours. The other Forest Renewal B.C. supported initiatives include those undertaken by the Zairai Lumber Partnership (an association of several British Columbia coastal firms, which works to promote the use of hemlock), the Canadian Plywood Association (composed of one Alberta, one Saskatchewan and eight British Columbian firms that sell plywood, veneer and veneer composite products) and the Interior Lumber Manufacturers Association, which focuses on spruce, fir and pine promotion.

72 "Quintette Coal Mine," Teck Corporation:
http://www.teckcorp.com/ops/coal_quin.html

73 Canada-Japan Trade Council, *Canada-Japan Trade Council Newsletter*, May–June 1999, 2.

74 Correspondence and survey results from Donald J. Bobiash, counselor and consul, Canadian embassy, Tokyo, 25 June 1999.

75 Andrew Smith, second secretary (Commercial), Canadian embassy, Tokyo, letter to author, 23 June 1999.

76 DFAIT, "Team Canada Japan Results in $409 Million in Deals for Canadian Firms," Press Release, 16 September 1999.

77 Heather Scoffield, "Canada-Japan trade deal backed," *The Globe and Mail*, 17 May 2000, B3.

78 Alan Toulin and Ian Jack, "Opposition expected from Japan on trade deal," *The National Post*, 17 May 2000, A7.

79 Rod McQueen, "Who is the guy making promises?" *National Post*, 17 May 2000, A7.

80 International Monetary Fund, Direction of Trade Statistics (Washington: IMF, 2000). For a review of political and governmental efforts to promote Canada-Japan trade, see Section III, Managing the New Relationship, in Michael Fry et al., eds., *The North Pacific Triangle: The United States, Japan, and Canada at Century's End* (Toronto: University of Toronto Press, 1998). See, in particular, the essays by the former Canadian ambassador to Japan, James Taylor, "Managing Canada-Japan Relations" and by Michael Fry, "Canada-Japan Forum 2000: A Novel Exercise in Diplomacy."

81 Patrick Cook, "Kiwi Kapers," *The Bulletin*, 7 December 1999, 114.

Index